# The Sociology of Sport and Physi[cal] Education



*The Sociology of Sport and Physical Education* is the fi[rst] one-stop introductory guide for undergraduate students of Sport and Physical Education in the UK. With contributions from the leading names in its field, *The Sociology of Sport and Physical Education* examines the most important current issues in this area.

The first section of this book will enable students to understand and contextualise the issues discussed by looking at the theoretical background and research methods used in the sociological study of sport. The book also covers a wide range of contemporary concerns, centring on the notion of difference in physical education and sporting contexts.

Topics discussed include:

- Gender, race and ethnicity.
- The sporting body.
- Participation and socialisation.
- Critical pedagogy and the hidden curriculum.
- Politics, sport and the mass media.

Each chapter concludes with questions for discussion, and a selection of tasks and suggested further reading, making this an ideal basis for either individual study or for a lecture series.

*Anthony Laker* is Degree Director in Physical Education in the Department of Exercise and Sport Science at East Carolina University in the USA.

With contributions from Bob Chappell, Gill Clarke, Matthew Curtner-Smith, Brian Davies, John Evans, Barrie Houlihan, Barbara Humberstone, David Kirk, Doune Macdonald, Gareth Nutt, Dawn Penney, George Sage and Sandra A. Stroot.

# The Sociology of Sport and Physical Education

## An Introductory Reader

Edited by
**Anthony Laker**

LONDON AND NEW YORK

First published 2002 by Routledge
2 Park Square, Milton Park, Abingdon, Oxon, OX14 4RN

Simultaneously published in the USA and Canada
by Routledge
270 Madison Ave, New York NY 10016

*Routledge is an imprint of the Taylor & Francis Group*

Transferred to Digital Printing 2007



Typeset in Times New Roman by GreenGate Publishing Services,
Tonbridge, Kent



*British Library Cataloguing in Publication Data*
A catalogue record for this book is available from the British Library

*Library of Congress Cataloging in Publication Data*
The sociology of sport and physical education: an introductory reader / [edited by]
Anthony Laker.
p. cm.
Includes bibliographical references and index.
1. Sports–Social aspects. 2. Physical education and training–Social aspects. I. Laker,
Anthony, 1951-

GV706.5'.S645 2001
306.4 83–dc21 2001019961

ISBN 0–415–23593–6 (hbk)
ISBN 0–415–23594–4 (pbk)

**Publisher's Note**
The publisher has gone to great lengths to ensure the quality of this
reprint but points out that some imperfections in the original
may be apparent

# Contents

# Tables

# Contributors

**Anthony Laker** is the Degree Director in Physical Education in the Department of Exercise and Sport Science at East Carolina University. He has taught in primary and secondary schools, and has been involved in training teachers of both primary and secondary physical education. Anthony is the editor of the *Journal of Sport Pedagogy* and the author of *Beyond the Boundaries of Physical Education: Educating Young People for Citizenship and Social Responsibility* and *Developing Personal, Social and Moral Education Through Physical Education: A Practical Guide for Teachers*, both published by RoutledgeFalmer. His current research interests include personal and social development through physical activity, and understanding and interpreting the physical education curriculum and sport experience from a global, cultural perspective. Anthony enjoys sailing, surfing and long-distance trekking.

**Robert 'Bob' Chappell** works in the Department of Sport Sciences at Brunel University, London. He was educated at Loughborough, Western Kentucky, London and Leicester Universities, and has made contributions to academic journals in the areas of race, ethnicity and sport, and political ideology. He has travelled extensively throughout the world making presentations at academic conferences. His passion is basketball for which he is team manager of the Great Britain team for the World University Games.

**Gill Clarke** lectures in physical education and biographical studies at the University of Southampton in the Research and Graduate School of Education. Her research interests centre on the lives of lesbian physical education students and teachers and the development of sport education in schools. Additionally, her interests are in sporting auto/biographies. Currently she is researching the experiences of lesbian and gay athletes and the history of the Women's Land Army. She has published widely on lesbian physical education teachers and recently co-edited *Researching Women and Sport* (Macmillan). She has just retired from international hockey umpiring having officiated nearly 150 international matches, including the Barcelona, Atlanta and Sydney Olympic Games.

**Matthew Curtner-Smith** is an Associate Professor in the Department of Kinesiology at the University of Alabama. His responsibilities include supervising graduate students working on master's and doctoral degrees in sport pedagogy and teaching undergraduates training to be physical education teachers. His research interests include teacher socialisation, teacher effectiveness, and curriculum change.

**Brian Davies** is Professor of Education, School of Social Sciences, Cardiff University, Wales. His recent research has included work on school sport and nationalism in Wales, reform in pre-service nurse education, a comparison of training procedures in small and medium enterprises in selected occupations in SE Wales and Rhine-Westphalia and the effects of Key Stage 3 testing in Maths in English and Welsh secondary schools. His most recent writing has been on the contribution of Basil Bernstein to research in the Sociology of Education.

**John Evans** is Professor of Physical Education and Head of the Department of Physical Education, Sports Science and Recreation Management at Loughborough University. He is the author of *Teaching in Transition: the Challenge of Mixed Ability Grouping*, editor of *PE, Sport and Schooling: Studies in the Sociology of PE*; *Teachers, Teachers and Control*; and *Equality, Education and Physical Education* (all by the Falmer Press) and he has published widely in the sociology of education and physical education. He is also editor of a special edition of the *Curriculum Journal, International Perspectives on Physical Education,* and co-editor of the international journal *Sport, Education and Society*. His research interests centre on the study of policy, teaching and equity issues in the secondary school curriculum.

**Barrie Houlihan** is Professor of Sport Policy at Loughborough University, UK. His research interests include the domestic and international policy processes for sport. He has a particular interest in sports development, the diplomatic use of sport, and drug abuse by athletes. His most recent books include *Sport and International Politics* (1994), *Sport, Policy and Politics: A Comparative Analysis* (1997) and *Dying to Win: the Development of Anti-doping Policy* (1999). Recent articles have been published in *Public Administration* (1999), *Journal of Sport Management* (1999) and *European Physical Education Review* (2000). He is currently preparing a book on sports development with Anita White to be published by Routledge and is also preparing a second edition of *Dying to Win*.

**Barbara Humberstone** is Professor of Sociology of Leisure (Sport and Outdoor Education) at Buckinghamshire Chilterns University College, High Wycombe, Buckinghamshire, UK. She teaches gender, difference and leisure, and outdoor education and adventure recreation. Her research interests include: social and environmental equity/justice and leisure, (eco)-feminist theories, cultural diversity and research methodologies. Barbara is a board member of the European Institute for Outdoor Adventure Education and Experiential Learning and UK representative for the International Association of Physical Education and Sport for Girls and Women. Her other leisure interests include windsurfing, walking, climbing and the environment.

**David Kirk** is currently Professor of Youth Sport at Loughborough University. After completing his education in Britain, he worked at the University of Queensland and Deakin University in Australia for fourteen years. His research interests include young people in sport, curriculum change in physical education, and the social construction of bodies in and through schooling. David won the International Olympic Committee President's Prize in 2001 for his contribution to research and development in physical and sport education. He believes his best work so far is the 1998 book *Schooling Bodies*, published by Leicester University Press, which very few people have ever read.

**Doune Macdonald** is an Associate Professor in the School of Human Movement Studies, The University of Queensland. She coordinates the health and physical education (HPE) teacher education programme and teaches the undergraduate curriculum studies courses. Prior to her university work she taught in primary and secondary schools and in 2000 returned to some part-time school teaching to be reminded of how challenging and complex teaching is. Her research interests include curriculum development and change, teacher education, and the place of physical activity in the lives of young people. While writing this chapter, Doune came to share a home with Steven, Erika and Sophie, from whom she learns a great deal every day.

**Gareth Nutt** is a Senior Lecturer in the Faculty of Education and Social Sciences at the Cheltenham and Gloucester College of Higher Education where he is the PGCE (Secondary) Course Leader for the Gloucestershire Initial Teacher Education Partnership. His research interests include the study of innovation and change within physical education and the changing nature of teachers' work. Before taking up his appointment at Cheltenham in 1989, Gareth taught physical education in Berkshire for 14 years. During this period he also held a variety of posts with pastoral responsibilities.

**Dawn Penney** is a Senior Research Fellow at the Department of Physical Education, Sports Science and Recreation Management, Loughborough University. Dawn has previously held research positions at the University of Southampton, the University of Queensland and De Montfort University, and is the reviews editor for *Sport, Education and Society*. Outside of her academic work, Dawn trains and competes in long-distance running, duathlons and triathlons.

**George Sage** is Professor Emeritus of Kinesiology and Sociology (joint appointment) at the University of Northern Colorado. He has published 15 books (including revisions) as either author, co-author or editor. His most recently authored book is the second edition of *Power and Ideology in American Sport: A Critical Perspective*. He has also written over 40 articles which have appeared in such journals as *Sociology of Sport Journal*, *Journal of Sport and Social Issues*, *Quest*, *Sociology of Work and Occupations Journal*. George has been president of the North American Society for the Sociology of Sport. He was an avid runner for 25 years, but more recently he has turned to golf for recreation and exercise.

**Sandra A. Stroot** is a Professor in the School of Physical Activity and Educational Services at The Ohio State University. She teaches in both the undergraduate and graduate programmes and supervises masters and doctoral dissertations. Sandra serves on the United States Physical Education Program and was previously a member of the editorial board of the *Journal of Teaching in Physical Education*. In addition to presenting widely at conferences, she has published extensively in the area of physical education teacher education. Her most recent research interests have included collaborative work between universities and school districts and induction programmes for newly qualified teachers.

# Introduction

The original idea for this book was born some years ago when I was teaching 'sociology of sport and physical education' to undergraduates in Plymouth, most of whom were training to be teachers. I noticed that my references and recommendations for additional reading were from both British and American authors. This was fine when I was referring students to specific topics, as both countries have fine traditions of sport sociology research and writing. I was able to cite particular chapters or articles that my students could go away and study. My problem came when asked to recommend one text that could be used as a course reader. There were many such books from American authors, but British authors had been much more specialised in their writing and there wasn't a 'one stop' book reference that I could supply. This book is intended to fill that gap and is therefore aimed at undergraduate students of sport, physical education, recreation and leisure; indeed, it is for any student interested in sport as a social phenomenon.

The result is a compilation of writings from the leading academic authors of their generation. I have been very fortunate that I was able to persuade these colleagues, friends and, in some cases, heroes to contribute to this book. I feel privileged to be able to write in their company.

There are twelve topics, each covered by one of the twelve chapters. At the end of each chapter there are some questions for students to reflect on. These could also be used as test, or examination, questions. The tasks suggested are designed to encourage students to engage with the material and to develop a personal context in which to interpret the subject matter of the chapter topic. Most of the tasks can be done in groups to encourage the social interaction so important in the constructivist, and social learning, formation of knowledge and understanding. Students who develop a particular interest will find the recommended further reading useful when pursuing their interest.

The way this book is used is, of course, entirely up to the course tutor or lecturer. However, the concept and layout lend themselves to being used as a course reader, an introductory text that supplements a series of lectures. The first three chapters cover what might be called the necessary background information of the importance and place of sport in culture, the theoretical background and the research methodologies prevalent in sport and physical education research. This provides a sound theoretical context on which to base the topic chapters that follow.

Although this is not an exhaustive account of all things sporting and sociological, the topics selected encompass most arenas of topical debate. Issues such as gender, the sporting body, race and ethnicity, and equality and equity are addressed and analysed from a macro and micro viewpoint. How these factors affect participation and socialisation are then considered. The critical perspective comes to the fore when the hidden curriculum and critical pedagogy are elaborated on. Finally, we look at the larger issues of political influence and globalisation and how they have an effect on sport and physical education.

I begin by discussing the relationship between sport, education and culture. These concepts are all interwoven and are very important to the way we live and conduct our lives. We all have experience of all of them and they impact our lives on a daily basis. Education promotes and maintains our culture, and sport is a part of that education and a part of our culture. This is also true of many cultures worldwide and there is a global language and community that has sport as its binding force. John Evans and Brian Davies then deal with the paradox of educational research in Britain. It has been claimed that such research is too theoretical and not relevant, yet universities are partially funded according to their high quality research output. Professors Evans and Davies briefly outline the development of research in physical education and conclude that it definitely has had an impact on classroom practice. They call for more, not less, theory and innovation in research and teaching. Chapter 3 looks at the different methodological approaches to educational research. Positivism, the interpretive paradigm and critical theory are explained by Matt Curtner-Smith. For each of these research paradigms Dr Curtner-Smith provides a description, a look at the evolution, and some examples of published studies. The references following this chapter are a valuable resource to all readers interested in continuing with any form of sport pedagogy research.

Barbara Humberstone investigates the issues of femininity and masculinity in sport. The construction of notions of femininity and masculinity is a result of social interaction, dominant ideology and institutional bias. Professor Humberstone explains the concept of patriarchal hegemony and begins to investigate how 'difference' is interpreted in gender forms. David Kirk also celebrates 'difference' in his chapter on the sporting body. As with gender, the body and how it is viewed is a social construction. Professor Kirk explains the cult of slenderness, how we 'school' our bodies to conform to dominant ideas of acceptability, and how the media promote normative body shape values. School physical education and sport in general are sites where this 'body construction' takes place and some alternative approaches for teachers and coaches are suggested.

Race and ethnicity are sometimes wrongly used as interchangeable terms. Bob Chappell explains these terms in Chapter 6. One of the critical points of the book is his attribution of the success of black athletes to socialisation and not to race differences. He then takes a cross-cultural look at black sports people in the USA and Britain, concluding with an examination of the involvement in sport of the Asian population in Britain. Dawn Penney's chapter on equality and equity suggests that the way 'difference' is interpreted and accommodated is the key to equity of provision, accessibility and opportunity. Dr Penney draws on her substantial investigation into the National Curriculum in physical education to point out that we still have a long way to go in promoting real equality for our young people in education. Too often 'difference' is seen as a problem requiring a solution, whereas it should be see as a state of being that deserves recognition and acceptance.

Sandra Stroot draws heavily on Bandura's social learning theory when writing about socialisation and participation in sport. She explains that the family, teachers and coaches are crucial in getting children involved in sport. However, Professor Stroot points out that continued participation is dependent on many other factors such as gender, social class, commitment, sporting identity, and race and ethnicity.

The notion of a 'hidden curriculum', in addition to the regular school curriculum, has received much attention from educational sociologists. Gareth Nutt and Gill Clarke help us understand how such a 'hidden curriculum' is constituted and transmitted in the school environment. They point out that the social relationship between teacher and students is a conduit for this transmission and that the 'power' of the teacher and the peer group is vital in transmitting these covert social values and messages. Teachers are also subject to a 'hidden curriculum' of sorts and the nature of teachers' work is changing. 'Deprofessionalisation', initial teacher training and examinations in physical education are shown to account for some of this change. Doune Macdonald continues the critical theory theme with her account of critical pedagogy. She analyses what it is and why it is important. Her description of three case studies provides fine examples of action research in teacher education, school physical education and a community physical activity programme. Dr Macdonald provides a model for reflective practice in these locations and her explanation of the cycles of action research should be valuable to any students considering such a project as part of their studies.

The final two chapters take a much broader look at sport in a political and global context. Barrie Houlihan investigates the various motives for governments adopting sport as a cause. These motives are various and not always the most altruistic. National prestige, control of social problems and health promotion are three that Professor Houlihan documents. The National Curriculum for physical education, soccer player transfer and eligibility, and anti-drug taking policy are used as examples of government involvement in sport. In a world of instant communication, domestic sports policy is often conditioned by the prevailing international climate and interests. George Sage takes up this theme in his chapter on the globalisation of sport and the media. Historically, the media has supported the status quo and been resistant to change. But the world's media is coming under the control of a decreasing number of corporations and individuals. Professor Sage writes about the symbiotic relationship between sport, business and the media. All serve the interests of the others. The media adapts and creates sports. What we see, hear and read is a mediated version of the real event. We are living in a global village, and sport and the media are global phenomena.

This book was originated to meet the needs of students and lecturers. I believe it serves that function very well. However, as I have conversed with the authors, read the chapters, and become involved in the content I have reformed my opinion of the way we should explore the sociology of sport and physical education. We put topics in boxes; I am as guilty of that as anyone. This book is designed that way; it is easy to study and understand that way. But it really isn't the way it should be. All of the topics are inter-related and should not be separated from each other. When you read this book try to make connections across the topics; that is what the tasks are for. Try to understand what you are reading from an intellectual and personal viewpoint. It is only by personalising the knowledge that you will truly understand it.

In a globalising, post-modern society, change is said to be the only constant. In editing this book I have come to realise that, in sport sociology and across all the topics, concerns and issues, 'difference' is the only similarity. This book then, is really an examination and exploration of difference in the human sporting condition.

Anthony Laker
March 2001

# 1 Culture, education and sport

*Anthony Laker*

## Introduction

The purpose of this chapter is to place sport in a social, cultural and educational context. This implies definitions of culture, education and sport, and the academic juxtaposition of each to the others. However, it will be seen that culture, education and sport have commonly-held meanings which, in some cases, eradicate the need for further clarification. So, apart from defining these important concepts, this chapter will also deal with the pervading nature of sport in society, sport as a system of sub-cultures and the degree to which sport has become an important symbol for individuals and societies worldwide. Sport has a variety of functions for different segments of society and therefore different meanings to those different populations.

Everyone knows what a culture is. Everyone knows what education is. And everyone knows what sport is. But everyone has slightly different definitions of culture, education and sport. What we require are commonly understood definitions of terms for the purpose of this chapter. The mere fact that we need to define these terms for the purposes of this analysis highlights the problem that definitions and meanings are context specific and will vary as the contexts of their usage changes. The potential differences in the meanings of sport have already been touched upon, but culture as a term can evoke different interpretations.

There is an inevitable and symbiotic relationship between culture, education and sport. Education and sport are two of the major institutions of our society. As such, they interact with each other, and of course other institutions, to contribute to what we commonly regard as culture and society. In this way, neither education nor sport are ideologically neutral because they have implicit values which we incorporate into recognition of both culture and society. This incorporation of sport and education into the meaning of society and culture legitimates them and gives them both a value and a place. Although we have only referred to sport and education here, it can be seen how the various societal and cultural components (such as religion, work and the family) are constructed through systems of meaning that are legitimated through practice and adoption and perpetuate the commonly-held view of culture and society.

The above argument indicates the real value of sport and education; that is, they have importance in many of our everyday lives, and they are a part of the fabric of our society. The emotions, particularly those of parents, raised by education and the number of newspaper pages devoted to sport are a testament to this importance.

## Culture

There is a commonly-held view that culture is art; paintings, sculptures, drama and the like, but that is mistaken. The artistic view of culture is limited by its narrowness of application – it is only one aspect of culture, and is sometimes referred to as 'high' culture. The converse is that a 'low' culture also exists and refers to football, pop music, and TV. This élitist view has little appeal in academic debate and, as the boundaries between these two opposing cultural dichotomies becomes ever more blurred, the currency of this framework is devalued.

A culture is a system of shared values, meanings and symbols that enables societies and individuals to operate effectively without continually redefining these values, meanings, symbols and points of reference. Imagine the impossibility of having to say what we meant by religion, for example, every time we used the term; or what morality meant to us; or what we understood by the word sport. Take the symbol of the cross. In one context it indicates religion, spirituality, and the religious claim that Jesus died on a cross to grant us salvation. In another context, as a traffic sign, a cross means two roads intersecting, and we must therefore drive with care. A cross on its side, in yet another context, indicates that something is wrong, incorrect and possibly needs to be done again. The meaning of the symbol clearly depends upon the context in which the symbol is placed.

As well as being things and items, symbols can be found in actions and language. Hand gestures, facial expressions, body language and head movements sometimes have specific meanings in different cultural contexts. In western society, we commonly throw paper and small pieces of household rubbish on a fire. However in Nepal, the Hindu and Buddhist household gods live in the hearth and it is an insult to throw rubbish at them. Giving or receiving items with one's left hand is poorly regarded in some Asian and eastern cultures because of the sanitary function for which the left hand is used. It is far better to offer and receive with both hands. Nearer to our own western experience, Churchill's V for victory hand gesture has come to be interpreted as a peace symbol. Although connections can be made between victory and peace, these are different concepts located in different times but represented by the same symbol.

These differences within shared meanings are what make separate cultures unique. People within the culture do not have to define their symbols at every social interaction. The commonly-held perception of meaning lubricates the social process. Within cultures there are sub-cultures. These smaller groupings of individuals also share systems of values and meanings and this develops their clear and separate identities. Some of the most obvious examples are surfers and bikers. Each of these groups has very distinctive ways of dressing, talking and behaving that are clearly identified as being peculiar to the group. The distinct nature of language, appearance and actions is what binds the fabric of sub-cultures together and makes them strong in their separateness and individuality. A sub-culture must have at least one unifying characteristic. For the surfing sub-culture, one of the unique characteristics of that community is that they go into the sea and ride waves, they surf. There is also an exclusionary nature to sub-cultures which means that without possessing the unique characteristic one could never join the sub-culture. So one could never be included in the surfing sub-culture if one did not surf. There are undoubtedly privileged groups who enjoy limited access to the sub-culture. In the case of surfing, board and wetsuit manufacturers, journalists, photographers and the like will be allowed this access, but they will not be part of the core group, the essential sub-culture.

## Education

We all have a view of what education means. In one role or another, we have all experienced education. We have been children at school so we know what it is like to be a pupil. We know what goes on in schools, even if only superficially, so we know what schools are like to work in. And many of us have seen school through our own children's eyes, so we think we know a lot about school, and therefore about education. This interpretation is similar to other people's interpretation because they have also been through the same process and experiences. Therefore, this interpretation gets reinforced and every time we use the word education, we do not have to explain what we mean. The meaning of education is a commonly-held meaning that is the culturally acceptable one.

Mention education to most people and they will get a mental image of a school; a lesser number will also think of higher education, perhaps in a university. Even fewer will picture adult education, job training, pre-school groups, taking up a new sport, reading a book, or going on holiday. All these activities are educational in that they encourage learning. So although the common perception of education may be limited, the possibilities for inclusion are many and would have a consensus of approval.

Dictionary definitions can be illuminating when considering cultural meanings. To educate derives from Latin and literally means to lead forth. In theorising about the education process in general, this literal meaning has an attraction to those who will be doing the leading, i.e. the teachers. It invests them with authority, power and control. It implies that knowledge is a product held by a few, to be packaged and made available to the many who are then led to this knowledge as if it were an enlightenment. Critical theorists take this view and have produced a wealth of commentary on just this aspect of the education process, some of which is reported in later chapters. This sociological interpretation of education illustrates why definitions vary and why sometimes technical definitions are required.

For many, education is what we get at school; for teachers, education is an enlightening teaching and learning process; and for critical theory sociologists, education is a socially controlling mechanism. It could be assumed that this would lead to confusion. However, the context in which the term is used refines the definition and allows a commonly-held meaning to prevail. So, in general terms, parents talking with each other about education would probably be referring to the package of knowledge that children receive at school; teachers in a staff meeting would be discussing the process of teaching and learning; and critical theorists writing in academic journals would refer to the sociologists' meaning of education.

## Sport

As with education, sport has a common core of shared meaning and a periphery of additional meanings that are very much context-dependent. In other words, although most of us have a common understanding of what sport is, it can still mean different things to different people. In general terms we recognise that football is sport, but that ballroom dancing is not; motor racing is sport, but driving to work is not; sailing a boat on an ocean is sport, but sailing on a tanker delivering oil is not. It is not necessary to define what we mean by sport whenever the word is used. However, the same sport can have different meanings to different groups of people. As an example of these differing meanings let us consider the sport of tennis. To a professional tennis player tennis is a job; to a club player, however competitive, tennis is essentially a recreation; to a spectator at Wimbledon, tennis may be a temporary diversion or an all consuming vicarious passion. In short, a sport, and sports, mean different things to different people even though there is an over-riding perception of what a sport is, and what sports are.

If we look more closely at a set of meanings of the sports experience, we can more closely approach the function of sport. Sport for a group of hillwalkers will mean things like freedom from everyday worries, possibly a sense of awe and wonder, and an exhilaration at being in a natural and remote environment. Sport for a group in an aerobics class could mean getting and staying healthy, socialising and stress reduction. The groups mentioned here have positive interpretations of sport. Unfortunately for some children, the experience of sport is not always positive and can come to mean getting wet and cold and being exposed to failure, and may lead to a complete lack of enthusiasm and enjoyment. It can clearly be seen that in promoting the benefits of sport and an active lifestyle, school sport and physical education have a major contribution to make. Thus, sport has different connotations for different groups in different contexts.

Outside school, sport has a number of different functions. The most obvious of these is as a form of recreation. The vast majority of those who take part in sport outside an educational environment do so as a form of recreation. The amateur footballer, the ten-pin bowler and the hillwalker pursue their activities for recreation. There is a sub-category of these recreational sports people; those for whom physical activity is merely body maintenance, a way of keeping fit to preserve or improve their health. This group may or may not find enjoyment in their participation. However, if enjoyment is not part of their experience, they are unlikely to remain participants for long. The enjoyment of the body maintenance group usually comes from the knowledge that they are fit and healthy and possibly from improvements in physical performance and fitness levels.

The sense of enjoyment in sport is what motivates recreational participants. Joy in movement, joy in the surroundings and shared joy in shared company are powerful motivators in encouraging and maintaining sporting participation. This carries a strong message for those involved in recreation and sports provision and also for those involved in sport in education i.e. physical education and school sport. That is, that enjoyment has to be at the heart of the process if continued participation is to be a realistic aim.

The basis for taking part in sport is linked to the notion of attaining some kind of benefit from that participation. As discussed, the benefit for recreational participants is, most notably, enjoyment. Professional sports people obtain a different kind of benefit from their participation; they take part for monetary gain. Provision of an income is the benefit they invoke by being involved in sport. Of course this also applies to a variety of occupations that revolve around sport and is not limited to active, professional sportsmen and sportswomen. So sports coaches, recreation managers, physical education teachers, agents, promoters, and a whole variety of associated occupations use sport and physical activity as a provider of income. Of course, there are also a number of drawbacks, or costs, to sports participation for these groups. Recreational sports people pay for their enjoyment both financially and with the use of their time; they have rationalised that their participation is worth the balance of costs. Professionals pay in other ways. Obviously, they devote their time to sport, as others devote their time to their jobs, but in many sports there is a risk of long-term injury and possible delayed disability. Although professionals work for an employer, either for themselves or for a team owner, they inevitably become public property in terms of media exposure, of public relations work and in the miriad of trivial ways demanded by fans of their heroes. This is a cost often forgotten when the big salaries of sports stars are discussed. So, although participant groups perceive a benefit from sport, there are also costs that must be accounted for.

## Sport in education

School sport and physical education are defined by a commonly-held perception. Physical education means playing games. That, unfortunately, is the most prevalent interpretation of the school subject. However, viewing a curriculum within a school very clearly dispels this notion and it can be seen that physical education is an educational process that uses human movement as its medium. Pupils will learn physical skills; they will learn about human movement and through human movement. The activities that constitute physical education will vary according to the context. In England and Wales there is a National Curriculum that dictates what state schools must do in physical education so there is very little variation between schools. Physical education uses games extensively, but not exclusively, as its medium of instruction. Gymnastics, dance, track and field athletics, swimming and outdoor pursuits are also all used to one degree or another as part of physical education programmes in many schools.

These common definitions are reinforced by the hegemonic process that pertains in many societies and institutions. Kirk and Tinning (1990: 1–21) suggest that physical activity programmes in educational institutions are instrumental in promoting a socially acceptable form of sport and activity. Very early in our development, physical education in schools begins to form what will become our view, and therefore eventually the societal view, of what sport, recreation and physical activity are. The selection of activities in any curriculum implies that those activities have some benefit over other activities and are therefore of more value than other activities. In this way a dominant segment of society constructs an authorised view of sport and physical education. This version represents the privileging of one set of ideas over other sets of ideas. When these privileged versions are challenged the authority quickly acts to impose the authorised view. In the mid-1980s, teachers of physical education challenged the emphasis on competitive games in the National Curriculum of England and Wales. They claimed that it did not lead to a balanced physical education for all pupils. The response came in the form of *Sport. Raising the Game* (DNH, 1995) which stated that sport should return to the heart of school life. Opposition had been eliminated and the authorised version imposed.

In light of the above, it is now understandable why school sport usually refers to organised, competitive contests between groups of pupils either within a school, as in house or tutor group matches, or between schools in the form of representative teams. This is much the same meaning that sport has in a wider context, the major difference being that school sport claims an educational component.

Sport, in the educational guises of physical education and school sport, has a major role to play in the education of young people. In spite of the restricted offering of socially acceptable forms of physical education and sport that constitute its educational manifestation, there are still a number of major cultural benefits to be gained from the experience of sport in school.

Society wants young people who can live within it, abiding by its regulatory codes of behaviour, conformity and productivity. Society wants people who have been inculcated into the nature of that society, and can be relied upon to act in a responsible way within a wider culture that incorporates notions of history, place and context. Sport, as a microcosm of society, helps with these aspects of inculcation. Not only do school sport and physical education attempt to teach physical activities, skills and so on; they are also instrumental in promoting personal and social characteristics such as fairness, cooperation, independence and teamwork. Playing the game by the rules allows the game to take place for everyone's benefit. In the wider context, the majority of the population abiding by the law of the land allows society to function. This development into social beings who have a sense of cultural affiliation cannot be attributed solely to educational sport, but educational sport (physical education and school sport) does have a great deal to offer as part of the whole educational package.

However, it is not only personal characteristics that can be encouraged through sport in education. Physical abilities and individual skills have already been mentioned, but there is also a whole world of knowing about sports that deserves some attention in an educational context. This is at least as important as psychomotor skills, and personal and social skills; this aspect enables young people to appreciate the place of sport in culture and the real importance that is attached to sport as a cultural phenomenon. A section of this chapter is entitled 'Tradition and myth', and the fact that sport can spawn and elicit such concepts is a tribute to its pervasive power. There is a wealth of history attached to sport, not only bare facts, but also how sport has changed and developed to take account of changing cultural circumstances, For example, why do cricketers wear white in some matches and colours in others, why do some soccer matches begin at 11.30a.m. on a Sunday morning and not at 3p.m. on a Saturday afternoon as they traditionally did, and why do Rugby League teams have 13 players per side and Rugby Union teams have 15 players per side?

Much of this type of information only becomes available when one becomes immersed in the world of sport. When one begins to learn a sport, to take part and to become part of that particular sub-culture, then one learns about the legacy of that sport. One learns its language, its history, its etiquette, its rules and its customs; in short, one begins to absorb its culture. Some of this is achieved in schools but only in a minor way. The predominant curriculum model, i.e. multi-activity, does not lend itself very well to this type of physical education. Sport education with its attention to team affiliation, seasons, recording, varying roles for participants, and the celebration of sport through culminating festivals is far better at promoting sport in this way (see Siedentop, 1994, for a comprehensive description of sport education). Schools can play a part in using physical education and school sport to inculcate this well-rounded sporting development; so that not only are psychomotor skills and talents developed, but so are ideas of sport's place in society and sport as an important part of our cultural heritage.

## Sport's function in culture and society

### *Experience of emotion*

Sport has been likened to religion. The fervent following of football teams, the stadium as a place of worship, and pilgrimage to the game on the sabbath are easily interpreted by sociologists as a replacement for a true religion. This is a misinterpretation and ignores the crucial point of religion, that it deals with existence in an afterlife and is, to a large degree, to do with sustainability of experience. Sport, on the other hand is here and now and is immediate. As much as we remember sports experiences from years past, there can be no pretence that they will benefit us in the afterlife.

However, sport does invoke emotions of utter joy and absolute despair and these emotions can be enjoyed and experienced in a relatively safe sporting environment. In real life these emotions are aroused by events such as birth and death.

But apart from a few exceptions such as climbing or motor racing, nobody dies because of sporting success or failure. Sport therefore enables us to experience these emotions in a vicarious way. We experience the emotions but none of the real consequences. We escape from the real world and live in our sporting world where we can touch on the spirituality of life, death and existence.

Sport brings joy to those who accept its challenge. It also brings sadness and frustration. Perversely, these extremes of emotion are dependant upon each other. The joy would not be as sweet if the disappointment had not been so bitter. The one puts the other in contrast and places a value on its experience. Sport provides our culture with an acceptable avenue for that celebration of human endeavour. If religion exists because man needs to have an expression of faith, then sport could exist to fulfil the need for the celebration of the human body and spirit. Although this logic does not answer questions such as 'why do mountaineers risk their lives on hostile peaks?', 'why have extreme sports experienced a huge rise in popularity?' it does provide a clue as to why these types of risk behaviour are indulged in.

Many of those who compete in endurance events such as marathons and triathlons experience very strong emotions at the event's end. Feelings of satisfaction and triumph, whatever their position, come to the surface. These emotions are rarely felt in everyday life and often words are useless for their expression. The occasion becomes important. Those privileged to take part in a festival of sport, a major championship or a final can recall emotions of being special and of being part of something bigger than just the sport or the game.

### *Social interaction and language*

The language of sport pervades our everyday existence. Sport provides a common ground, a safe arena for interaction in a wide variety of social settings because sport is a constant in the cultural milieu. Sport pervades culture, not only in terms of media content and coverage, but also in terms of language and metaphor. We all know what sport is and we are all exposed to its influence, whether we like to be or not.

As a means of social interaction, sport provides a safe topic. Most people would have a view on the fortunes of the local professional football team, or the Olympics when they are covered on TV, or the aerobics class that friends attend together. In that ultimate social setting, the local pub, landlords try to avoid conversations about religion and politics, but actively encourage sporting debate. Indeed, many are happy to provide sporting opportunities for their patrons; darts, and pool, and the pub football team. In other social settings, 'did you see the game last night?' is a neutral, safe opening gambit in a casual conversation.

We encounter sporting metaphor in everyday life. To extol our friends to 'play the game' is to demand fair treatment; if someone is 'for the high jump', they are likely to be in some kind of trouble; and we must not 'rock the boat' by upsetting an established procedure, but we should hope for the 'plain sailing' which makes all our endeavours easier. These phrases drawn from the lexicon of sport demonstrate that the language of sport is in common usage and has a shared meaning that does not have to be qualified and interpreted on every occasion.

### *Tradition and myth*

As Inglis (1977) shows, sport also provides some of the cultural histories and stories that are told and retold, so becoming part of a legend. The rehearsal of these stories, usually to the same audience, adds a patina of mellowness to them and they become part of a tradition. If one view of sport as an important part of culture has to be selected, I believe this to be one of the most powerful. It shapes our idea of tradition as part of a common culture and it provides the substance of that tradition, becoming part of a comfortable contentment that can enthuse, invigorate and inspire us long after the event has happened and long after the 'actors' have lost the physical capabilities to re-enact the scene. The myth becomes as important as the act. So sporting achievements and stories become part of a cultural fabric.

The tendency of parents and grandparents to say, 'I was there', when talking to their children about some long ago sporting accomplishment adds to the telling of the story an emotional level that embellishes the telling, and makes it more meaningful and personal. This symbolic storytelling often carries connotations of heroic struggle against the odds; machismo and combative elements are sometimes included to add to the essentially male view of sport as an endeavour and an elemental struggle. But not always so. The success in the early 1980s of British ice skaters Jayne Torvill and Christopher Dean was not combative, or male, or an elemental struggle (even though they skated to *Bolero*); it was about grace, form and beautiful movement and has become a part of British sporting culture and is embedded in the tradition of the Olympics.

The events that are converted to traditions, myths and legends do not always have to be Olympic successes, or world championships. They could just as easily be friendly matches between two local soccer clubs, or Sunday evening walks on the nearest common. What sets them apart as traditions is that there has to be something unique about them to justify the telling and the retelling. So, a great goal scored completely out of the blue in a local soccer match, or a view of the sun setting in a beautiful, colourful sky can become mythical as easily as England's soccer World Cup win of 1966, or Ian Botham's exploits in the cricket internationals of the 1981 season, or Pete Goss's rescue of Raphael Dinelli in the Southern Ocean in 1996. And what is equally as important is that the more personal stories have just as much worth and validity as tradition as do the stories of more global proportions.

### *Cultural reproduction*

#### *Functionalism*

One of the most powerful criticisms of the cultural function of sport has been by Brohm (1978). He suggests that sport embodies all the elements of a functionalist tool to reproduce the pertaining culture and social context. The argument is that recreational sport promotes economic exploitation, patriarchy, hegemony, élitism and an imperialist work ethic that likens sportsmen and women to components in the production process of a capitalist society. Similarly, professional sport locates the performers firmly in the context of 'workers', owned by the clubs, agents, and to some extent the public. They produce their performances for the consumption of the viewing public.

An extension of this thesis leads to a view that sport played an active part in the imperial process. It is a truism that Britain exported some of the most popular sports to other parts of the world. The patriarchal hegemony of the Victorian era held that men exercised domination and control over all aspects of life in society, except raising children and running the home. It also held dear the work ethic, respect for authority and one's betters, and the idea that emotions and displays of emotion should be kept firmly under control. This hegemonic process promoted the values of imperialism and the notion of empire: sport was a part of that process and thus played a role in supporting those values. Thus sporting imperialism, or sport as a component of imperialism, provides strong evidence of a structural functionalism that was, and is, culturally reproductive.

### *Play and conformity*

When young children play they very rarely measure, compete formally, or celebrate winners and denigrate losers. Play is play – no more, no less. Play is outside normal everyday existence, it has a special quality that is its essence. It is escapism and fairy tale as well as being anything the participants want it to be. There are no rules, apart from those imposed by the players, no boundaries apart from the imagination, and no consequences.

Huizinga (1955: 18–21) provides a similar set of conditions that characterise play. He identifies that play is completely free and voluntary and exists outside normal life. Once play becomes functional and 'everyday' it ceases to be play, or it becomes a poor imitation of real play. Play exists within its own world, in its own time and space and it proceeds in an orderly manner developing its own rules. In spite of this created 'order', play has a tension and an uncertainty about it. Lastly, and importantly in the context of this text, play encourages a common shared experience within its own community.

However, play soon becomes corrupted by structure and the imposition by adults of their own ideas of what children need. The increasing trend to involve children in 'educational' interactions at earlier and earlier ages restricts play and replaces it with embryonic games and sports, albeit in the guise of educational activities. What children freely play and do is a response to their own needs and inclinations. This becomes replaced by what adults deem necessary for the attainment of appropriate physical, social and academic development. So acceptable activities are imposed at an early age. What constitutes play and knowledge is no longer defined by the needs of the children, but by a society that dictates that young children will benefit from what adults say is beneficial and needed. While accepting that this might be done with the most altruistic of motives in mind, children must be allowed to be children and not just small adults to be socialised as soon and as efficiently as possible. In his classic work *Homo Ludens*, Huizinga (1955) suggested that civilisation works gradually to eliminate play as humans progress through their lives. In worst case scenarios adults no longer play; some take their play vicariously by being watchers of play, i.e. sports spectators, and some become involved in sport as recreation. Work becomes predominant and play is replaced by socially acceptable ways of relaxation. Thus, the joyful running of children becomes the track events in school, then the jogging to keep fit, then the watching of track events on TV, and sadly, perhaps ignorance and apathy.

Schmitz (1979) takes a more kindly view of the evolution of play into sport. He claims that sport is an extension of play and that it adopts its central values from play. In both forms of human behaviour we indulge in them pleasurably and suspend the normal rules and conventions of everyday life and behaviour for the duration of the participation. Where else is it acceptable to tackle a fully-grown adult to the ground, except on the playing field?

The cultural reproductive functions of sport discussed so far – functionalism and play and conformity – have somewhat negative connotations attached. They represent one viewpoint. Not all the functions of sport in culture are negative. Sport has a vast amount of good to offer. Consider the strength of the argument that follows as it describes the place that sport has in popular culture.

### *Sport as a cultural strand*

The significance of sport is not any more at issue. To be an effective citizen requires that one has an understanding of the culture in which one exists and operates, and sport is an integral part of that culture. Therefore one's knowledge of one's culture is greatly enriched by a knowledge of sport. This knowledge of and about sport also extends to the ability to take part in sport of some kind thus indicating physical and kinesthetic development.

Not only does it pervade our culture, but it has an important place in a multitude of other cultures. Thus, sport provides a commonality of experience on a global scale. Sport provides a common language which can be used to communicate within, and between, cultures. This shared experience is therefore important on a small scale locally and in community settings; it is important on a national, cultural scale; and it is important on an international, global scale. An increasing ethnic diversity in western cultures enriches the experience and has much to offer in broadening a culturally diverse appreciation. Sporting acculturation is enhanced by such diversity and extends the boundaries of personal development and cultural awareness.

Young people, or indeed any informed, rational and educated people, need to know about the society and the culture of which they are a part. This 'necessary knowledge' covers huge areas of custom, tradition and history as well as more recognisable areas of knowledge. Thus, knowing about academic subjects, taking part effectively in the democratic process, knowing about current affairs, and knowing about the place that sport holds in culture are some of the disparate elements of the informed, rational and educated person. Too often this knowledge is limited to school knowledge; the accepted, but restricted, and restrictive, diet of an authorised curriculum. Young people have a variety of talents, abilities and intelligences, and school can only serve a limited number of these.

If we accept that there are a variety of potentials in young people, and indeed in people of any age, then Gardner's proposition of multiple intelligences (Gardner, 1983) appears a very attractive interpretation. Gardner suggests that individuals have seven intelligences in one degree or another. They are linguistic–verbal, mathematical–logical, visual–spatial, musical, interpersonal, intrapersonal, and kinesthetic. An individual who is educated and developed in all of Gardner's areas would indeed be a true renaissance wo/man. But different people will have different strengths and ought to be encouraged to develop their strengths and build on their weaknesses. For this reason it is vital that teachers and all those involved in the learning process at school, in the community, and in a variety of settings, have at least a working knowledge of this multiple intelligence concept. Unfortunately, the vast majority of school education is largely restricted to just two of the seven intelligences; the linguistic-verbal and the mathematical-logical. However, schools do teach music, art and design, design and technology, and physical education which correspond approximately to musical intelligence, visual-spatial intelligence, and kinesthetic intelligence. Schools also increasingly address the inter- and intrapersonal qualities through personal, social and health education, and citizenship. However, literacy and numeracy hold a dominant place in the curriculum, and many other subjects; science, history, geography, and information and communication technology for example, are taught in a way that necessitates the mastery of linguistic–verbal and mathematical–logical skills. This may, to some extent, be unavoidable; literacy and numeracy are the conduits of educational transmission.

All of these intelligences contribute to a well-rounded individual. To omit one or more from a person's development would be to restrict that person's development. In a similar way, these intelligences approximate the qualities necessary to understand one's own culture. It is necessary to have a knowledge of literature; and music has an important place in a culture; art is important in enhancing cultural richness; and a knowledge of sports and their histories and traditions has a place as well. In this way, one can make an argument for the potential of any of Gardner's intelligences to contribute significantly to one's knowledge of one's own culture.

## Conclusion

Culture, education and sport have strong links with each other. The relationships between them demonstrate the importance of sport in education and culture. Each of these concepts have commonly-held definitions that enable discourse and debate on an academic level, but also contribute greatly to the social interactions of everyday life. In addition to enabling discourse and interaction, sport has a number of functions in society. It allows the relatively safe experience of emotional extremes, it adds to and embellishes our language, and it contributes a traditional and mythical component to our existence. Sport aids in the process of cultural and social reproduction. In this, it can possibly be seen as a functionalist mechanism leading to conformity and control. Alternatively, sport can be viewed as a cultural strand that enhances our sense of community and provides a vehicle for cross-cultural understanding on a global scale. Sport has a place in schools because society has determined that the aspect of intelligence that is kinesthetic has value and is worthy of inclusion in school education. This educational manifestation of sport should not limit itself solely to the psychomotor component of the subject but should explore all aspects of sport. Similarly, the complete beneficial potential of sport will only be understood by taking note of the full role of sport in culture and society.

## Reflection questions

1. What are 'high culture' sports and what are 'low culture' sports? Do you think these labels are appropriate? Is so, why? If not, why not?
2. Why is sport, in the form of physical education, included in the school curriculum? Discuss the function of school sport, as opposed to physical education.
3. Huizinga says that civilisation works to eliminate 'play' as people mature. How is this happening in your life?

## Tasks

1. What sub-cultures do you belong to? Describe the group norms and how they are applied.
2. In groups of four, recount to the rest of the group a personal sporting myth, legend or tradition – a moment that will live with you for ever. Question the narrator about why this is so important, how it has affected their lives, what it meant at the time, what it means now, etc.

## Further reading

Bonington, C. (2000) *Quest for Adventure: Ultimate Feats of Modern Exploration*. Washington, DC: National Geographic Society.

Inglis, F. (1977) *The Name of the Game: Sport and Society*. London: Heinemann.

Morgan, W.J. and Meier, K.V. (1988) *Philosophic Inquiry in Sport*. Champaign, IL: Human Kinetics.

## References

Brohm, J-M. (1978) *Sport – A Prison of Measured Time*. London: Ink Links.

Department of National Heritage (1995) *Sport. Raising the Game.* London: DNH.

Gardner, H. (1983) *Frames of Mind: The Theory of Multiple Intelligences.* New York: Basic Books.

Huizinga, J. (1955) *Homo Ludens.* London: Routledge & Kegan Paul.

Inglis, F. (1977) *The Name of the Game: Sport and Society.* London: Heinemann.

Kirk, D. and Tinning, R. (1990) 'Introduction: physical education, curriculum and culture', in Kirk, D. and Tinning, R. (Eds) *Physical Education, Curriculum and Culture: Critical Issues in the Contemporary Crisis*, 1–21. London: Falmer Press.

Schmitz, K.L. (1979) 'Sport and play: Suspension of the ordinary', in Gerber, E.W. and Morgan, W.J. (Eds) *Sport and the Body: A Philosophical Symposium*, 22–29. Philadelphia: Lea & Febiger.

Siedentop, D. (1994) *Sport Education: Quality PE Through Positive Sport Experiences.* Champaign, IL: Human Kinetics.

# 2 Theoretical background

*John Evans and Brian Davies*

## Introduction

Critics sometimes accuse sociology of being too abstract, too theoretical, too far removed from the interests of practitioners and irrelevant to the task of improving the quality of education in schools. This chapter suggests that these claims are largely unfounded; it emphasises the place and importance of theory in research and in the wider educational practices of Initial Teacher Education physical education (ITT PE) and teaching in schools. Looking back over the socio-cultural research of the last decade we suggest that sociological research in physical education has much to contribute to the understanding of teaching and learning in schools and ITT physical education, especially if it draws deeply on insights from social theory. The chapter draws attention to areas of achievement in research in physical education, concentrating on studies of teaching and teacher education, identity (social class, gender and ethnicity), grouping, pupil learning, curriculum organisation, policy and innovation, before going on to highlight the lacunae that remain and suggest some new directions for research on physical education. We conclude by stressing the fact that teachers face many challenges in a 'post-modern' age, not least the task of dealing with children and young people who may hold attitudes, expectations and relationships that are often markedly different from their own. Unless we have a thriving research community generating research that advances understandings of the social composition and consequences of pedagogy in physical education, teachers may be as unable to sustain their status as 'professionals' as they are of developing the kind of physical education that children and young people need.

In recent years educational research in Britain has come under attack from a number of quarters; most notoriously from former Her Majesty's Chief Inspector (HMI) Chris Woodhead (he resigned in November 2000), and also from 'new right' think tank spokespersons; occasionally criticism has come from within the ranks of educational research itself (Mortimore, 1998). The main thrust of such criticism is that the bulk of work produced by academics is too abstract, too far removed from practitioners, unusable by politicians and too much aimed at fellow academics. It is, therefore, deemed irrelevant and fundamentally flawed. The outpourings of research grounded in the social sciences, especially the sociology of education, has putatively given greatest cause for concern. Indeed there seems to be a direct line of inexplicable anxiety running from the Conservative Party Secretary of State Kenneth Baker's 1982 dictum that all teacher educators (because of their interest in social theory) ought to be 'hung from the entrails of every last educational sociologist' (Evans, Penney and Davies, 1996: 10) to Chris Woodhead's innuendo that much educational research could be lost down the pan. There may, of course, be a measure of truth in these critical comments. Perhaps educational researchers in the UK have become too esoteric, too far removed from teachers' concerns; perhaps their work has become insufficiently 'applied'. No researcher in higher education in the UK in recent years will have escaped the influence of the Higher Education Funding Council's (HFCE) 'Research Assessment Exercise', which now determines the level of research funding to be distributed to Institutes of Higher Education largely on the basis of an assessment of their research outputs. This has had a narrowing and deeply damaging effect on the development of applied educational research. We may have slipped dangerously towards a situation in which, if the findings of research cannot and are not to be published in international 'scholarly journals', then they are not considered worthy of publishing at all. In short, the more abstract the research, the better it is deemed to be. But educational researchers can hardly be blamed for this tendency towards 'abstraction', nor would many criticise the merits of this kind of work in education and physical education. They would, I suspect, baulk only at the notion that there is only one worthwhile way of doing research and one worthwhile way of disseminating findings. But whether educational researchers, including researchers in physical education, are any better or worse than their counterparts in other fields of research at disseminating their findings and relating them to policy, or addressing the interests of practitioners in the field is questionable and a matter worthy of discussion and debate. Few could accuse researchers in physical education for not trying to make their findings available to politicians. They certainly cannot be blamed if the response of government ministers driven by political agendas rather than the benefits of children in schools, do not want to hear what researchers have to say.

There is no logic to the claim that research in or on education should be geared straightforwardly to fulfilling purely instrumental ends or to informing teachers how its findings should be translated into pedagogical action in schools. Perhaps these critiques are simply expressions of a consumer culture (including governments that define us all as merely consumers of their policy products) that increasingly define only the immediately relevant and consumable as useful and really worthwhile, while anything of more enduring quality is deemed inherently worthless or fundamentally flawed. Or, alternatively, they may be expressions of a more post-modern epistemological tendency towards believing that, as all knowledge is inevitably transient and ephemeral, then no form of research, educational or otherwise, is worth doing at all (Smith, 1998). Neither are views to which we would subscribe and all open the door to mere school improvers. Unsurprisingly, in the UK, the former view has given rise to a new cliché in the political discourse on educational policy and practice; 'evidence based'. Evidence-based teaching, evidence-based management, evidence-based curriculum development, health, etc., etc. Nothing is now worth knowing or doing in education unless it is 'evidence based'. Pity help a bright, innovative idea, or those elements of education (for example, enjoyment, satisfaction, empowerment, equity, dignity, responsibility, independence) that are not easily measurable, quantifiable, or amenable to an evidence base. Montessori, Dewey, J.S. Mill; there would be no place for any of you, or your risk-taking inspirational theory and practice, in the education discourse of today. Like all good clichés, this latest one feels and sounds reasonable, intrinsically good, until squeezed for its meaning and validity; then it begins to seem fragile and as difficult to pin down as a swallow on the wing. While no educational researcher would baulk at the claim that, where possible and desirable, actions should be grounded in empirical research and inquiry as well as in other forms of advice (for example, moral judgements) few, we suspect, would want to go on to suggest that we treat complex educational problems (relating to learning, teaching, etc.,) as if they were solvable simply by throwing quick-fix data at them, like mud at a wall. To do so would be to engage in the kind of instrumental empiricism that is as disreputable in research terms as it is unlikely to lead to improvements in education and the achievement of worthwhile educational goals. We know that if research is to be of enduring value it has to be theoretically rigorous, cumulative and comprehensive in focus and, perhaps above all else, critically reflexive not only in relation to its own actions and the problems that either it wants, or others want it to explore, but also to questions such as, what problems are worth addressing? what is research for? who is setting the agendas? and whose interests does research serve? We need independence and risk-taking in research environments just as we do in teaching, classrooms and schools. The perspectives offered in this book might help take us further along that road.

It has also to be pointed out that in the UK, historically, much of the research in and on education and physical education has had an indirect impact on teaching in schools. That is to say it has traditionally been used to inform the knowledge base of teaching in physical education and in this way inform the development of pedagogy in schools. Research findings, for example, on child development, sexism and racism, curriculum innovation, the fitness and health of children, along with the more enduring ideas of philosophy and sociology, have filtered into the pedagogical process through the practices of initial teacher education and via programmes of In-service training (Inset) and continuing professional development. These opportunities for research to impact upon teaching and for students and teachers to reflect on and critique their use, value and merits have, however, all but disappeared in the UK in recent years, not because of the inadequacies of researchers but because central government policies on education have driven them out of these arenas. The content of ITT in the UK is now determined almost entirely by the instrumental requirements of a government quango, the Teacher Training Agency (TTA), while Inset opportunities for continuing professional development have all but disappeared for teachers of physical education. One can, therefore, hardly blame researchers for the consequences of government policies or, as suggested above, ministers' refusals to let the empirical insights of available research get in the way of their ideologically driven policies and their visions of how children, the curriculum, or schools, ought to be.

So why is educational and sociological research in particular singled out for special attention? Why are empirically-informed ideas and theory-driven research considered so dangerous? What is there to fear from the insights of sociology or any other brand of educational research in education and physical education?

It may be the case that these critiques have more to do with the successes of research, with what empirically-driven theory has to offer by way of an understanding of education, than with what purportedly they fail to deliver to teachers in schools. In our view, criticisms of educational research have less to do with the interests of securing 'better' educational research, 'better' policy and improving the quality of educational practice in schools, than with removing theory and critical reflection from educational research, teaching and ITT; a project initiated and championed by the narrow instrumental thinking of previous Conservative governments in the UK and which now, sadly, under New Labour, shows little sign of decline.

We would go further and suggest that the problem with research and teaching in physical education, particularly in the UK, is not that it is too abstract, too conceptual, but rather it is not theoretical enough. We stress, we use the term 'theory' here not in an elitist way to refer to something that is the commodity product of an intelligentsia in academia, but to those organised sets of ideas which endeavour to explain the nature of relationships in the social and natural world and which, in so doing, generate opportunities not just for further reflective action but also social and educational amelioration and change, and which, ideally, are generated as routinely by academic theorists as by teachers and others working in schools and ITT. Unfortunately, the instrumentalism of government policies on education in the UK has driven a sizeable wedge between these two intellectual domains when there should be greater synergy between them. Consequently, ironically, despite the many vibrant developments in social theory emanating from within Europe in recent years, which proffer significant understandings not only of the dramatic social changes that are occurring in a post-modern age but also of educational practice in schools, with few notable exceptions (for example, Fernandez-Balboa, 1997) very little of this work has been reflected in research and related literature on physical education and consequently in the thinking and practice of teachers in schools.

## 'Old ground'

Let us retrace our steps for a moment to say a little more of the relationships between theory and research and physical education, before going on suggest how more recent developments in social theory may add to our understanding of pedagogy in physical education and perhaps improve its quality.

It is now well over a decade since the publication in the UK of *Physical Education, Sport and Schooling* by the Falmer Press (Evans,1986). It was a modest text which attempted to outline an agenda of critical socio-cultural research for physical education informed notably by the interpretative social theories of Mead, Schutz and Garfinkl and the structuralist perspectives of Althusser and Marx; theories which were then being expressed in a vibrant sociology of education in the UK. It was suggested amongst other things that while the sociology of sport both in the UK and the USA had begun to address important social issues, neither mainstream sociology, then only beginning to discover the significance of 'the body' as an object of sociological enquiry (see the seminal work of Featherstone, 1982; Shilling, 1993, and David Kirk in Chapter 5), nor the embryonic and overly descriptive studies of teaching in physical education, had much to say about the complexities of physical education and the identities of children and young people in schools. By contrast the 'new sociology', as it was then somewhat misleadingly called, implored educational researchers and teachers not just to 'take' the educational problems that had become the stock in trade subject matter of much educational and sociological research of the 1950s and 60s, or the ways of approaching them methodologically, but rather to 'make' educational problems in order to look at schooling and education in new and challenging ways. For us this has meant fixing our gaze afresh on the physical cultures of schooling and their representation in the form and content of the curriculum and pedagogy of physical education.

As we have pointed out, the predominant concern of the sociology of education in Britain and the USA in the early 1950s and 60s was whether the educational system met the changing needs of an expanding industrial society. Within this framework of sociological and socio-economic thought, education was conceived as an important commodity, as a consumer good, a mark of status, and a means of personal mobility. The problem with education lay not so much with what it was or what it did but how it was distributed. Tacitly it held that the traditional curriculum was unproblematically worthwhile and educational policy was to maximise access to it. The school was seen as a complex system functioning to service the parts which other sub-systems like the family and the church also reached, and the needs of the broader society. Schools functioned to socialise children into values and norms necessary for the effective performance of their roles in society; differentiate their academic achievements and allocate their human resources to the adult role system. The person in this perspective often seemed to be little more than an amalgam of the expectations, values and attitudes handed down to them by one of a variety of socialising agencies. Deviance, or failure to succeed, was too easily explicated as an individual, familial, or sectional pathology; a view of schooling which continues to pervade the thinking of many politicians and teachers in schools.

The 'New Sociology' invited us to re-examine these issues, especially those relating to social class and educational success and failure in schools, and approach them in new ways. This, amongst other things, meant problematising (not accepting at face value) taken-for-granted assumptions about knowledge and values and about children and their families, especially the view that they were solely responsible and 'to blame' for their own success or failure in schools. Instead, we were encouraged to consider that educational processes, especially the form and content of the curriculum and the nature of pedagogy and evaluation, were also culpable. The unthinkable became thinkable. We were forced to consider that for a great many young people, particularly those from working-class homes, for girls and young women, and people from 'non mainstream' cultural groups, education, in content and conventional organisation, was neither worthwhile, nor in terms of empowerment, a very good thing. To grasp this was to challenge the most powerful of educational rhetorics – 'that education does you good'. Then (as now) nowhere was this ideal more endearingly coveted or readily propagated – usually in the form of the more you have of 'it' (fitness or physical activity) then the more it is doing you good – than within the physical education community. This signalled that we needed to consider seriously that what passes for physical education in the school curriculum is neither arbitrary nor immutable. It is a social construct laden with values that not all would adhere to or want to share. Consequently, physical education, as with the educational process more generally, inevitably makes both friends and enemies; it inspires and it alienates, it conditions and reconditions class, cultural and power structures. This, as we have pointed out, is nice for some (disproportionately middle-class, male pupils) and nasty or others. The price which has to be paid by many for their meagre receipt of knowledge (and we used this concept to refer not only to the cognitive but also physical skills, abilities and competence) is the heavy cost of knowing more sharply one's lowly place (Evans and Davies, 1986).

On the one hand then, the theoretical insights of interpretative social theory compelled us to problematise conventional ways of thinking. It involved exploring the conventions of curricular hierarchies and deconstructing the ways in which common sense categories of, for example, the 'good' and 'able' child, the 'athlete' and the 'troublemaker', of 'intelligence', 'physical ability', 'skill', 'educability', and how the social ranking of subjects, or disciplines (for example, games or dance) which might routinely be employed within physical education contexts, come to organise and constrain social reality in education and physical education. We believed that deconstructing categories (for example of 'ability', 'gender' and 'race' ) that were taken for granted in education and physical education would help reveal their socio-cultural and economic origins and enable teachers to see more clearly the potential consequences of their curriculum and pedagogical actions for the learning opportunities and identities of pupils in schools.

On the other hand the theoretical interests and insights of Marx and Althusser encouraged researchers and teachers to seek understandings of pupils' success and failure in physical education not just with reference to what went on inside classrooms in terms of the interactions between teacher and taught, or the organisation and content of the curriculum, but rather in the relationships between these phenomena and the socio-cultural and economic interests, hierarchies and ideologies prevailing both in the wider school settings and also outside them in the societies schools served. This, fundamentally, was to explore issues of power, authority and control. It meant adopting a relational view of educational processes; to consider how the actions of teachers and taught both frame and construct the social world of classrooms and the opportunities therein and how they are themselves framed and constrained by wider socio-cultural, political and ideological forces. It was to ask of education: whose voice and values matter and where lies the locus of power, authority and control?

In essence this was to do no more than suggest we take seriously the central sociological dictum that we understand the relationships between agency and structure, human action and social constraint, in contexts of education between the personal actions and interests of teachers and pupils, their school settings and wider socio-cultural and economic forces, or we do not understand human action at all. Unsurprisingly these questions seemed nihilistic and damaging to conventional ways of understanding education, especially so either to those with vested interests in sustaining an inequitable *status quo* or in fixing them up in a hurry. All educational realities, categories, subjects, stood in need of explanation. The task became to explore which persons, groups and processes, forms of knowledge and organisation, status and identity, became established in schools. We came to the view that only a Durkheimian view of necessity mediated by Basil Bernstein's brilliant focusing upon educational discourse and pedagogy (Bernstein, 1996), gave sufficient purchase on the complexity of educational struggles in physical education and sport.

We also claimed that research driven by the physical, biological and behavioural sciences in physical education, while providing an invaluable source of information for physical educators, left as many questions unanswered about the nature and purposes of educational processes as they had asked. In the research on teaching emanating from the USA and Europe, the focus was predominantly on physical education teaching, using observational schedules as the main method of describing and analysing what actually happens in physical education. Its emphasis, placed upon the measurable, the observable and the quantifiable, left us ill-informed about curriculum issues, processes of teaching and learning, and the consequences of these phenomena for children's social, physical and educational identities in schools. This tradition continues to inform the research activity of many scholars in the UK, USA and Europe (Carreiro Da Costa and Pieron, 1997). At its best freed from the crude behaviourism of an earlier era and guided by recent developments in either cognitive and constructivist psychology (Mortimore, 1999) or socio-cultural perspectives (Kirk and Macdonald, 1998) on learning, this research is beginning to provide deeper and more profound insights into how and why teachers teach; and perhaps more radically still, into how and what it is that pupils learn and meta-learn in contexts of physical activity and physical education (Hardy and Mawer, 1999).

## So what's new?

A decade on we might now consider the extent to which this research agenda has been met and what progress has been made in the sociology of physical education in the UK and elsewhere? We might also ask, with Hargreaves (1999), whether the central concerns of the sociology of education, for example, in selection, differentiation, identity, equity, the nature of socio-cultural reproduction, order and control, reflected in our 1986 text, remain valid in a post-modern age? As a good many social theorists and our own experiences have told us, in the last decade we have witnessed massive socio-economic and cultural changes. These have often been accompanied by 'monumental efforts to undertake significant educational reform' (Hargreaves, 1999: 340) in schools and in ITT. Fundamental changes in the form and organisation of economic activity throughout the western world, aided by rampant neo-liberalism, have been reflected in political policy and expectation that educational systems should operate more on the lines of the market, treat parents and pupils as 'consumers' of education and the curriculum more as a package of quality-controlled consumable goods to be acquired than as a set of rights to educationally worthwhile experiences. At the same time, as Hargreaves (ibid.) points out, the globalisation of knowledge, information and entertainment has created moral and scientific uncertainty. Conventional belief and value systems (including, for example, the once powerful grand narratives of socialism, feminism, religion and morality) are, if not breaking down, then being subjected to critical scrutiny and disbelief. Concomitantly, a resurgence of interest in notions of 'community' and national identity has emerged perhaps reflecting a search for social and psychological certainty/security and as ways of countering these globalising trends. Paradoxically, the spectres of fascism and democracy simultaneously rear their heads. Furthermore, changes in the economic base are having a profound impact on the socio-cultural infrastructure of society, dramatically altering relationships between men and women and making problematic conventional conceptions of masculinity and femininity, of what it is to be male and female in the work place, at home, and at leisure. Some of these changes have been reflected in significant educational reforms among many countries, including 'movement towards more locally managed schools, National curricular and curriculum requirements being defined less in terms of content to be covered and time to be allocated to that content, than in terms of standards, targets or outcomes that must be achieved' (ibid. 340). Responses to the more difficult socio-cultural changes relating for example, to how social class inequities and 'ability' are to be re-conceptualised and dealt with and how young men and women are to think about themselves and each other in respect of these new and changing times have, however, yet to be adequately addressed. All these changes have impacted upon teachers' work making it more complex, more demanding and, as Hargreaves (1999) and others have pointed out, in some senses more professional, in others more technical, managerial and isolating. What is not clear is just how far these changes have penetrated into the core practices of teaching and learning in classrooms and physical education. How able are teachers to cope with and either resist, adopt or adapt these changes in the interests of all the pupils in their care? Equally demanding is the question of what sort of research agenda is required to help teachers and pupils meet these modern day needs?

In our view, despite the achievements of recent years there remain serious areas of neglect in research in physical education. A number of questions need attention if we are to meet the challenges of these new and modern times. In approaching them we share Hargreaves' (1999) view that there remains no better place to begin in formulating such a research agenda than in the traditional concerns of the sociology of education and the sociology of physical education. We acknowledge that the 'new' discourses of contemporary social theory may lead to us to ask and approach old questions in new and innovative ways.

In a recent overview David Kirk (1997) identifies two significant gaps remaining in socio-cultural research in physical education: students' learning – where he calls for studies of how children learn, what children learn and how physical education contributes to the making of identity; and socio-cultural work that focuses on health education in schools. We agree, much remains to be done in each of these fields. The first echoes and extends the traditional sociological concern with the ways in which schools and physical education teachers within them select, sort and occasionally 'mix' children based on merit, achievement and ability, and/or by social class, gender, 'race' and disability (see Evans, 1993). It may be, as Hargreaves (op. cit.) contends, that in contemporary classrooms, for example in the new curricular of physical education (e.g. in the competency-driven National Curriculum of physical education or health-related exercise, or physical education examination classes) the processes of sorting and selecting pupils has become more subtle and less obvious. How are pupils identified, selected, defined and sorted in these contexts? by what and whose criteria? who is benefited and dis-benefited? Are old hierarchies of, for example, social class and physical ability dismantled or reconstructed in new ways? How do social class, gender, race and 'ability' co-mingle in these processes? We remain some way removed from having achieved detailed understandings of these processes and how teaching relates to academic and social learning, how both are constructed discursively and practically within contexts of physical education and impact upon children's sense of self, citizenship and nationality. We also need to show how these processes are mediated through forms of curriculum organisation and content, grouping policies and the pedagogies of physical education and relate discursively and materially to wider socio-economic trends. And on issues of racism, ethnicity and disability (with very few exceptions, for example the work of Tansin Benn, 1996) the silence is deafeningly loud.

In the intervening years some of the lacuna in our understandings of the forementioned processes have been filled, at least in part, by the endeavours of researchers in physical education. David Kirk (1998), for example, draws attention to some of the inroads that have been made particularly into teaching and teacher education, the social construction of gender, and curriculum policy and practice. These three broad topics, he suggests, have now attracted a critical mass of socio-cultural researchers in physical education. In the first area he highlights developments in research on teacher socialisation, recruitment into teaching, teacher education, entry into the workforce and attrition, teachers' work, lives and careers, that have been influential in steering researchers towards more recent interest in teachers' lives and careers. Furthermore, research on the social construction of gender has thrown light on the ways in which Initial Teacher

Education, historically, has been deeply gendered. It has also highlighted the continued and pervasive sexism in contemporary physical education, nurtured through sex differentiated forms of organisation and curriculum provision, curriculum planning, patterns of interaction, and the form and content of teacher talk. This research has also prompted new avenues of exploration, for example on issues of masculinity (Brown, 1999), femininity and sexuality (see Clarke, 1998; Griffin and Genasci, 1990; Oliver and Lalik, 2000; Squires and Sparkes, 1996), while leaving many enduring issues, for example, relating to the relationships between government policies, grouping policies, teaching and sexism in physical education to be further explored. Indeed it is particularly regrettable at a time when social and economic changes are dramatically altering the expectations and relationships between boys and girls and men and women, in ways that have a direct bearing on educational processes and the practices of physical education, that very little of this research is entering the thinking of policy-makers in government or is fed into the practices of ITT and schools in the UK. Recent debate surrounding New Labour's endeavour to repeal 'section 28' (the previous Conservative government's legislation prohibiting the 'promotion/treatment' of homosexuality in schools) has brought to the surface the homophobia which is endemic in society and is offering a stark reminder of the work to be done in education and physical education to contest the prejudices and intolerance that persists in society. The same may also be said of research on curriculum policy and practice. This, in recent years, has had much to say about the limits and possibilities of innovations relating for example, to the emergence of health-based physical education in Australia and the National Curriculum for physical education in England and Wales, but which has had little or no impact on the direction of government policies in education, at least not in the UK. These research developments, in drawing on social theory for their direction and understandings, have contributed not only towards theoretical issues within the sociology of education but also practical understandings of innovation and pedagogy in physical education and its consequences for what children receive in educational terms.

However, it is perhaps also worth noting that the majority of the references given in David Kirk's review of the literature suggest that much of this work has emanated from researchers in the USA, Australia and (to some degree) in Britain, rather than elsewhere in Europe, or in other countries. Perhaps this is an illusion, an artefact of the Australian vantage point from which the review was written, rather than a real lacuna in the European intellectual field of physical education. There is a substantial literature on teacher behaviour emanating, for example, from France, Portugal and Spain, which tends still to be driven by psychological theories, utilising psychometric instrumentation or similar techniques for data collection, which tells us much of what children learn but little of how or why. It does seem ironic that, while researchers elsewhere are driven by developments in social theory which are quintessentially European, much of the European research on physical education seems to remain uncontaminated and unconvinced by what these theories have to offer our understandings of physical education; a distinctive way of looking at the social world and making sense of how 'new times' are mediated by the perspectives and relationships that pupils and teachers bring to school. These criticisms, by the way, do not apply to sociological researchers in Europe who focus essentially on sport.

It is perhaps also worth noting, with David Kirk, the recent establishment of journals such as *Sport, Education and Society, Journal of Sport Pedagogy*, new outlets for socio-cultural research, along with *Quest, European Physical Education Review,* and the new *European Journal of Physical Education, Journal of Teaching in Physical Education* and *Research Quarterly for Exercise and Sport,* which are now publishing more socio-cultural material. David Kirk properly notes that these developments augur well for a field of research that is fast growing to maturity. A real momentum is developing in research in physical education generating data that can and should inform developments in schools and ITT but which in the UK is in danger of being ground to a halt by education policies and ill-conceived criticisms that may be of short-term sound bite significance to the interests of politicians but of little enduring value or relevance to the task of raising standards in education and physical education.

## Future directions

To our previous agenda for research in physical education, we, therefore, add the insights of recent social theory as proffering new directions for research for the forthcoming years. In so doing, we repeat that observations and, consequently, descriptions of classroom events are always selective, regardless of whether the method of data collection is by systematic observational schedule, impressionistic note taking or life-history story telling, as are our interpretations of the data collected. Theoretical positions, whether functionalist, interpretative, structuralist, post-structuralist or post-modern, can and do determine what is to be looked at, how data are to be collected and how they are to be explained. In the new grand narratives of post-modernism, just as in the old ones of Marxism or Feminism, this can mean that the questions raised by one position and the methods used to answer them are ignored by another position. Things can and should be otherwise if our understanding of the nature and purposes of physical education is to progress and if we are to avoid producing accounts which claim not only to have discovered the truth and the whole truth but reveal processes and positions in the social world of education to which there are no alternatives (Constas, 1996).

In recent years, a number of social theorists (for example, Lyotard, Rorty, Jameson, Foucault; for an excellent overview see Best and Kellner, 1991; Lyon, 1994), whose work has variously been referred to broadly as either post-modernist or post-structuralist, have begun to exert a considerable influence on social science and educational research in the UK and elsewhere and, gradually, on the direction of socio-cultural research in physical education (see Fernandez-Balboa 1997; Kirk, 1998). Each of these writers has something distinct to offer understandings of life in physical education classrooms and together, they provide a substantial challenge not just as to how we think (and write) about the social world but also to how it is we claim to know it and to the status and nature of the knowledge itself. Issues of representation are brought to the fore. The work of Foucault, in particular, has captured the imagination of educational researchers in the UK, prompting a rich vein of writing on the body, education policy, and the social construction of identities in classroom life. This work is not without its critics (see Hargreaves, 1999; Constas,1996; Young, 2000). One has, for example, to be a little concerned at the inherent relativism of post-modern theory, well reflected in a Foucaultian perspective and its tendency to evade, if not dismiss altogether, structural issues relating for example, to racism, gender, ability and social class. As Hargreaves (ibid.) points out in relativist theories of post-modernism, which centre 'discourse' as the main object of analysis, language is not seen as being able to bring us together and create community, it does not connect us, it constitutes us.

> Language condemns us to a cacophonous world in which all voices are different and no voice is, on rational grounds, more valid than any other. Postmodernists therefore become fascinated with the irreconcilable differences of colour, gender, sexual orientation, disability, etc. and the respective discourses through which each of these identities are constituted. In postmodernism, all of us are knowable 'others'. In post-modern theory, it is not human subjects that create language, but discourse that constitutes subjects and identities. In all this material realities of income, wealth, occupation, opportunity and class that structure people's lives differently and significantly affect how they experience education and what they gain from it, are pushed to the background or denied. Power is collapsed into the fashionable politics of discourse, identity and lifestyle and experience.
>
> (338–9)

Without wishing to sound conservatively regressive, we would also suggest that recent theoretical developments have simply shed new light on enduring issues rather than generate new questions for researchers to address. Notwithstanding these problems and leaving them aside for discussion elsewhere (see Young, 2000), we would claim that the discourses of post-modernism demonstrate the kind of commitment to 'the ideal of doubt' (Constas, 1996) that was once the trademark of the 'new' sociology of education in the UK. In this sense as Constas points out, 'postmodernism represents the reinvigoration of a sceptical attitude and should cause us to raise questions about the veracity of the frameworks used to make sense of the world' (1996: 31). We would also stress that, whether the theoretical inclinations of researchers are towards interactionist, structuralist, post-structural or post-modern, they all continue to annotate the most significant single notion produced within the sociology of education to date, namely that the form and content of educational practice both matter greatly in determining the life chances and identities of pupils in schools. What children learn from the school curriculum in general and physical education in particular derives not only from the content of the curriculum but also from the manner and mode in which it is organised and then provided and from how learning is assessed. There is no conceivable content without transmission. The work of Foucault, especially when combined with that of other social theorists and particularly when anchored to a Bernsteinian grammar of the pedagogic field (see Bernstein, 1996 and 1999) may help us look at these processes afresh.

For example, as Skelton (1997) points out, a Foucauldian perspective rejects the use of totalising theories of explanation and transformation, such as Marxism and Feminism, that were the stock in trade backdrop explanations of educational processes of the new sociology of physical education. In so doing it denudes the significance of 'structural forces' (such as capitalism or patriarchy) as explanatory tools. Instead power is viewed as multifarious and multi-located, not to be reduced to a conspiratorial group or entity, such as class interests and the state, or patriarchy (ibid. 189). The strength of this view, however, is that we are compelled to study the role of education in cultural reproduction and social control via a focus, essentially, on the 'exercise of power' and the relationships between power and knowledge. This prompts consideration of how certain values, attitudes and norms come to be identified as appropriate for education and through what mechanisms people come to accept them as legitimate. It generates questions such as, what and whose discourses are privileged in the curriculum of physical education? and how and why are certain discourses, for example, of health-related exercise and games teaching, rather than say aesthetics, dance and outdoor education, privileged and heard at this juncture in time? What are the origins of these discourses in wider 'regimes of truth' and whose interests do they serve?; and how is power, as a resource, drawn on and used by pupils and teachers to determine how and what teachers and pupils can think, teach and learn? As Skelton points out, a Foucauldian perspective invites us to look at schools as disciplinary institutions, organising physical space and time with structures which are designed to change people's behaviours along designed lines and to reinforce those behaviours using techniques of surveillance such as testing, observing and documenting aspects of students personal dispositions and feelings. In this process, students become objectified and often accept institutional definitions of themselves, which enable them, subsequently, to be politically dominated as docile beings (Skelton, 1997: 187). For Foucault then, 'the hidden curriculum of schooling would refer to those disciplinary practices that reduce individuals to docility'. If the goals of democracy and equity through education and physical education are our 'good things', the work of Foucault, and other like-minded social theorists, allows us to advance some way in the direction of answering questions of this kind, but also brings us to points where, conceptually and empirically, we are drawn to a halt by the limits of the theoretical frame and its failure to speak to our issues.

As already mentioned, many criticisms have been levelled at post-modern theory, particularly the notion that power is pluralistic and can be used by anybody at any time, in any place; particularly at a time of increasing state intervention in the education system which seems pretty widespread in the western world (Evans, Davies and Penney, 1994; Penney and Evans, 1999). In our view Foucault's work alone neither provides sufficient explanations of the social world of education and physical education or the conceptual tools to enable us to draw connections between what happens outside schools and the social construction of pedagogy and identity within them. It is to the work of Bernstein that we have turned for a more enlightening conceptual scheme. Post-modern theories invite us to consider the possibility that power resides in knowledge, that discourse can be reproduced or contested in a multiplicity of sites and is not held centrally by the state or a conspiratorial group (Skelton, 1997: 189). But how are particular forms of knowledge and discourses translated into pedagogical practices, and with what consequences for identity and consciousness? We share Bernstein's view that Foucault's analysis of power, knowledge and discourse is a mighty attempt to show the new forms of the discursive positioning of subjects. Yet there is no substantive analysis of the complex of agencies, agents, social relations through which power, knowledge and discourse are brought into play as regulative devices, nor any discussion of modalities of control. In a way it is a discourse without social relations. Further, Foucault ignores almost completely any systematic analysis of the common denominator of all discourses, education and the modalities of its transmission (Bernstein, 1996: 134).

Our research (Penney and Evans, 1999; Tomlinson, 1993) certainly confirms Bernstein's view that understanding which discourse is appropriated depends more and more today upon understanding the dominant ideology in fields of political and educational decision-making outside schools and education (e.g. inside government agencies such as the Department for Education and Employment, the Office for Standards in Education in the UK) and the complex range of sites, agencies and communities of practice, which both mediate and comprise discursive practices in education and PE (Penney and Evans, 1999; Young, 2000). The point we stress here, however, is that, with few notable exceptions (Fernandez-Balboa, 1997; Kirk *et al.*, 1997; Kirk, 1998; Penney and Evans, 1999; Tomlinson, 1993; Tinning, 1997), very little of this post-structural work, with or without the more pedagogically specific and challenging work of Bernstein added, has been applied to curriculum theory or the study of pedagogy and identity in education and physical education. In our view the insights of recent social theory give rise to macro and micro questions of the following kind.

Firstly, at the level of macro (systems) and meso (local/organisational) level analysis it would mean interrogating how the discourses (languages, ways of thinking, speaking and acting) for example, of patriarchy, social class, nationalism, 'race' and ability, or those of science and ideology, are embedded in the physical cultures (see Kirk *et al.*, 1997) of contemporary society; and how they are then mediated and shaped by local and national environments as well as by the global changes taking place on the socio-cultural and economic terrain. It would also mean interrogating how such discourses, operating outside schools, are appropriated, fused and selected through for example, processes of teacher education or government policy, for transmission within them. Whose, and what, discourses are privileged in the process? What are the sites and contexts though which they are mediated, how, if at all, are they changed in the process, and have they led to teachers becoming more or less professionalised and better or less able to deal with the contexts of complex and rapid change (Hargreaves, 1999)?

At the micro and meso level of analysis it would mean interrogating how social, economic and political changes influence the details of school and classroom practice. Inside schools we might ask, does the curriculum and the pedagogic discourses of physical education reproduce existing inequalities or do they offer a medium for lessening the inequalities of opportunity, power and knowledge in our society? If so what does innovative and progressive practice look like? How are they engendered in contexts of physical education? Are the discursive practices of physical education strongly determined by wider ideological, economic and cultural forces, or do they have a significant degree of autonomy? What are the contemporary conditions of practice that permit some schools and physical education teachers to achieve the ideal of a physical education for all, while others fail to do so? How are discourses translated into structural relations and constraints inside schools? Do they generate continuities that facilitate or limit the actions of teachers and pupils in physical education? What elements of discourse (for example of patriarchy and social class) cross-cut pedagogic discourses, old, innovative and 'new' to foster either change or stability in education and physical education?

As well as creating opportunities for children and young people schools also frame and limit them. They also socialise as they skill or de-skill. What actually happens within the physical education curriculum and classrooms, in the social relations of teaching and learning? How are discursive rules, resources and practices 'used'/implicated in the social construction of citizenship and identity? Whose and what physical cultures and identities are valued in contexts of physical education? Hargreaves makes the telling point that the curriculum and pedagogy of many public schools have tended to treat matters of cultural difference with silence. For schools to be sensitive to cultural difference, to acknowledge rather than ignore cultural identity, and to foster a belief among cultural minorities in their potential for educational achievement, requires significant modifications to all aspects of practice (for example, see the work of Benn (1996) in contexts of ITTPE and schools). Do schools and physical education teachers acknowledge and capitalise on the rich array of physical cultures that children bring to schools? As Hargreaves notes, in contexts of cultural diversity and sophisticated imagery, student identities are themselves both varied and shifting. The challenge for teachers and schools is how to accommodate these flexible identities and also what to make of them (Hargreaves,1999: 345).

Specifically we might ask, into what and whose values, norms and attributes are pupils socialised? How are pupils differently positioned by the discourses of physical education in relation to their class, gender, ability and ethnicity? What social, emotional and physical predispostions are required of pupils for them to take part in and succeed at learning in physical education. What forms of habits do schools and physical education teachers think pupils need? And how do the practices of teachers and schools square with what pupils and their communities think they need? In Hargreaves' words 'To what extent and in what ways are schools serving communities, building communities and being communities, within the complex and diverse conditions of the post-modern age?'(ibid. 347). What is the relationship between the physical cultures that children experience in their communities and those transmitted in physical education? What and how do children learn within the discursive regimes of PE classrooms? Whose voices, which pupils, what communities are and can be heard and privileged; whose voices, which pupils, what communities are silenced or ignored in contexts of physical education?

Whether these processes are evident in all communities, all schools, irrespective of their organisational contexts, the content of the curriculum, or the ethnic, class or gender of their clientele, are matters that come to the fore, as do the social relations that intersect and become complicated with class and status hierarchies such as gender and ethnicity. We need research that asks for example, do schools alienate all working-class pupils, all teenage girls, all black or Asian boys? Simply posing these questions clearly insinuates that the cultural worlds of classrooms are not contexts which are simply constructed for pupils by teachers. Both play their part in framing classroom relations, while being themselves framed, materially and discursively, by factors such as levels of resourcing, the requirements of curriculum and policy texts, organisational rules and requirements, and so on, over which they may have little or no control. Issues of agency and structure must be considered if we are to understand how processes of teaching produce particular outcomes in terms of patterns of success and failure, involvement and under-involvement, and why certain negative features of schooling and education may persist, despite the best intentions of teachers. Recent developments in social theory help us raise these questions and explore these relationships, not least those between the forms of citizenship implicating the 'good', or 'successful' pupil that teachers seek to 'produce' in their classrooms and the form and content of wider discursive frames.

All this raises questions about the nature of society being reproduced through processes of schooling, about the cultural origins of physical education teachers and about class and cultural interests, power and control. Ten years ago the 'new sociology's' curious mixture of humanistic Marxisms and interpretative sociologies helped us raise these questions and more recent sociological insights sharpen and toughen their focus and give added impetus to their exploration in exciting new ways. The enduring requirements of doing the sociology of education, whether expressed in old or new ways however, is that we examine the social bases of conventional practices and decision-making processes including those which grant or withhold access to valued forms and practices in contexts of physical education. It means interrogating the criteria which underpin curricular selections, the rationales which are used to justify them, and locating these not only within subject communities but also the particular organisational, social and political contexts of which they are more widely a part. This requires theory and methods capable of making the connections between consciousness, human agency, culture and social structure. In the study of schooling we must seek the relations between the complexities of teachers' and pupils' cultures, their actions and intentions and their relationships with forms of curricula organisation and content, the organisational contexts of schools and the communities and wider societies in which they are located. In Hargreaves terms this would require adopting a more sophisticated view of micro-macro relationships, 'avoiding the artificial conceptual boundaries' between what is inside classrooms and what is 'out there' in the world beyond. As he notes, 'What is "out there" is already "in here" in the ethnocultural diversity of students, in the technological world of virtuality through which students live their lives and which they bring to schools, in the ways that the passions and desires of minority students are relegated from the curriculum and regulated within the classroom by a Eurocentric tradition of rationalised control and so on' (1999: 351).

Our central idea two decades ago is as now: that we may only arrive at an understanding of the activities of teachers and teaching and of what pupils learn in physical education, if we view them relationally and locate them historically, organisationally, institutionally and intentionally. And we remain a long way from having exhausted these projects in the study of physical education.

## Conclusion

Let us return, then, to the question of why research generative of and dependent on social theory may seem so dangerous, so threatening to education. We share Stephen Ball's (1994) view that it is because, at its very best, theory is not just a catalytic agent of understanding but also of educational and social change. It is a vehicle for thinking otherwise, a platform for outrageous hypotheses, and for unleashing criticism. It offers a language of challenge and modes of thought other than those articulated by dominant others. Critically, it makes the familiar strange. As Goodson (1995) points out, the purpose of theory is to de-familiarise present practices and categories, to make them less self-evident and necessary, and to open up spaces for the invention of new forms of experience. He also notes that once that is taken away, once research ceases to inform teachers and teaching, teaching becomes, and can be presented as, essentially a task for technicians (ibid. 16). As we have been at pains to stress elsewhere, any demise of research on education would not then be just a problem for academia. If teaching physical education is to be seen as a profession then it will be because it is based on a set of research expertise and theoretical bodies of knowledge. We erode these elements of our practice at our peril. The message is clear, in physical education we should make research and teaching more, not less, complex, and 'theory', ideas and innovation, not our enemies but friends.

## Note

Earlier versions of this paper were presented at the European Sports Science Conference, Manchester, 1998 and at the Summer University course on Physical Education at the End of the Century, in Gandia, Spain, 1998.

## Reflection questions

1 Can there be such things as 'theory free' practice, or 'theory free' explanations of practice?
2 Is it possible to explain how students fail or succeed, with reference only to what goes on inside physical education 'classrooms'? In short, do we need micro and macro theories to make sense of what we do and see in schools?
3 What does it mean 'to problematise' our thinking about education and physical education; can theory help us do this, to be more imaginative, to 'think otherwise'?

## Tasks

1 Schools socialise as they skill children; they are as much about instruction as they are about social control (see Bernstein, 1996, intro and chapter 1). Ask a colleague to describe the students in one of their physical education lessons. What hierarchies emerge? See if you can uncover in their responses, the social and physical traits and attributes required of students, if they are to be defined as 'good and/or successful'. How do the social norms and values of the physical education classroom relate to the social mores and values of the wider school context and the communities they serve?
2 Can theories of the 'post-modern' (see for example, Hargreaves, 1994; Best and Kellner, 1991) help inform the development of practice in physical education? Explore, in particular, whether, and how, ideas about the 'post-modern identity' (e.g. Peterson, 1998) are reflected in the curriculum of physical education.

## Further reading

Bernstein, B. (1996) *Pedagogy, Symbolic Control and Identity, Theory, Research, Critique.* London: Taylor and Francis.
Oliver, K.L. and Lalik, R. (2000) *Bodily Knowledge, Learning about Equity and Justice with Adolescent Girls.* New York: Peter Lang.
Jones, R.L. and Armour, K.M. (2000) *Sociology of Sport, Theory and Practice.* London: Longman.

## References

Ball, S. (1994) Intellectuals or technicians? The urgent role of theory in educational studies. Annual Address to the Standing Conference for Studies of Education, RSA, 4 November 1994.

Best, S. and Kellner, D. (1991) *Postmodern Theory – Critical Interrogations.* London: Macmillan.

Benn, T. (1996) Muslim women and physical education in initial teacher education. *Sport, Education and Society*, 1, 1, 5–23.

Bernstein, B. (1996) *Pedagogy, Symbolic Control and Identity: Theory, Research and Critique*. London: Taylor and Francis.

Bernstein, B. (1999) Vertical and horizontal discourse: an essay. *British Journal of Sociology of Education*, 20, 2, 157–175.

Brown, D. (1999) Complicity and reproduction in teaching physical education. *Sport, Education and Society*, 4, 2, 143–161.

Carreiro Da Costa and Pieron, M. (1997) Teaching the curriculum: policy and practice in Portugal and Belgium. *The Curriculum Journal*, 8, 2, 231–249.

Clarke, G. (1998) Queering the pitch and coming out to play: lesbians in physical education and sport. *Sport, Education and Society*, 3, 2, 145–161.

Constas, M.A. (1996) The changing nature of educational research and a critique of postmodernism. *Educational Researcher*, 27, 2, 26–33.

Evans, J. (1986) *Physical Education, Sport and Schooling: Studies in the Sociology of Physical Education*. London: The Falmer Press.

Evans, J. (1993) *Equality, Education and Physical Education.* Lewes: Falmer Press.

Evans, J. and Davies, B. (1986) 'Sociology, Schooling and Physical Education', in Evans, J. (Ed.) *Physical Education, Sport and Schooling: Studies in the Sociology of Physical Education,* 11–41. London: The Falmer Press.

Evans, J., Davies, B. and Penney, D. (1994) Whatever happened to the subject and the state in policy research in education. *Discourse: the Australian Journal of Educational Studies*, 14, 2, 57–65.

Evans, J., Penney, D. and Davies, B. (1996) 'Back to the future: education policy and physical education', in Armstrong, N. (Ed.) *New Directions in Physical Education,* 1–19. London: Cassell.

Featherstone, M. (1982) The body in consumer culture. *Theory, Culture and Society*, 1, 2, 18–33.

Fernandez-Balboa, J-M. (1997) *Critical Postmodernism in Human Movement, Physical Education and Sport.* Albany: SUNY.

Goodson, I. (1995) 'Trendy Theory and Teacher Professionalism', in *Re-Thinking UK Education: What Next?,* 15–28. London: CEDAR, Roehampton Institute.

Griffin, P. and Genasci, J. (1990) 'Addressing homophobia in physical education: responsibilites for teachers and researchers', in Messner, M.A. and Sabo, D.F. (Eds) *Sport, Men and the Gender Order.* Leeds: Human Kinetics.

Hardy, C.A. and Mawer, M. (1999) *Learning and Teaching in Physical Education.* London: Falmer Press.

Hargreaves, A. (1994) *Changing Teachers, Changing Schools: Teachers' Work and Culture in a Postmodern Age.* London: Cassell.

Hargreaves, A. (1999) Schooling in the New Millennium: educational research for the post-modern age. *Discourse: studies in the cultural politics of education,* 20, 3, 333–357.

Kirk, D. (1997) 'Socio-cultural research in physical and health education: recent trends and future developments', in Wright, J. (Ed.) *Researching in Physical and Health Education,* 5–23. University of Woolongong.

Kirk, D. (1998) *Schooling Bodies: School Practice and Public Discourse 1880–1950.* Leicester University Press.

Kirk, D. and Macdonald, D. (1998) Situated learning in physical education. *Journal of Teaching in Physical Education,* 17, 3, 376–387.

Kirk, D., Macdonald, D. and Tinning, R. (1997) The social construction of pedagogic discourse in physical education teacher education in Australia. *The Curriculum Journal,* 8, 2, 271–299.

Lyon, D. (1994) *Postmodernity.* Buckingham: The Open University Press.

Mortimore, P. (1998) A concerted offensive in quango land. *The Times Higher Education Supplement,* April, 3, 13.

Mortimore, P. (1999) *Understanding Pedagogy and its Impact on Learning.* London: PCP.

Oliver, K.L. and Lalik, R. (2000) *Bodily Knowledge, Learning about Equity and Justice with Adolescent Girls.* New York: Peter Lang.

Penney, D. and Evans, J. (1999) *Politics, Policy and Practice in Physical Education.* London: E. and F.N. Spon/Routledge.

Peterson, A. (1998) *Unmasking the Masculine, 'Men' and 'Identity' in a Sceptical Age.* London: Sage.

Shilling, C. (1993) *The Body and Social Theory.* London: Sage.

Skelton, A. (1997) Studying hidden curricula: developing a perspective in the light of post modern insights. *Curriculum Studies,* 5, 2, 177–195.

Smith, J.K. (1998) 'Learning to Live with Relativism', in Hodkinson, P. (Ed.) *The Nature of Educational Research: Realism, Relativism or Post-Modernism?.* The Manchester Metropolitan University.

Squires, S.L. and Sparkes, A.C. (1996) Circles of silence: sexual identity in physical education and sport. *Sport, Education and Society,* 1, 1, 77–103.

Tinning, R. (1997) 'Performance and Participation Discourses in Human Movement: Towards a Socially Critical Physical Education' (op. cit.), in Fernandez-Balboa (Ed.) *Critical Postmodernism in Human Movement, Physical Education and Sport,* 99–121. Albany: SUNY.

Tomlinson, A. (1993) Interrogating the policy text, in education, sport and leisure: connections and controversies. *CSRC Topic Report 3*, Chelsea School Research Centre, 85–93.

Young, M.F.D. (2000) Rescuing the sociology of educational knowledge from the extremes of voice discourse: towards a new theoretical basis for the sociology of the curriculum. *British Journal of Sociology of Education*, 21, 4, 523–536.

# 3 Methodological issues in research

*Matthew Curtner-Smith*

## Introduction

The main aim of this chapter is to provide an overview of the methods employed by those who do sport pedagogy research. This research includes studies of physical education teaching and coaching, physical education teacher and coach education, physical education teachers and coaches, pupils in physical education programmes and those who participate in sport and physical activity, and physical education and coaching curricula. Additional goals for this chapter are to outline some of the major research findings from this body of work and to provide examples of specific types of research. Despite these aims, readers should be aware that this chapter does not include an exhaustive literature review or even an extensive review of research methods. Rather, it is intended as a starting point for those who are new to the research process and to help promote understanding of the chapters which follow in the rest of this book.

## Paradigms for sport pedagogy research

To date, researchers of sport pedagogy have operated within one of three paradigms: the positivist paradigm, the interpretive paradigm, and the critical paradigm. Each of these paradigms provides a different lens for viewing and understanding the world of human activity (Sparkes, 1994a). Not surprisingly then, researchers working within each paradigm seek to answer different types of questions about physical education and sport. Moreover, they often employ different methods for gathering information (data collection) and making sense of this information (data analysis), the two processes which they hope will allow them to arrive at answers to their questions. In the following three sections, I will describe the main goals of those working within the positivist, interpretive, and critical paradigms as well as the methods by which they collect and analyse data. In each section specific examples of recently conducted studies will be provided and some of the main contributions made to the field by researchers working within each paradigm will be described.

## The positivist paradigm

Those doing research within the positivist paradigm seek to examine the social world in the same manner as natural scientists have investigated the physical world (Sparkes, 1994a). They believe that human activity (in our case, physical education teaching and coaching) can be broken down into discrete and measurable components (Schempp and Choi, 1994). Their goals are to describe, predict, and change these components (Silverman, 1996) (see Table 1). To achieve these goals, researchers focus on specific aspects of teaching or coaching and attempt to analyse them in as much detail as possible (Lee, 1996). Once patterns of actions or thoughts are discovered within one group of teachers, coaches, pupils, or players, the belief is that other groups will act and think in the same way. Moreover, if researchers are successful in their attempts to alter the actions or thoughts of one group of teachers, coaches, pupils, or players, the assumption is

*Table 1* Paradigms for research in sport pedagogy

| | *PARADIGMS* | | |
|---|---|---|---|
| | *Positivist* | *Interpretive* | *Critical* |
| **Goals** | To describe, predict and change components of human activity | To understand human activity in specific situations from the participants' perspective | To understand power within society and facilitate the emancipation of oppressed groups and individuals |
| **Methods** | Tend to use **quantitative** methods | Tend to use **qualitative** methods | |
| **Designs** | Descriptive<br>Correlational<br>Experimental | Ethnographies<br>Case studies<br>Life histories<br>Critical incident<br>Ethnographic fiction | |
| **Data collection** | Surveys<br>Inventories<br>Questionnaires<br>Tests<br>Focus groups<br>Systematic observation | Observations (field notes)<br>Formal interviews<br>Informal interviews<br>Stimulated recall interviews<br>Thinking aloud<br>Journal writing<br>Document analysis<br>Critical incident writing<br>Story-writing<br>Open-ended questionnaire<br>Projective slide viewing<br>Video commentary<br>Case discussions | |
| **Data analysis** | Statistical description<br>Statistical testing | Search for categories and themes | |

that they would also succeed were they to try the same types of interventions with other similar groups.

Positivist sport pedagogy researchers employ many of the same methods used by natural scientists. This means that they tend to use quantitative methods to gather numerical data. Their work is aimed at providing numerical illustrations of teaching/coaching (descriptive studies), discovering relationships between components of teaching/coaching (correlational studies), or attempting to change some aspect of teaching/coaching (experimental studies).

Positivist sport pedagogy researchers aim to be as objective as possible by attempting to rule out any human bias during data collection and analysis. Data collection techniques include the use of surveys, inventories, and tests which yield numerical scores to various questions or items. In addition, a technique called systematic observation (see Darst, Zakrajsek, and Mancini, 1989) is often used to quantify the behaviours of teachers, coaches, pupils and players. For example, many researchers have recorded the amount of time teachers/coaches and pupils/players spend in various behaviours (e.g. demonstration and skill practice) while others have recorded the number of times that teachers/coaches and pupils/players have used or been engaged in various behaviours (e.g. feedback statements and practice trials). Data analysis usually includes the production of a statistical description of the actions, thoughts, or behaviours of the group (or various sub-groups within the group) being studied. It can also involve the use of statistical tests designed to tease out relationships among various actions, thoughts, or behaviours or differences between the actions, thoughts, or behaviours of various sub-groups.

### *Evolution*

Positivism has been, and arguably still is, the dominant paradigm for sport pedagogy research (Sparkes, 1994a). Indeed, until relatively recently it was the only paradigm within which sport pedagogy researchers worked.

The first efforts at serious pedagogical research in the classroom began in the 1940s (Lee, 1996). At this stage, researchers asked administrators (e.g. headteachers or their equivalent) and pupils to identify their best teachers and then set about trying to discover whether highly rated teachers possessed common personal characteristics (e.g. sex, age, I.Q., appearance) (Graham and Heimerer, 1981). These so-called ‘best teachers’ were found to be warm, caring, and organised but, since no attempt was made to measure pupil learning or observe them in their work, nothing was learned about their effectiveness.

A second phase of research followed during which the test scores of pupils taught by one method were compared with those of pupils taught by another (Lee, 1996). Again, teachers using either method were not observed. Instead, it was assumed that they employed significantly different behaviours (Graham and Heimerer, 1981). In general, the results of these studies were also disappointing since their authors often found that the academic performances of pupils taught by either method were similar. One suggested reason for this finding was that, in actuality, the methods employed by the teachers in these experiments did not differ a great deal (Lee, 1996).

Mirroring the efforts of classroom researchers, some of those who conducted early studies in sport pedagogy unsuccessfully attempted to identify the common personal traits of highly-rated physical education teachers (Placek and Locke, 1986). Others, often working within the framework of motor learning, compared methods of teaching the subject in laboratory settings (Nixon and Locke, 1973). As noted by Locke (1977), these efforts, and those of researchers who ventured out of their motor learning laboratories and into schools, also generally ended in failure because the gymnasium had been treated like a 'black box':

> The standard drill has been to feed teachers, kids, hardware, curriculum or organization in at one end of the gym, and to observe various consequences at the other end. It was assumed that you could safely ignore the process events which went on inside. Those points at which teachers, kids, hardware, curriculum and organization collided were presumed irrelevant, or at least beyond serious contemplation
>
> (10)

By the mid-1970s, sport pedagogy researchers had largely given up on black box methods experiments and, again following the lead of those who studied the pedagogy of classroom subjects, began to observe instruction in the gymnasium and on the playing field directly. The development of systematic observation instruments to code, categorise, and quantify the behaviours of teachers, coaches, pupils and players at this stage proved to be revolutionary and, for many, marked the beginning of productive sport pedagogy research (Placek and Locke, 1986).

The initial aim of researchers equipped with systematic observation instruments was to provide quantitative illustrations of how teachers and pupils spent their time during physical education lessons. The data produced during this early descriptive work provided the basis for studies in which researchers attempted to discover links between the actions of teachers and pupils during lessons and pupils' motor skill learning. These process-product studies, in turn, provided the foundation for intervention studies during which attempts were made to change the behaviours of practising and preservice teachers and those of their pupils during lessons in order to increase pupils' learning (Metzler, 1989). As noted by Silverman (1991), key findings from this type of 'effectiveness' research were that teachers who provided good demonstrations and clear explanations, allocated time for skill practice, and organised practice so that pupils were engaged successfully promoted learning. Unfortunately, much of the descriptive work indicated that pupils spent relatively little time engaged in successful practice and, instead, spent a great deal of time waiting to take part in activity (Metzler, 1989). On the upside, researchers found that it was relatively easy to change the behaviours of practising or student teachers for the better (Smith, 1992).

The successful employment of systematic observation instruments and what Rosenshine and Furst (1973) called the 'descriptive, correlational, experimental loop' in physical education meant that some researchers also attempted to use the same formula within the coaching setting.

A reasonable amount of work describing the behaviour of coaches and players during practice and game play is now available (e.g. see Aicinena, Steffen and Smith, 1992; Curtner-Smith, Wallace and Wang, 1998; Lacy and Martin, 1994). As yet, however, only a few attempts have been made to conduct correlational and experimental studies in this area (e.g. Curtner-Smith, Wallace and Wang, 1999).

Research on physical education teacher and coach effectiveness may well get a boost in the near future due to a relatively new form of systematic observation developed by Sharpe (see Sharpe, 1997a, 1997b; Sharpe and Hawkins, 1992). This computerised procedure, known as field systems analysis, is more flexible than, and technologically superior to, traditional forms of systematic observation. For example, it allows the researcher to measure and graph frequency, rate, and duration of the behaviours coded and is capable of predicting sequences of behaviours (e.g. see Fabian Lounsbery and Sharpe, 1999).

At the same time as some sport pedagogy researchers were developing and collecting data with systematic observation instruments, others began to design more sophisticated questionnaires, inventories and surveys to study different aspects of instruction (Schempp and Choi, 1994). For example, several researchers have used the Value Orientation Inventory (Ennis and Chen, 1993; Ennis and Hooper, 1988) to study practising and preservice physical education teachers' beliefs about curricular goals (e.g. Curtner-Smith and Meek, 2000; Ennis and Chen, 1995). Others have tried to examine physical education teacher development with the Teacher Concerns Questionnaire (George, 1978) and the Student Teacher Anxiety Scale (Hart, 1987) (e.g. Capel, 1998; Meek, 1996). Finally, a number of researchers have employed variations of the Task and Ego Orientation in Sport Questionnaire (Duda, 1993) to investigate the factors which motivate children and youth to participate in physical activity and sport (e.g. Carpenter and Morgan, 1999).

### *Examples of positivist studies*

#### *Description*

Some of the work that I have been involved with provides a straightforward example of descriptive research (e.g. Curtner-Smith, Hasty and Kerr, in press; Curtner-Smith, Todorovich, Lacon and Kerr, 1999). During this work, my colleagues and I videotaped teachers while they were teaching a variety of activities before and after the National Curriculum for Physical Education (NCPE) was introduced. We then coded these videotapes with a series of systematic observation instruments so as to provide numerical descriptions of the teachers' teaching styles and managerial systems and their behaviours related with pupils' skill, psychosocial, and health-related development. Results indicated that the introduction of the NCPE had little impact on the teachers' instruction. In addition, findings revealed that the teachers favoured direct styles of teaching, had well-established managerial routines and expectations, used behaviours likely to enhance pupils' self-esteem and skill learning, but did not incorporate health as a permeating theme.

Another good example of descriptive research was produced by Cale (2000). During this study, forty-two heads of physical education departments in central England completed a questionnaire designed to gather information about their capacity to promote physical activity. Data generated during this study included the average time allocated for pupils to engage in compulsory physical education and the percentage of schools offering specific health-related and extracurricular activities.

### *Correlational*

Silverman and his colleagues have produced a number of process-product studies in the last fifteen years (e.g. Silverman, 1985; Silverman, Kulinna and Crull, 1995). In his often cited study of 1985, a group of university students was pre-tested on their ability to execute the survival float (a swimming skill), given instruction on that skill, then post-tested. The instructional periods were video-taped and systematically coded. Statistical analyses revealed that the more times the students practised the skill successfully during the instructional periods, the more their performance of it improved from pre- to post-test.

### *Experimental*

Since the early 1980s, a number of sport pedagogy researchers have been successful in their attempts to change the behaviours of individual practising or preservice teachers (e.g. Meek and Smith, 1998; Smith, Kerr and Meek, 1993). For example, Smith, Kerr and Meek (1993) conducted a ten-lesson experiment aimed at increasing the number of feedback statements made by one experienced British physical education teacher while teaching swimming, track, and rounders to pupils in Years 5 to 8. During the early lessons of the study, the number of feedback statements given by the teacher which were intended to improve pupils' performances and aimed at motivating pupils was counted and the rates of feedback statements per minute were calculated. Following the fourth and seventh lessons, these data were presented to the teacher in graphic and written form during thirty-minute meetings. At the completion of each lesson after the initial intervention meetings had taken place, the rates per minute at which the teacher used each of these types of feedback were also relayed to him verbally and in writing. Results of the study indicated that, collectively, these interventions produced a considerable increase in the amount of feedback the teacher gave to his pupils during the practice phases of his lessons.

Relatively few experimental studies involving groups of teachers or pupils have been conducted by sport pedagogy researchers in the last ten years. One such experiment, however, was completed recently by Todorovich (1999). The main purpose of this study was to find out whether pupils' goal orientations (i.e. how pupils determine whether or not they are successful) could be influenced by manipulating the orientation climate of their physical education lessons. The young primary-aged pupils in the study were randomly assigned to one of three groups. A task-oriented group was taught a ten-lesson modified hockey unit within a climate designed to promote a task orientation (i.e. success is determined by whether or not and by how much one can improve one's own performance). An ego-oriented group was taught a ten-lesson modified hockey unit within a climate designed to develop an ego orientation (i.e. success is determined by comparing one's performance with others). In addition, a control group was taught a ten-lesson modified softball unit in which no effort was made to modify the instructional climate. All thirty lessons were videotaped and coded with a systematic observation instrument which verified that task, ego, and mixed instructional climates had been created. Pupils completed the Task and Ego Orientation in Sport Questionnaire before and after their respective ten-lesson units. This pencil and paper inventory measured their dispositions for the task and ego orientations. Statistical tests showed that the pupils taught within the task-involving climate strengthened their task orientations while those taught within the ego-involving climate strengthened their ego orientations. Todorovich concluded, therefore, that it was possible for physical education teachers to alter pupils' goal orientations by creating different instructional climates.

## The interpretive paradigm

Those who conduct research within the interpretive paradigm do not believe that the social world can be studied in the same manner as the physical world (Sparkes, 1994a). Since human activity is based on intentions and beliefs which may differ from culture to culture, person to person, or from one time period to another, they believe that it is impossible to develop a set of universal rules which explain why humans act, think, and behave in specific ways (Borg and Gall, 1989). Rather, they believe that 'multiple interpretations' of human activity are possible (Sparkes, 1994a). For this reason, interpretive sport pedagogy researchers attempt to understand physical education and coaching in specific settings and at specific times from the perspectives of teachers, coaches, teacher educators, pupils and players (Silverman, 1996). To realise this goal, they use 'a wider angle lens' (Lee, 1996) than positivists and emphasise that the whole setting, including historical, political, social, and cultural influences, must be taken into account (Borg and Gall, 1989).

Interpretive sport pedagogy researchers use many of the same methods employed by social scientists working in the fields of anthropology and sociology (Schempp and Choi, 1994). This means that they tend to use qualitative techniques to gather data in the form of text (i.e. the written or spoken word). Unlike positivists, interpretive researchers usually rely on their own skills and wits to collect and analyse data since they believe that non-human instruments are not sophisticated or flexible enough to adapt to complex social settings (Borg and Gall, 1989). As explained by Sparkes (1994a) 'interpretive research is an intensely interactive and personal process of engagement that relies heavily on the social skills and creative capacities of the researcher' (14).

Also in contrast to positivists, interpretive researchers argue that it is impossible not to be biased during the research process. Although they strive not to contaminate the setting and participants they are studying so that their findings and conclusions are developed from or 'grounded' in the data (Sparkes, 1994a), they realise that this is a goal that is virtually impossible to accomplish. When writing reports of their research, therefore, they will generally go out of their way to explain relevant aspects of their own backgrounds (e.g. beliefs, values, race, socio-economic status, politics, relationships with participants) so that readers will have an idea of their biases and how these might have affected data collection and analysis.

The primary data collection methods used by interpretive sport pedagogy researchers to date have been observations of the setting being studied (e.g. a particular physical education class) during which copious notes are taken (e.g. Sage, 1987), formal interviews of key participants (e.g. teachers, coaches) which are generally tape-recorded and transcribed (e.g. Armour and Jones, 1998), and informal interviews (e.g. conversations with teacher or coach educators) which are usually recorded in writing as soon after they occur as possible (e.g. Curtner-Smith, 1999). In addition, some interpretive sport pedagogy researchers have collected documents (e.g. lesson plans, exams, student teacher evaluations, newspaper articles about a school) which might help explain participants' thoughts, dispositions and actions (e.g. Curtner-Smith, 1997) while others have asked participants to complete open-ended questionnaires (e.g. Nugent and Faucette, 1995) or keep a journal (e.g. Curtner-Smith, in press).

A few sport pedagogy researchers working within the interpretive paradigm have also employed focus groups during which small numbers of participants (e.g. three or four pupils or players) are formally interviewed at one time (e.g. Carlson and Hastie, 1997). Fewer still have used case discussions in which a group of practising or preservice teachers discusses a fictional but authentic story or 'case' about physical education teaching or coaching (e.g. Bolt, 1998).

A number of researchers have used stimulated recall interviews to generate data (e.g. Byra and Sherman, 1993). This technique might involve a student teacher observing one of his/her videotaped lessons and attempting to explain to an interviewer why particular courses of action were taken at specific stages during the lesson. A data collection technique sometimes used in conjunction with stimulated recall involves a coach or teacher being audiotaped 'thinking aloud' while planning a lesson, practice or single task (e.g. Allison, 1990).

Two techniques which are similar in nature to stimulated recall are video commentary (see Byra, 1996) and projective slide viewing (see Behets, 1996). According to Byra and Goc Karp (2000), the first of these techniques involves a practising or preservice teacher viewing a videotape of one of his/her lessons in its entirety before answering in writing a set of questions predetermined by the researcher. Researchers using the projective slide viewing technique, on the other hand, ask participants to make written or verbal statements while viewing a series of slides or a single slide depicting teaching or coaching events.

Another qualitative data collection technique that has been used with some success by sport pedagogy researchers is critical incident writing (e.g. see Curtner-Smith, 1996). This technique, developed by Flanagan (1954), involves participants reporting, in writing, incidents which they find particularly significant during a set time period (e.g. a physical education lesson, extracurricular sports practice, school day).

Finally, in more recent years, a small number of sport pedagogy researchers have argued that narrative analysis or story-writing could help provide a deeper understanding of the cultures of sport and physical education (see Oliver, 1998; Sparkes, 1997, 1999). Using this technique involves a researcher drawing on qualitative data in an attempt to construct an authentic but fictional account of the lives of teachers, coaches, pupils, players, teacher educators, or coach educators complete with characters and a plot.

Interpretive sport pedagogy researchers often employ more than one data collection technique. For example, they might use a combination of observations, formal and informal interviews, and document analysis. Using multiple data collection techniques enables researchers to be more confident that their interpretations of the data are accurate or 'trustworthy'. Analysis usually involves researchers coding and categorising their data and searching for themes. Some use computer programs to complete this task (e.g. QSR NUD*IST, 1995) while others use more basic methods such as colour coding or literally cutting and pasting pieces of data. Analysing qualitative data, then, is an untidy business which many argue is more of an art than a science.

Interpretive sport pedagogy researchers have used several different designs. Obviously, those who have asked participants to report critical incidents have employed the critical incident design and those who have dabbled with fictional story-writing have produced 'ethnographic fiction'. A number of researchers have also employed the life history design during which participants' (e.g. teachers, teacher educators, coaches) perspectives and practices are explained by examining their 'life stories' for political, social and historical influences (see Sparkes, 1994b).

A more often used qualitative design is ethnography, defined by Borg and Gall (1989) as 'an in-depth analytical description of an intact cultural scene' (387) (e.g. one school's physical education department or one physical education class). Typically, this type of study involves long periods of observation or 'field work' as well as many informal and some formal interviews and document analysis (Schempp and Choi, 1994).

For some, another design, known as the case study (see Stake, 1988), is virtually synonymous with ethnography (Borg and Gall, 1989). For others, the difference between these two designs appears to be explained by the complexity, size and number of participants in the cultural scene the researcher is attempting to understand. For example, case studies are more likely to involve the investigation of individual or small groups of physical education teachers while ethnographies might involve all the physical education teachers in one community.

***Evolution***

Interpretive research methods were first used in earnest by a few sport pedagogy researchers in the late 1970s and early 1980s (e.g. Templin, 1981) who were interested in physical education teacher socialisation. That is, they sought to explain why physical education teachers acted, behaved, and thought as they did (Lee, 1996). The number of sport pedagogy researchers interested in how teachers (e.g. Sparkes and Mackay, 1996; Templin, Sparkes and Schempp, 1991), and to a lesser extent coaches (e.g. Sage, 1989) and teacher educators (e.g. Dodds *et al.*, 1999), are socialised has grown considerably in the last fifteen years. Using theory originally developed by those studying classroom teachers (e.g. Lacey, 1977; Lortie, 1975) and employing a variety of interpretive methods, these researchers have examined the effects of biography, teacher education programmes, and the school culture on the perspectives and practices of the participants in their studies. Despite generating a fair amount of data and several well-written accounts which synthesise what is known about the socialisation of physical education teachers, teacher educators and coaches (e.g. Stroot, 1993), some scholars believe that much more of this kind of research is needed (e.g. Evans, Davies and Penney, 1996).

Since the early 1980s, the focus of sport pedagogy research has widened considerably (Lee, 1996) and many different aspects of physical education/coaching have been studied using interpretive methods (Byra and Goc Karp, 2000). For example, researchers have examined the thought processes involved in teacher planning (e.g. Barrett, Sebren and Sheehan, 1991); curriculum change (e.g. Evans and Penney, 1993); pupils' views about physical education (e.g. Pugsley, Coffey and Delamont, 1996), pupils' participation styles (e.g. Bennett, 2000); the managerial, instructional, and social systems which exist in the gymnasium (e.g. Carlson and Hastie, 1997); teachers' values and beliefs (e.g. Ennis, 1994); pupils' thoughts and feelings during instruction (e.g. Hare and Graber, 2000); young players' competitive anxiety (e.g. Peach and Thomas, 1999); and how teachers acquire the knowledge to teach specific content (e.g. Rovegno, 1994).

Byra and Goc Karp (2000) suggested that the dramatic increase in the amount of interpretive sport pedagogy research in the last decade is the result of several factors. First, in the mid-1980s, a number of highly-regarded educational researchers argued that studying instruction from a single perspective (i.e. positivism) was limiting (Evertson and Smylie, 1987; Shulman, 1986). Second, at the same time, the editorial boards of some leading sport pedagogy journals went out of their way to encourage the use of interpretive methods (e.g. Templin and Griffey, 1987). Finally, a number of well-known sport pedagogy and sport sociology researchers published commentaries on the interpretive paradigm which were widely read (e.g. Earls, 1986).

## *Examples of interpretive studies*

### *Ethnography*

As noted above, I have spent a good part of the last eight years examining the influence of the NCPE on teachers and their teaching. Part of this investigation involved carrying out an ethnographic study with the aim of describing twenty-three teachers' differing interpretations of the new curriculum and identifying the factors which led to these interpretations (see Curtner-Smith, 1999). These teachers worked in eight secondary schools situated in three towns in the south of England. I collected data by observing the teachers and taking field notes, conducting formal and numerous informal interviews, and collecting relevant documents. I then searched for categories and themes in the mountain of data I had gathered. This process revealed that the teachers' interpretations of the NCPE were either innovative, conservative or eclectic. The factors which led to these interpretations included the teachers' genders, experience, participation in sport and physical activity, colleagues, teacher education and experiences of school physical education and sport as pupils.

### *Case study*

Two other researchers interested in the effects of the NCPE were Laws and Aldridge (1995). During their study of one urban secondary school's physical education department, they collected data by observing and interviewing the five teachers in the department, employing an open-ended questionnaire, and collecting relevant documents such as the department's policy statement and timetable. Key findings were that the teachers were reluctant to alter their teaching at all following the introduction of the NCPE because they believed that they were already meeting its requirements or were complacent. Moreover, while two of the teachers thought that the new curriculum might be beneficial, two thought it undervalued their efforts, and two thought that it caused them to engage in work that was unnecessary.

### *Life history*

During a year-long study, Armour (1997) observed and interviewed the four physical education teachers working in one secondary school located on the outskirts of a large English city. In addition she asked the teachers to complete open-ended questionnaires. Her aim was to explore these teachers' life histories in order to explain their differing personal philosophies about physical education teaching and the practices they employed. Results indicated that the teachers' perspectives and practices were heavily influenced by their families, experiences of school as pupils, teacher education, and the culture of the school in which they were employed. Moreover, sport had been important to all four teachers throughout their lives and had played a major part in the development of their beliefs and values.

### *Critical incident*

As part of a study of the effects of a secondary early field experience, O'Sullivan and Tsangaridou (1992) asked thirty-nine undergraduate physical education students to write critical incident reports after each of four lessons which they had taught and following the completion of the course. These data were analysed with the goal of discovering which issues the students focused on while learning to teach and whether these issues changed during the course of the early field experience. In contrast to most of the previously conducted research, results of the study indicated that the students focused on elements of teaching related to pupil achievement and learning.

### *Ethnographic fiction*

As yet, very few sport pedagogy researchers have attempted to write ethnographic fiction (Oliver, 1998; Sparkes, 1999). Sparkes (1999) noted, however, that one researcher who has employed this design is Denison (1996). He went on to explain that Denison examined the lives and experiences of twelve high level athletes from New Zealand once they had retired through interviewing and the writing of field notes. Rather than reporting the actual categories and themes that emerged during the course of the study, Denison drew on his data to write three short fictional stories about the effects of retirement on athletes.

## The critical paradigm

Those who conduct research within the critical paradigm also tend to use qualitative methods to collect and analyse data (Schempp and Choi, 1994). Their main goals, however, are to understand power within society and improve the lot of oppressed individuals and groups by facilitating their emancipation and enabling them to take charge of their own lives (Sparkes, 1994a). Critical researchers, then, are interested in documenting privilege, repression, and the dominance of one group over others. In addition, they try to create change which leads to greater social justice. They aim to expose perspectives and practices that, to most, seem normal but when subjected to closer inspection clearly promote inequality and are unfair (Schempp and Choi, 1994). Not surprisingly, critical researchers often have an obvious social and political agenda which is aimed at empowering the participants in their studies (Silverman, 1996).

Some sport pedagogy researchers have attempted to uncover or draw attention to privilege and injustice that is peculiar to physical education and sport (e.g. the marginalisation and low status of physical education teachers). Others have attempted to tie inequalities which occur in the gymnasium to broader social structures and attitudes (e.g. racism, sexism, élitism) or sought to understand how physical education and sport help to promote and maintain inequalities (e.g. homophobia) which are prevalent in the wider society (Schempp and Choi, 1994). Regardless of whether researchers have taken a micro or macro perspective, their aim has been to produce improved learning, working and playing conditions for teachers, coaches, teacher educators, pupils and players.

### *Evolution*

Sport pedagogists did not begin doing critical research until comparatively recently (Silverman, 1991). The critical paradigm is, therefore, the least developed of the three paradigms in which sport pedagogy researchers have worked. Schempp and Choi (1994) suggest that this is primarily because sport pedagogists have tended to be relatively conservative when compared to those who conduct research in some other fields.

According to Schempp and Choi (1994), interest in conducting critical research was first sparked by the writing of a small group of well-known sport pedagogy researchers in the mid-1980s and early 1990s including Kirk and Tinning (1990), Scraton (1992), and Dewar (1987). In the last ten years there has been a gradual increase in the volume of critical research being produced in the field, a trend that is likely to continue judging by the number of sport pedagogists now promoting this paradigm (see Fernandez-Balboa, 1997). Topics studied by these researchers include school politics (e.g. Fernandez-Balboa, 2000), gender equity (e.g. Evans, Davies and Penney, 1996), homophobia (e.g. Squires and Sparkes, 1996), ethnicity and racism (e.g. McGuire and Collins, 1998), and religion (e.g. Macdonald and Kirk, 1999).

Again, the catalyst for the increase in the volume of this kind of research appears to have been the general acceptance by the sport pedagogy community that the critical paradigm could open up new possibilities for improving or reforming physical education and sport and the fact that a number of journals (most notably *Sport, Education and Society*) have encouraged the submission of critical research reports.

### *Examples of critical studies*

#### *Ethnography*

Griffin (1984, 1985) conducted some of the earliest critical research in sport pedagogy when she examined sex equity and pupils' participation styles during physical education lessons. In her classic study of boys' participation styles in middle school physical education, Griffin (1985) collected data by observing fifty-five team game lessons and formally and informally interviewing the teachers of those lessons. Data analysis revealed five styles of participation. These were machos, junior machos, nice guys, invisible players, and wimps.

Machos were highly skilled, in the centre of the action, loud, aggressive, often ridiculed their peers, yet were viewed as leaders by other pupils. Junior machos were similar except they were smaller, less skilled, and realised that they were a rank below machos. In addition, junior machos often put down highly-skilled girls while machos simply ignored them. Nice guys were often as skillful as machos, tended to treat girls as equals, and did not physically or verbally abuse other pupils. Invisible players appeared to be involved in games but didn't actually participate. Moreover, they rarely interacted with other pupils and were not passed to or marked. Wimps were unskillful, took peripheral roles in games, and were teased and abused by machos, junior machos, and some girls.

Based on these findings Griffin observed that boys who do not exhibit traditional male characteristics (e.g. tough, competitive) are, like girls, victims of gender-role stereotyping. Furthermore, she argued that children whose self-worth depends on humiliating others who are different are in as much need of help as those who are tormented. Without this help, she noted, physical education would be a place where low-skilled boys and girls are subjected to misery and failure and high-skilled boys gain a perverted sense of superiority.

### *Case study*

Recognising that in order to survive in schools new physical education teachers need to be reasonably skilled politicians as well as instructors, Fernandez-Balboa (2000) interviewed nine student teachers with the intention of finding out what they knew about school politics and how they intended to operate within a school's political system once employed. Key findings were that the student teachers had a vague understanding of the main players and issues in school politics but were generally deficient in political skills, strategies and knowledge. Fernandez-Balboa argued, therefore, that teacher education programmes could help empower preservice teachers by paying more attention to school politics during coursework.

### *Life history*

Squires and Sparkes (1996) explored the life histories of five lesbian physical education teachers through a series of formal interviews. Data revealed that the homophobic school cultures in which these teachers worked shaped their interactions with other teachers and pupils and denied them the type of freedom enjoyed by heterosexual teachers. For example, these teachers felt forced to hide their real private lives or fabricate heterosexual ones for fear of adverse reactions to the truth. In addition, they felt the need to distance themselves from their pupils simply because they were gay, felt awkward in the changing rooms, and struggled when confronted with homophobia during lessons. Based on these findings, Squires and Sparkes recommended that homophobia be challenged by all teachers regardless of their sexual orientation.

### *Ethnographic fiction*

Interested in examining the issue of sexual identity with the undergraduate physical education students enrolled in one of his courses, Sparkes (1997) could find nothing describing what it was like to be a gay male physical education teacher.

Drawing on his own experiences of playing rugby, being a physical education student, and his knowledge of the discrimination faced by gay friends, Sparkes constructed the fictional story of Alexander. This story traced Alexander's experiences of homophobia as a schoolboy, college student, rugby player, and teacher. The intent of the story was to raise awareness about the misery and inner turmoil caused by homophobia and the taken-for-granted privileges of being heterosexual. The ultimate aim, of course, was to make life more socially just for gay male physical education teachers.

## Conclusion

To date, sport pedagogy researchers have worked within the positivist, interpretive and critical paradigms. Each of these paradigms involves looking at the social world through a different lens and trying to answer different types of questions. Positivist researchers have tended to use quantitative methods while interpretive and critical researchers have tended to use qualitative methods.

In concluding, however, I should make it clear that, often, things are not quite this simple in sport pedagogy research! For example, some researchers, although obviously working within the interpretive paradigm, have also employed quantitative data collection techniques (e.g. Evans and Penney, 1992) while some researchers who employ qualitative methods appear to be more positivistic in terms of the goals of their research. To make matters more confusing, a number of researchers are conducting mixed methods of research and using both qualitative and quantitative methods to collect data (see Borg and Gall, 1989).

Finally, I should acknowledge that, in some circles, there has been heated debate about whether one paradigm is superior to the others (e.g. see Schempp, 1987, 1988; Siedentop, 1987). However, I believe that most sport pedagogy researchers agree that work in multiple paradigms is needed if physical education and sport are to improve and that researchers working in one paradigm should seek to understand and be sensitive to those working in another (Sparkes, 1991, 1994a).

### Reflection questions

1. Compare and contrast the goals, methods, research designs, data collection strategies, and data analysis procedures of positivistic, interpretive and critical research in sport pedagogy.
2. Select a sport pedagogy topic in which you are interested and outline how you would study it from a positivistic perspective.
3. Outline how you would study the topic you selected in question 2 from an interpretive or critical perspective.

**Tasks**

1. Taking a positivistic perspective, collect some quantitative data by observing a physical education lesson and recording (a) the amount of time allocated for the whole lesson, (b) the amount of time for which more than half the pupils are engaged in activity (i.e. skill practice or game play), (c) the number of technical feedback statements made by the teacher aimed at improving pupils' skills or strategies, and (d) the number of motivational feedback statements made by the teacher designed to encourage pupils. Analyse your data by calculating the percentage of lesson time during which pupils were engaged in activity and the rate per minute of technical feedback and motivational feedback provided by the teacher. Discuss the quality of the lesson you observed based on these data.
2. Taking either an interpretive or critical perspective, collect some qualitative data by observing a physical education lesson and writing field notes which describe in detail what is occurring. Analyse your data by searching for categories and themes. List these categories and themes together with examples and discuss the quality of the lesson you observed based on these data and your research perspective.

**Further reading**

Fernandez-Balboa, J.M. (Ed.) (1997) *Critical Post-modernism in Human Movement, Physical Education and Sport*. Albany: State University of New York Press.

Silverman, S.J. and Ennis, C.D. (Eds) (1996) *Student Learning in Physical Education*. Champaign, IL: Human Kinetics.

Sparkes, A. (Ed.) (1992) *Research in Physical Education and Sport: Exploring Alternative Visions*. Lewes: Falmer.

## References

Aicinena, S.T., Steffen, J.P. and Smith, M.D. (1992) A comparison of the behaviours of physical education teachers in curricular and extra-curricular settings. *Physical Education Review*, 15, 2, 148–156.

Allison, P.C. (1990) Classroom teachers' observations of physical education lessons. *Journal of Teaching in Physical Education*, 9, 272–283.

Armour, K.M. (1997) Developing a personal philosophy on the nature and purpose of physical education: Life history reflections. *European Physical Education Review*, 3, 1, 68–82.

Armour, K. and Jones, R.L. (1998) *Physical Education Teachers' Lives and Careers: PE, Sport and Educational Status*. London: Falmer Press.

Barrett, K., Sebren, A. and Sheehan, A.M. (1991) Content development patterns over a 2-year period as indicated from written lessons plans. *Journal of Teaching in Physical Education,* 11, 79–102.

Behets, D. (1996) Comparison of visual information processing between preservice students and experienced physical educators. *Journal of Teaching in Physical Education,* 16, 79–87.

Bennett, G. (2000) Students' participation styles in two university weight training classes. *Journal of Teaching in Physical Education,* 19, 182–205.

Bolt, B.R. (1998) Encouraging cognitive growth through case discussions. *Journal of Teaching in Physical Education,* 18, 90–102.

Borg, W.R. and Gall, M.D. (1989) *Educational Research: An Introduction* (5th ed.). New York: Longman.

Byra, M. (1996) Postlesson conferencing strategies and preservice teachers' reflective practices. *Journal of Teaching in Physical Education*, 16, 48–65.

Byra, M. and Goc Karp, G. (2000) Data collection techniques employed in qualitative research in physical education teacher education. *Journal of Teaching in Physical Education,* 19, 246–266.

Byra, M. and Sherman, M. (1993) Preactive and interactive decision-making tendencies of less and more experienced preservice teachers. *Research Quarterly for Exercise and Sport*, 64, 46–55.

Cale, L. (2000) Physical activity promotion in secondary schools. *European Physical Education Review*, 6, 1, 71–90.

Capel, S. (1998) A longitudinal study of the stages of development or concern of secondary PE students. *European Journal of Physical Education*, 3, 2, 185–199.

Carlson, T.B. and Hastie, P. (1997) The student social system within sport education. *Journal of Teaching in Physical Education*, 16, 176–195.

Carpenter, P.J. and Morgan, K. (1999) Motivational climate, personal goal perspectives, and cognitive and affective responses in physical education. *European Journal of Physical Education*, 4, 1, 31–44.

Curtner-Smith, M.D. (1996) The impact of an early field experience on preservice physical education teachers' conceptions of teaching. *Journal of Teaching in Physical Education,* 15, 224–250.

Curtner-Smith, M.D. (1997) The impact of biography, teacher education, and organizational socialization on the perspectives and practices of first-year physical education teachers: case studies of recruits with coaching orientations. *Sport, Education and Society*, 2, 73–94.

Curtner-Smith, M.D. (1999) The more things change the more they stay the same: factors influencing teachers' interpretations and delivery of National Curriculum Physical Education. *Sport, Education and Society,* 4, 75–97.

Curtner-Smith, M.D. (in press) The occupational socialization of a first-year physical education teacher with a teaching orientation. *Sport, Education and Society.*

Curtner-Smith, M.D., Hasty, D.L. and Kerr, I.G. (in press) Teachers' use of productive and reproductive teaching styles prior to and following the introduction of National Curriculum Physical Education. *Educational Research.*

Curtner-Smith, M.D. and Meek, G.A. (2000) Teachers' value orientations and their compatibility with the National Curriculum for Physical Education. *European Physical Education Review,* 6, 1, 27–45.

Curtner-Smith, M.D., Todorovich, J.R., Lacon, S.A. and Kerr, I.G. (1999) Teachers' rules, routines, and expectations prior to and following the implementation of the National Curriculum for Physical Education. *European Journal of Physical Education,* 4, 1, 17–30.

Curtner-Smith, M.D., Wallace, S.J. and Wang, M.Q. (1998) Behaviors of girls' high school basketball coaches and their players during early season, mid-season, and late season practices. *International Sports Journal*, 2, 1, 79–93.

Curtner-Smith, M.D., Wallace, S.J. and Wang, M.Q. (1999) Relationship of coach and player behaviors during practice to team performance in high school girls' basketball. *The Journal of Sport Behavior*, 22, 2, 203–220.

Darst, P.W., Zakrajsek, D.B. and Mancini, V.H. (Eds) (1989) *Analyzing Physical Education and Sport Instruction* (2nd ed.). Champaign, IL: Human Kinetics.

Denison, J. (1996) Sport narratives. *Qualitative Inquiry,* 2, 3, 351–362.

Dewar, A. (1987) The social construction of gender in physical education. *Women's Studies International Forum*, 10, 453–466.

Dodds, P., Gubacs, K., Placek, J.H., Griffin, L., Supaporn, S., Parker, J., Banville, D. and Miller, R. (1999) Training prospective teacher educators as researchers: insiders' perspectives. *Journal of Sport Pedagogy*, 5, 1, 65–78.

Duda, J. (1993) 'Goals: A social cognitive approach to the study of achievement motivation in sport', in Singer, R.N., Murphy, M. and Tennant, L.K. (Eds) *Handbook on Research in Sport Psychology*, 421–436. New York: Macmillan.

Earls, N. (Ed.) (1986) Naturalistic inquiry: interactive research and the insider-outsider perspective [monograph]. *Journal of Teaching in Physical Education*, 6, 1–101.

Ennis, C.D. (1994) Urban secondary teachers' value orientations: delineating curricular goals for social responsibility. *Journal of Teaching in Physical Education*, 13, 163–179.

Ennis, C.D. and Chen, A. (1993) Domain specifications and content representativeness of the revised Value Orientation Inventory. *Research Quarterly for Exercise and Sport*, 64, 436–446.

Ennis, C.D. and Chen, A. (1995) Teachers' value orientations in urban and rural school settings. *Research Quarterly for Exercise and Sport*, 66, 41–50.

Ennis, C.D. and Hooper, L.M. (1988) Development of an instrument for assessing educational value orientations. *Journal of Curriculum Studies*, 20, 277–280.

Evans, J., Davies, B. and Penney, D. (1996) Teachers, teaching and the social construction of gender relations. *Sport, Education and Society*, 1, 165–184.

Evans, J. and Penney, D. (1992) Investigating ERA: Qualitative methods and policy oriented research. *British Journal of Physical Education Research Supplement*, 11, 2–7.

Evans, J. and Penney, D. (with Bryant, A.) (1993) Physical education after ERA? *British Journal of Physical Education Research Supplement*, 13, 2–5.

Evertson, C.M. and Smylie, M.A. (1987) 'Research on teaching and classroom processes: views from two perspectives', in Glover J. and Ronning, R. (Eds) *Historical Foundations of Educational Psychology*, 349–371. New York: Plenum.

Fabian Lounsbery, M. and Sharpe, T. (1999) Effects of sequential feedback on preservice teacher instructional interactions and students' skill practice. *Journal of Teaching in Physical Education,* 19, 58–78.

Fernandez-Balboa, J.M. (Ed) (1997) *Critical Post-modernism in Human Movement, Physical Education and Sport.* Albany: State University of New York Press.

Fernandez-Balboa, J.M. (2000) Prospective physical educators' perspectives on school micropolitics. *Journal of Sport Pedagogy*, 6, 2, 1–33.

Flanagan, J.C. (1954) The critical incident technique. *Psychological Bulletin*, 4, 327–358.

George, A.A. (1978) *Teacher Concerns Questionnaire.* Austin, TX: The University of Texas at Austin.

Graham, G. and Heimerer, E. (1981) Research on teacher effectiveness: a summary with implications for teaching. *Quest,* 33, 14–25.

Griffin, P.S. (1984) Girls' participation patterns in a middle school team sports unit. *Journal of Teaching in Physical Education,* 4, 30–38.

Griffin, P.S. (1985) Boys' participation styles in a middle school physical education team sports unit. *Journal of Teaching in Physical Education*, 4, 100–110.

Hare, M.K. and Graber, K.C. (2000) Student misconceptions during two invasion game units in physical education: a qualitative investigation of student thought processing. *Journal of Teaching in Physical Education*, 20, 55–77.

Hart, N.I. (1987) Student teachers' anxieties: four measured factors and their relationships to pupil disruption in class. *Educational Research,* 29, 12–18.

Kirk, D. and Tinning, R. (Eds) (1990) *Physical Education, Curriculum, and Culture: Critical Issues in the Contemporary Crisis.* Lewes: Falmer Press.

Lacey, C. (1977) *The Socialization of Teachers.* London: Methuen.

Lacy, A.C. and Martin, D.L. (1994) Analysis of starter/nonstarter motor skill engagement and coaching behaviors in collegiate women's volleyball. *Journal of Teaching in Physical Education*, 13, 95–107.

Laws, C. and Aldridge, M. (1995) Magic moments, myth or millstone – the implementation of national curriculum physical education. *British Journal of Physical Education Research Supplement,* 16, 2–12.

Lee, A.M. (1996) 'How the field evolved', in Silverman, S.J. and Ennis, C.D. (Eds) *Student Learning in Physical Education*, 9–33. Champaign, IL: Human Kinetics.

Locke, L.F. (1977) Research on teaching physical education: new hope for a dismal science. *Quest,* 28, 2–16.

Lortie, D. (1975) *Schoolteacher: A Sociological Study*. Chicago: University of Chicago Press.

Macdonald, D. and Kirk, D. (1999) Pedagogy, the body and Christian identity. *Sport, Education and Society*, 4, 131–142.

McGuire, B. and Collins, D. (1998) Sport, ethnicity, and racism: the experience of Asian heritage boys. *Sport, Education and Society*, 3, 79–88.

Meek, G. (1996) The teacher concerns questionnaire with preservice physical educators in Great Britain: being concerned with concerns. *Journal of Teaching in Physical Education*, 16, 20–29.

Meek, G.A. and Smith, M.D. (1998) A field study of supervisory intervention of preservice physical education teachers via data-based feedback: feeding back feedback. *Journal of Sport Pedagogy,* 4, 1, 43–55.

Metzler, M. (1989) A review of research on time in sport pedagogy. *Journal of Teaching in Physical Education*, 8, 2, 87–103.

Nixon, J.E. and Locke, L.F. (1973) 'Research on teaching physical education', in Travers, M.W. (Ed.) *Second Handbook of Research on Teaching,* 1210–1242. Chicago: Rand McNally & Company.

Nugent, P. and Faucette, N. (1995) Marginalized voices: constructions of and responses to physical education and grading practices by students categorized as gifted or learning-disabled. *Journal of Teaching in Physical Education*, 14, 418–430.

Oliver, K.L. (1998) A journey into narrative analysis: a methodology for discovering meanings. *Journal of Teaching in Physical Education*, 17, 244–259.

O'Sullivan, M. and Tsangaridou, N. (1992) What undergraduate physical education majors learn during a field experience. *Research Quarterly for Exercise and Sport,* 63, 381–392.

Peach, S.J. and Thomas, S.M. (1999) Young, gifted and anxious: the role of significant others in mediating the experience of competitive anxiety. *Journal of Sport Pedagogy,* 5, 2, 54–70.

Placek, J.H. and Locke, L.F. (1986) Research on teaching physical education: new knowledge and cautious optimism. *Journal of Teacher Education*, 37, 24–28.

Pugsley, L., Coffey, A. and Delamont, S. (1996) Daps, dykes and five mile hikes: physical education in pupils' folklore. *Sport, Education and Society*, 1, 133–146.

QSR NUD*IST (Nonnumerical Unstructured Data Indexing Searching and Theory-Building) 3.0 [Computer software] (1995) Melbourne, Victoria, Australia: Qualitative Solutions & Research Pty Ltd.

Rosenshine, B. and Furst, N. (1973) 'The use of direct observation to study teaching', in Travers, R. (Ed.) *Second Handbook of Research on Teaching,* 122–183. Chicago: Rand McNally.

Rovegno, I. (1994) Teaching within a zone of curricular safety: school culture and the situated nature of student teachers' pedagogical content knowledge. *Research Quarterly for Exercise and Sport*, 65, 269–279.

Sage, G.H. (1987) The social world of high school athletic coaches: multiple role demands and their consequences. *Sociology of Sport Journal*, 4, 3, 213–228.

Sage, G.H. (1989) Becoming a high school coach: from playing sports to coaching. *Research Quarterly for Exercise and Sport,* 60, 81–92.

Schempp, P. (1987) Research on teaching physical education: beyond the limits of natural science. *Journal of Teaching in Physical Education*, 6, 111–121.

Schempp, P. (1988) Exorcist II: a reply to Siedentop. *Journal of Teaching in Physical Education,* 7, 79–81.

Schempp, P.G. and Choi, E. (1994) Research methodologies in sport pedagogy. *Sport Science Review*, 3, 1, 41–55.

Scraton, S. (1992) *Shaping up to Womanhood: Girls and Physical Education.* Milton Keynes: Open University Press.

Sharpe, T.L. (1997a) Using technology in preservice supervision. *The Physical Educator,* 54, 11–19.

Sharpe, T.L. (1997b) An introduction to sequential behavior analysis and what it offers physical education researchers. *Journal of Teaching in Physical Education*, 16, 368–375.

Sharpe, T.L. and Hawkins, A. (1992) Strategies and tactics for field systems analysis. *Journal of Teaching in Physical Education,* 12, 9–23.

Shulman, L.S. (1986) 'Paradigms and research programs in the study of teaching: a contemporary perspective', in Wittrock, M.C. (Ed.) *Handbook of Research on Teaching* (3rd ed.), 3–36. New York: Macmillan.

Siedentop, D. (1987) Dialogue or exorcism? A rejoinder to Schempp. *Journal of Teaching in Physical Education*, 6, 373–376.

Silverman, S. (1985) Relationship of engagement and practice trials to student achievement. *Journal of Teaching in Physical Education*, 6, 13–21.

Silverman S. (1991) Research on teaching in physical education. *Research Quarterly for Exercise and Sport,* 62, 352–365.

Silverman, S. (1996) 'How and why we do research', in Silverman, S.J. and Ennis C.D. (Eds) *Student Learning in Physical Education*, 35–51. Champaign, IL: Human Kinetics.

Silverman, S., Kulinna, P. and Crull, G. (1995) Skill-related task structures, explicitness, and accountability: relationships with student achievement. *Research Quarterly for Exercise and Sport*, 66, 32–40.

Smith, M.D. (1992) The supervision of physical educators: a review of American literature. *British Journal of Education Research Supplement,* 11, 7–12.

Smith, M.D., Kerr, I.G. and Meek, G.A. (1993) Physical education teacher behaviour intervention: increasing levels of performance and motivational feedback through the utilisation of clinical supervision techniques. *Physical Education Review,* 16, 2, 162–172.

Sparkes, A.C. (1991) Toward understanding, dialogue, and polyvocality in the research community: extending the boundaries of the paradigms debate. *Journal of Teaching in Physical Education,* 10, 103–133.

Sparkes, A.C. (1994a) Research paradigms in physical education: some brief comments on differences that make a difference. *British Journal of Physical Education Research Supplement,* 14, 11–16.

Sparkes, A.C. (1994b) Understanding teachers: a life history approach. *Educational Research Monograph Series,* No. 2, School of Education, Exeter University.

Sparkes, A.C. (1997) Ethnographic fiction and representing the absent other. *Sport, Education and Society*, 2, 25–40.

Sparkes, A.C. (1999) Exploring body narratives. *Sport, Education and Society*, 4, 17–30.

Sparkes, A.C. and Mackay, R. (1996) Teaching practice and the micropolitics of self presentation. *Pedagogy in Practice*, 2, 1, 3–22.

Squires, S.L. and Sparkes, A.C. (1996) Circles of silence: sexual identity in physical education and sport. *Sport, Education and Society*, 1, 77–101.

Stake, R. (1988) 'Case study methods in educational research', in Jaeger, R. (Ed.) *Complementary Methods for Research in Education,* 251–300. Washington, DC: American Educational Research Association.

Stroot, S. (Ed.) (1993) Socialization into physical education [Monograph]. *Journal of Teaching in Physical Education,* 12, 337–466.

Templin, T. (1981) Student as socializing agent. *Journal of Teaching in Physical Education*, Introductory Issue, 71–79.

Templin, T.J. and Griffey, D.C. (1987) Editorial. *Journal of Teaching in Physical Education,* 7, 1–4.

Templin, T., Sparkes, A. and Schempp, P. (1991) The professional life cycle of a retired physical education teacher: a tale of bitter disengagement. *Physical Education Review*, 14, 143–156.

Todorovich, J.R. (1999) Influence of physical education classroom motivational climate on third and sixth grade students' task and ego orientations. Unpublished doctoral dissertation, The University of Alabama, Tuscaloosa, AL.

# 4 Femininity, masculinity and difference: what's wrong with a sarong?

*Barbara Humberstone*

## Introduction

From birth the processes of sex differentiation occur through which appropriate and expected yet different behaviours may be learnt by each sex. The ways in which sport, physical activities and physical education provide informal and formal sites in which gender identities are constructed, reinforced and, on occasions, challenged are examined in this chapter.

This chapter considers concepts of gender and the ways in which the notion of cultural hegemony has been utilised to explore and explain dominant forms of masculinities and femininities in society. Sport is shown to be a significant culture in which hegemonic masculinities and restricted, inferiorised femininities are constructed and reinforced. But in certain circumstances, there may also be contexts through which gender boundaries may be transgressed or gender reformation achieved.

Patriarchal relations and institutional bias in sporting organisations provide for particular cultural contexts that tend overtly or covertly to exclude most women and some men. Normalising discourses and practices that reinforce cultural hegemony are explored. The ways in which cultural hegemony is resisted and challenged are considered through analyses of situated practices of participants and professionals. The implications and paradoxes of post-structural perspectives on analyses of gender and difference in sport are considered.

## Difference: the construction of 'masculinity and femininity'

Taken-for-granted assumptions about what it is to be a woman and what it is to be a man have varied throughout the aeons and in different cultures (Miles, 1989). In any particular time and culture, who decides and legitimates what it means to be a man and what it means to be a woman, how such notions are maintained and for what reasons have been matters over which there have been, and still are, considerable personal and political struggles. When a child is born the first exclamation is usually, 'it's a boy' or 'it's a girl'. This is the beginning of the differentiation between the sexes.

Traditionally, the girl may be dressed in pink and treated gently, whilst a boy may be dressed in blue and handled more energetically. Biological sex is the precursor to what is considered to be appropriate and expected, yet different, behaviours of girls and boys, and women and men. At the beginning of the twenty-first century, Oakley's (1972) analysis of some three decades ago is still pertinent.

> On the whole, Western society is organised around the assumption that the differences between the sexes are more important than any qualities they have in common. When people try to justify this assumption in terms of 'natural' differences, two separate processes become confused: the tendency to differentiate by sex, and the tendency to differentiate in a particular way by sex. The first is genuinely a constant feature of human society but the second is not, and its inconstancy marks the division between 'sex' and 'gender': sex differences may be 'natural', but gender differences have their source in culture, not nature'.
>
> (189)

Thus sex refers to the biological aspects of being male or female. Gender refers to learnt behaviour and is often categorised broadly as 'masculinity' and 'femininity'. Even today, everyday notions of biological sex and gender may be conflated. Femininity and masculinity are often viewed as immutable and natural arrangements. Although biological sex is usually fixed, masculinity and femininity are constructs of a particular culture or society and may therefore be open to change.

Conventional notions of what constitutes femininity and masculinity and associated expected behaviours and privileges took hold of everyday thinking largely as a consequence of the Enlightenment period in the eighteenth century. The Enlightenment tradition, which ushered in modernity, emerged as a 'rational' counter to faith and superstition, through the exercise of reason (Harding, 1986). It also spawned in Britain the humanistic project, which declared the legal entitlements of 'the Rights of Man'. Despite the demands by women to be included in these rights, they were excluded. 'Woman' as a category became defined as 'Other' and opposite to 'Man'. Man was associated with public life, whereas Woman was symbolically aligned with nature, birth and the private sphere. Through the construction of sets of binaries, masculinity became associated with science, rationality, objectivity and culture, whilst femininity became equated with emotionality, subjectivity, irrationality and nature. These hierarchical, dichotomising principles have done much to separate woman from man and to underpin taken-for-granted divisive assumptions of appropriate and expected behaviours and attributes of male and female. Such dualistic notions are also identified as implicated both in the continued separation and oppression of 'other' groups of people for example on the grounds of race, ethnicity, ability and so forth.[1] This dualism, with its associated privileging and exclusion, is deeply embedded in forms of western knowledge and may be implicated in the 'popular' perception of sport as in some way a 'masculine' cultural activity to which women are frequently denied access or have different and less privileged relationships from those of men, and in which particular forms of masculinity are valued and so dominate. These differences and privileges are emphasised in sport partly through derogatory name-calling. This is a common cultural practice whereby boys and men who do not perform 'well' or in an acceptable way are 'put down' through such comments as: 'Are you a poof or something?'; 'What a big girl's blouse!; 'you throw like a girl' and so forth.

## Ideology of femininity and leisure/sport

Sport is a particular manifestation of a cultural leisure form. Deem (1986) and Green *et al.*'s (1990) critical research into woman's leisure in the 1980s was pivotal in highlighting women's different leisure experiences from those of men, analysing these through Marxian feminist perspectives. 'Leisure', Green *et al.* (1990: 37) maintain, 'is not only an area where social divisions structure access and experience, but is also an area where inequalities are negotiated, reproduced or challenged'. Personal struggles that women experienced from day to day in gaining access to leisure were linked to the gender power relations in society (Deem, 1986). Capitalist patriarchal structures, and the 'ideologies of femininity', worked to exclude women from public places and maintain their servicing position within the home.[2] From these perspectives, men dominate in politics, work institutions and community and can control political and economic agendas, and notions of what constitutes femininity. The sexual division of labour, the need for women's leisure to fit their lives as mothers and carers and the 'policing' of women in public spaces were found to constrain most women's leisure more or less, at different periods of their lifecycle, and generally to structure a different experience from that of men. In addition, many women's leisure experiences were found to be limited by access to transport, costs, feelings of guilt, lack of confidence and isolation.

Talbot (1988), Wearing (1990), Wimbush (1988), highlight the ideology of motherhood which imposed constraints on mothers with young children, inhibiting their access to some leisure experiences. Not only were women's experiences more constrained than men's, but in some cases women were servicing men's sport and leisure experiences. Dempsey (1990) and Thompson (1999) both show the ways in which women were supporters and facilitators of male's sport at the expense of their own interests. In explaining these inequalities between the sexes in sport and leisure the concept of ideology of femininity is used to make sense of this apparent acceptance of and collusion with male interests and women's oppression. Ideology is taken by Green *et al.* (1990: 30) to be, 'the complex system of perceptions and representations through which we experience ourselves and come to make sense of the world'. It is also implicated in serving the interests of the dominant ruling group. For 'Ideologies are sets of ideas, assumptions and images by which people make sense of society, which give a clear sense of social identity, and which serve in some way to legitimise relations of power in society' (McLennan, 1995: 126).

The ideologies of femininity, like those of masculinity, thus 'work' by making the values incorporated into the ideas about what constitutes a 'real' woman, which are different from and inferior to those that constitute a 'real' man, appear natural and rational. It conceals or denies contradictions. Thus discourses of gender that normalise conventional relations between the sexes are embedded in and built on the biological distinction of sex, through the continued legitimisation of taken-for-granted notions of femininity and masculinity. Ideologies present themselves as universal or 'how it really is' for everyone, rather than the sectional interests of a particular group. Ideologies convey and normalise the values of the dominant group. The ideology of femininity is based on separation from and 'other' to man. The ways in which the differences between the sexes are constructed and gendered by society and in particular through sport render invisible the complexities and relations of power that serve the dominant white male interest. This is captured in Connell *et al.*'s (1982: 33–34) conceptualisation of gender as, 'a pattern of relations among people ... an extensive and complex pattern woven through all institutions they live in ... and shapes their lives at every level'. In sport the values and practices associated with dominant masculine culture are emphasised and reinforced. Referring to Carrigan, Connell and Lee's (1985) sociological work on masculinity, Wearing (1998: 84) points out, 'ideologies such as those of the family, motherhood, femininity and masculinity keep individual women believing in the naturalness and inevitability of their subordinate status. This combination of structural, institutional and ideological power enables hegemonic control through masculine culture which valorises and rewards physically aggressive, competitive, task-focused, achievement-oriented masculinity and inferiorises all forms of femininity'.

Thus dominant ideologies such as those associated with gender which find a 'voice' through sport cultures provide frameworks through which people can view the social world in a particular way and if this framework is adopted, certain consequences follow about lifestyle and attitudes. A dominant ideology helps individuals and groups to make sense of society within a framework of meaning and it provides security about ideas, giving a sense of identity. Clearly, biological sex is central to individuals' perceptions about themselves, their identity and about 'others' and these manifest themselves in dominant forms of femininity and masculinity.

Ideologies may be conveyed, circulated and reinforced with varying degrees of consciousness or deliberation (and differing levels of success) through a variety of public and private institutions and informal arenas. This can occur through the general process of socialisation within the family and schooling and through interaction in peer groups in community, leisure or work sites. Public and private institutions involved not only in sport but others such as the media and education operate to maintain and legitimate particular gender ideologies, together with business concerns, the professions and so forth (McLennan, 1995).

Explanations informed by marxian feminist traditions such as those of Deem (1986) and Green *et al.* (1990) maintain that those who control the means of production are also likely to control the vehicles for creating the ways in which people think, so influencing and creating the prevailing ideologies. Structures of power, as understood through such perspectives as patriarchal capitalism, are considered to constrain and subordinate some men and all women. In its extreme form, this perspective puts all women at the mercy of structural capitalist patriarchal power and all men as the perpetrators of this oppression. Clearly, although providing a significant macro framework through which to view patterns of inequality and structural differences between men and women in society and in sport, it is somewhat over-deterministic and does not adequately provide for understanding individual experiences or resistance. Not everyone is duped by dominant ideologies and the prevailing social order, relations of production and lifestyle that are their realisation. Consequently, some individuals or groups may become agents in resisting or challenging ideologies in a variety of ways.

Interactionist theories and cultural studies emerged to develop an understanding of the micro-social milieu of individuals and the cultural contexts within which they operate. Cultural studies took seriously the ways in which individuals make sense of and give meaning to their everyday lives but it was also concerned to locate these within broader structural features. The over-determinism of macro theories gives way to exploring the struggles over meaning and practices in particular social and cultural contexts.[3] The concept of ideology, with its notion of 'false consciousness' became superseded by Gramsci's (1985) concept of hegemony. As Wearing (1998: 61) points out, 'hegemony, then, is the control of the consciousness by cultural dominance through the institutions of society. Power and privilege are maintained through cultural hegemony, but struggles over hegemonic control are inevitable. Subcultures are often formed which challenge dominant cultural forms'. Ideology is implicated in and crucial to the struggle for hegemony.

Clarke and Critcher (1985) point out that leisure is a significant site in the struggle for hegemony. Sport then from this perspective can be seen as a significant cultural form which not only reflects the dominant values and ideologies but can also be a site of struggles over meaning and practices.

## Sport and culture

Culture in its simplest form is considered to be the shared experience, 'shared principles of life, characteristics of particular classes, groups or shared social milieux' (Griffin, 1985: 202) of specific groups of people. Cultures may be local, as in a school; regional, as in the Lake District; national as say Scottish; or global as McDonald's hamburger outlets or FIFA. These examples indicate that the idea of culture is considerably more complex than it may at first appear (see Williams 1981; 1988). In the twenty-first century, with increased trends in consumerism, mass communication and the continuation of social movements that, from the latter part of the twentieth century, organised around 'race', gender, sexuality, the environment and so forth, the concept of culture has received a critical re-reading. This re-conceptualisation of culture has emerged as a consequence of the development of cultural studies and analyses by a number social thinkers.[4] Culture is no longer assumed merely to be a set of shared values and beliefs, taken-for-granted assumptions and ways of acting. Rather it is also the ways in which ideologies and practices are constructed through systems of meanings, by webs of power and through the organisations and institutions that produce and legitimate them. Consequently, sport cultures are made up of these processes, practices, knowledges and categories that are understood to constitute them. Sport is no longer seen as a neutral arena providing positive recreational or competitive experiences uninfluenced by power and politics, but a space of hegemonic struggles.

Critiques of sport as necessarily 'a good thing' emerged in the 1970s and 1980s as responses to functionalist academic discourse in the sociology of sport. This discourse was male dominated and, as Hall (1996) and Hargreaves (1994) remind us, tried to make sense of the relationships between sport and other cultural formations but neglected the power relations between women and men. However, more recent investigations into sport drew attention to gender and its significance in critical analysis (see Birrell, 1988; Messner, 1992; Messner and Sabo, 1990). The field of sports studies was also critiqued for its scientism (Clarke and Humberstone, 1997a; Hall, 1997; Talbot, 1997); its heterosexism (Clarke, 1997; Griffin, 1990; Krane, 1996) and ethnocentrism (Birrell, 1989). These critiques further emphasise the significant role sport plays in conveying and legitimating ideologies and symbols of dominant forms of masculinity and emphasised or inferiorised femininity. Historically, in western cultures, 'sports constituted a unique form of cultural life: they were overwhelmingly symbols of masculinity and chauvinism, embodying aggressive displays of physical power and competitiveness' (Hargreaves, 1994: 43). Prevailing sport cultures and the ideological processes underpinning them thus played a significant part in valorising idealised forms of masculine character, at particular times in history.

## Sport as masculine culture or the culture of masculinity

### *Hegemonic masculinity and sport*

In the processes that construct and legitimate dominant forms of masculinity through sport what is to be excluded is also defined. The prevailing cultural messages both celebrate the idealised form of masculinity at the same time as inferiorising the 'other'; women and forms of masculinity that do not conform. This culturally idealised form of masculinity conveyed through sport to which many men may aspire, but which may not be the usual form of masculinity at all, is understood as hegemonic masculinity (Connell, 1990). Bryson (1990: 173) argues that 'Sport's very physical nature gives it special significance because of the fundamental link between social power and physical force. Sport is a major arena in which physical force and toughness are woven into hegemonic masculinity and the resultant ideologies transmitted.' Derived from Gramsci's analysis of class relations, the concept of hegemony is taken to be:

> the cultural dynamics by which a group claims and sustains a leading position in social life. At any given time, one form of masculinity rather than others is exalted. Hegemonic masculinity can be defined as the configuration of gender practice which embodies the currently accepted answer to the

> problem of the legitimacy of patriarchy, which guarantees (or is taken to guarantee) the dominant position of men and the subordination of women'.
> (Connell, 1995: 77)

Connell's (1990) life-history analysis of an Australian champion 'iron-man' (who competes in endurance events which include swimming, running, surf-riding) demonstrates the paradoxes and contradictions associated with the everyday experience of this male athlete who 'lives an exemplary version of hegemonic masculinity'. Although he lives it, Connell (1990: 94) claims that he does not understand his cultural position. When asked about masculinity, he has difficulty in defining what it means to him. For the 'iron-man', it is, 'not be(ing) gay' and 'be(ing) strong' and it is also about keeping his sport exclusively male. Through this life-history, the ways in which the processes of hegemony operate are vividly explicated. In analysis, Connell (1990: 94) shows that for

> a particular form of masculinity [to be] hegemonic means that it is culturally exalted and that its exultation stabilises a structure of dominance and oppression in the gender order as a whole. To be culturally exalted, the pattern of masculinity must have exemplars who are celebrated as heroes. Steve (the iron-man) certainly enacts in his own life some of the main patterns of contemporary hegemonic masculinity: the subordination of women, the marginalisation of gay men, and the connecting of masculinity to toughness and competitiveness. He has also been celebrated as a hero for much of his life, in school and in adult sport. He is being deliberately constructed now as a media exemplar of masculinity by the advertisers who are sponsoring him.

Clearly, the 'iron-man' needs to live out an idealised form of masculinity which, although celebrated by some, is unobtainable by most men. Connell's work on the diversity of men's experiences has shown the considerable pressure on individual men to conform to heterosexual hegemonic masculinity particularly in sport with its informal codes and powerful sanctioning mechanisms.[5] Tensions and contradictions are highlighted in men who move outside the norm when for example they enter ballet dancing, where they become the objects of gaze (Burt, 1994). Hegemonic masculinity is socially and culturally constructed and is arguably not the 'natural' condition for men. Its form varies over time but it continuously embodies, 'toughness, physical and sexual prowess, aggressiveness and the distancing of femininity'. For men to retain power at a societal level, especially with the considerable challenge by women at all levels of society, the maintenance of hegemonic masculinity is imperative.

A significant ethnographic study of competitive offshore sailing sub-culture in Australia moves forward our reading of the work of repeated cultural practices in the maintenance of hegemonic masculinities in sports culture. The study illuminates the ways in which for the male sailors, 'fears of intimacy play an over-determining role in the construction and embodiment of both corporeal and theoretical subjectivities as trouble' (Bricknell, 1999: 435).[6] Emotional attachment or the development of intimacy is set aside for dominant heterosexual attraction in which woman is generally viewed as sex object and in which non-hegemonic masculinities are marginalised.

### *Schooling*

> Organised sports is [*sic*] a 'gendered institution' – an institution constructed by gender relations. As such, its structure and values (rules, formal organisation, sex composition, etc.) reflect dominant conceptions of masculinity and femininity. Organised sports is [*sic*] also a 'gendering institution' – an institution that helps to construct the current gender order. Part of this construction of gender is accomplished through the 'masculinising' of male bodies and minds.
>
> (Messner, 1998: 119)

Most if not all the more popular sport cultural forms embody signifiers of hegemonic masculinity which convey messages to boys and young men and may be central to the early construction of dominant modes of masculinity (see Skelton, 2000). Ethnographic studies of British primary schooling evidence that football is central in constructing gender relations in school and in the construction of hegemonic masculinities (see Connolly, 1998; Murphy *et al.*, 1990; Renolds, 1997; Skelton, 2000). This is also apparent in studies of schooling in Australia suggesting a global impact of football (see Connell *et al.*, 1982). Delemont (1980) and Williams (1989) both observed that patterns of segregation between girls and boys seen in playgrounds stemmed from the fact that boys monopolised the main activity space to play football and excluded those girls who wished to participate. Similarly, this is evident in Claudia's determined account of her primary school experiences:

> At break ... at first ... [the boys] used to say, 'no you're not playing football with us'. So what I did to get around that was I bought a new football ... Then they [the boys] said, 'can we borrow your football?' and I said, 'yes you can play with me', and so that was how that was resolved.
>
> (quoted in Humberstone, 1993: 218)

Although time has past, very little seems to have changed in respect of playground domination by boys in primary school. Skelton (2000) identifies the ways in which, in one primary school, football, although not a significant element in the school national curriculum, took a pivotal position in lunch time, break time and as an extracurricular activity. Girls and some boys were excluded from the relationships that developed between the male teachers and the boy team players through the emphasis and celebration of football.

The following interview with 10 and 11-year-old girls of Skelton's (2000) research shows the barriers created for girls through the collusion of male teachers with the notion that football is only for boys:

HOLLY: The boys are sexist, Mr Naismith ... says boys would prefer playing football ... and sometimes I feel like having a little kick around but we can't.

MARIE: Mr Kenning says its like for the girls too, but it isn't like that ... He only lets us have one ball a class and the boys give it to Bob [caretaker] to look after and they rush their dinner so they can get there first.

(quoted in Skelton, 2000: 13)

### *Physical education and the preservation or transformation of hegemonic masculinity*

Physical education is a formal site that is strongly associated with messages and practices that bolster ideological forms of masculinity and exaggerated inferiorised forms of femininity. Historically, the image of the physical education teacher promulgated in writings and so forth was one displaying various characteristics of toughness, aggressiveness and competitive zeal. Implicitly linked with physical education teaching and classroom control were various modes of domination that encouraged physical and verbal attacks, diminishing pupil self-esteem and confidence (Whitehead and Hendry, 1976; Cohen and Manion, 1981). Arguably these descriptions were only partial and represented the paucity of pedagogical research in physical education at that time. However, such texts highlighted the symbolic nature of traditional physical education and the myths that surround it. Flintoff's (1993) research into physical education and initial teacher education, although not giving credence to the mythology of excessive physical or mental brutality in physical education teaching, clearly demonstrated the discourses and practices that reinforce traditional concepts of masculinity and femininity. Male students during dance classes worked hard to distance themselves from association with the activity and declined the possibility of male to male contact if asked to work with another male. Flintoff (1993: 194) found that in the institutions she studied normalising discourses of heterosexuality and ideologies of masculinity prevailed partly '[B]y retaining soccer and rugby as male-only activities, the institutions ensured the involvement of male students in ... "masculinising practices"'.

Likewise, traditional sex segregation in British physical education lessons does little to create greater understanding between girls and boys. Arguably it augments attitudes that announce and celebrate the stereotypical polarities of representations of masculinity and femininity prevailing in sport such that cooperation and the recognition of similarities between the sexes is stifled. All-male environments may be problematic for some boys. Such contexts may place boys under considerable pressure to conform to non-emotional, uncaring masculine stereotypes (Askew and Ross, 1988; Wright, 1997). Nevertheless, Scraton's work (1992, 1993) is significant in pointing to the enigmas for girls when their physical education lessons are organised on mixed sex/coeducational basis. For Muslim girls and women, all female environments are crucial for their involvement in sport or physical education (Zaman, 1997). Single-sex girl groups also provide scope for work that may not be possible within situations where boys are present. Issues pertinent to young women, such as those concerning personal relationships and health can more easily be addressed in 'safe' girl-only situations (see Baker-Graham, 1999; Barak *et al.*, 2000; Spratt, McCormack and Collins, 1998). This may also be true for boy-only groups. Furthermore, research suggests that girls lose out in mixed-sex groupings because of inabilities of teachers to bring about pedagogic change, together with persistent demand by many boys for the teacher's attention (Evans, 1989). Merely mixing boys and girls together without sensitive and careful integration and without a change in teaching approach may serve to exacerbate misconception and mistrust between the sexes and so reinforce masculine hegemony.

However, there is some evidence from an ethnographic study of one mixed-sex outdoor adventure centre that the form and content of the hidden and overt curricula held positive implications for pupil's learning and confidences. An unintended consequence of the teaching approaches realised through the material conditions, social relations and ethos was a shift in gender identities and relations during the coeducational experience (Humberstone, 1986; 1993). Behaviours demonstrating collaboration, responsibility and group support were valued and encouraged rather than those expressing aggressive, competitive individualism. The experience provided the opportunity for boys to rethink their views about girls' physical potential and competences. The programme visibly challenged stereotypical assumptions of gender and everyday notions of physicality. Girls' and boys' apparently more sensitive understanding of themselves and each other was a consequence of the contextual and ideological features characteristic of the outdoor centre – they were learning new skills together in relatively small numbers where they were positioned centrally in their learning and affective (emotional) communication was acknowledged. It is suggested that 'physical education experiences of these types could form a developmental basis for alternative masculine identities that neither celebrate the warrior ethos not identify co-operative endeavour, caring, and emotional expression as "wimpish" weakness' (Humberstone, 1990: 210).

Cultural hegemony is difficult to shift. Even when attempts have been made to create more equitable practices in school physical education lessons, there still seems to be a continued reinforcement of traditional gender relations and identities (Evans *et al.*, 1996; Wright 1997, 1999). Education can provide the basis upon which society can challenge and change not only personal self-perception and abilities (self-knowledges) but also social understandings and social relations, such as those to do with gender. Sport and physical activity in schooling are significant milieu in this respect. But uncritical and ill-considered discourses regarding single sex or coeducational practices may perpetuate the man/woman dualistic ideology, becoming woman/man privileging women's diversity of experiences above an apparent, yet untrue male mono-culture. The paradox for every marginalised group as well as women is highlighted in these debates in sports contexts. How to affirm a particular collective experience, maintain solidarity in the light of exclusion, whilst not resorting to essentialist notions of difference?

The celebration of girl-only groupings and denigrating mixed-sex teaching may deny many boys the opportunities to develop so called 'feminine' attributes whilst young women become more assertive and confident. Perhaps in its extremes, such strategies may reproduce aggressive, masculinist, hierarchical behaviours in young women without challenging such behaviours in young men. This may well reaffirm essentialist notions of differences between men and women. It seems it is largely men who perpetrate violence against women and peoples (as in war). Such actions represent the collapse of personal, social and environmental relations. Thus practices that reaffirm particular relations not only amongst girls and women and amongst boys and men, but also those between girls and boys and between men and women need to be explored, critically reflected upon and action taken. Some physical education contexts may provide challenges to hegemonic cultures and these need further research. But there seems little evidence to suggest that such possible reformations are permeating to any great degree adult life or media reportage and representation. We may want to ask questions such as: does the media include and take seriously women's views and experiences in sport? are alternative male and female images or configurations respected in the media?

## The media, sport and hegemonic struggles

Images presented through newspapers, television, music videos, advertisements, radio, computer games and so forth convey cultural meanings that are received by most people in society. Media mediate cultural messages that frequently reflect gender stereotypes but they may also be contested sites where struggles over gender hegemony may create alternatives to restrictive polarised notions of masculinity and femininity.

Transgressions from masculine 'norms' by popular sports 'heroes' are frequently ridiculed. For example, pictures of David Beckham dressed in a sarong, as he leaves a restaurant with 'Posh Spice', filled the front pages of the tabloids in June 1998. They were accompanied by headlines; 'Beckham has got his Posh frock on' (Whitaker, 1998: 1). 'Girlie gear sarong for sexy David. But does it work for women?' (Weathers, 1998: 3). Written by a woman, the latter headline goes on to further collude with hegemonic masculinity, with comments trivialising Beckham's unconventional image and relationship. The text implies that he is dominated by his partner Victoria, becoming feminised and emasculated: 'David's fashion statement is alarming for us women who prefer soccer stars in shorts not skirts. It's enough to make you weak with nostalgia for all things reassuringly macho and smelling of Brut'.

Cockburn's (1999) study of the ways in which teenage girls' magazines impact upon their sporting identities highlights the 'conflicting stereotypes' presented to young women. This analysis and other recent feminist analyses of women's magazines demonstrate changes in cultural hegemony where ideological representations have become more complex and paradoxical (Wearing, 1998). Nevertheless, Cockburn (1999: 15) finds: 'it becomes clear how inconsistent and unsatisfactory are the images offered by magazines'. They provide contradictory representations of girls' relations to sport but which are generally taken as childish and 'unfeminine' such that many girls and young women may come to reject physical education and sport as irrelevant.

Furthermore, media coverage of women's sport is shown to endorse a hegemonic masculinity and to inferiorise women. Missing from media reportage is the accomplishment of women both in team sport, individual sport and such outdoor activities as sailing, rock-climbing and so forth. For example, it is mainly men who are portrayed as 'heroes' involved in risk-taking adventurous activities in the outdoors. When women do engage in these activities, sometimes with fatal consequences, they are depicted not as heroines, but behaving inappropriately and selfishly. The ideology of motherhood was a significant feature in the reporting of the tragic death of the British climber Alison Hargreaves. Having successfully climbed a number of Himalayan peaks, she died in an accident on K2 in 1995. The media were scathing of her for depriving her children of their mother. Such criticism is rarely made of male climbers who deprive their children of a father (Humberstone, 2000).

Rowe (1995: 134) points out, 'The large scale absence of women's sport from 'serious' media coverage and the presence of sporting women's bodies as objects to be sexually appraised (as man-like/unattractive or woman-like/attractive) is a significant reproduction in culture of persistent social and material inequalities' (cited in Wearing, 1998: 77). Wright and Clarke's (1999: 228) examination of media representation of female rugby players takes this analysis further arguing that media discourse constructs 'Compulsory heterosexuality' [which] thereby acts as a form of social and sexual control through the naturalising and normalising of (hetero)-sexual relations'. They point to women rugby players whose actions might be seen as calling into question hegemonic masculinity as epitomised through rugby and so challenging traditional notions of what it is to be male or female. However, hegemonic processes are far more complex, subtle and pervasive, for female players are still assumed to conform to normalising sexual and gender ideologies (Wright and Clarke, 1999).

Clearly then the media does much to bolster dominant forms of masculinity and emphasise inferiorising forms of femininity, reinforcing discourses of hegemonic masculinity and traditional patterns of gender order. Challenges to conventional notions of what it is to be male or female or what are taken as everyday gender and sexual relations are frequently constructed as unnatural and are denigrated or even censured through dominant cultural practices and institutions, particularly in the reportage of sports cultural forms.

## Female permeation of male sporting space

All-women sport advocacy organisations are not immune from the influence of cultural hegemony. Whilst all-male sport organisations are perceived as the norm without question, life-history research of the female chairs of the Women's Sport Foundation (UK) highlights the dilemmas for them as they operate at the interface between structures (in sport) and agency (themselves). One chair drew attention to the possible destabilising effects on the organisation of charges of it being 'a lesbian organisation' (Clarke and Humberstone, 1997b). Clarke (1995: 9) points to the insidious ways that homophobia, a crucial aspect of hegemonic masculinity can act to 'separate[s] heterosexual women from their lesbian sisters and prevent[s] them sharing experiences and working together to challenge prejudices and discriminatory practices'.

Women's entry into all, or predominately male, sporting spaces arguably present possibilities for women to resist and contest dominant male definitions of and control in sport (see Bryson, 1987). However, research into sport and leisure as paid work for women highlights the ambiguities and considerable barriers experienced by women and the various strategies they use in negotiating these male-dominated spaces (see Allin, 1998; Yule, 1998). British professional boxer Jane Couch who won the World Women's Welterweight title in the USA in 1997 was denied by the British Boxing Board of Control (BBBC) its professional boxer's licence which would enable her to box in the UK. No women had previously been granted a licence by the BBBC and by her application and participation she transgressed the conventional boundaries of 'femininity'. When she took the BBBC to an industrial tribunal on the grounds of sex discrimination, the BBBC put forward spurious medical evidence in its contention that boxing held special and different dangers for women than for men. Couch won her case and was give a licence partly on the grounds that, 'the "medical grounds" [offered in defence] are all gender based stereotypical assumptions [and are] not capable of amounting to [a] valid defence' (McArdle, 1999: 18). Couch, through her desire to box professionally, threatened the masculine authority of the boxing world in the UK. Mennesson's (2000) study of women boxers in France shows the ways in which the existing gender order is challenged through women's participation, but it also highlights the paradoxes as many of the women boxers displayed traditional modes of femininity.

Harris's (1996) analysis of women collegiate footballers also evidences paradoxes for women participating in perceived male team sport in the UK. On the one hand they challenge male hegemony by playing football but on the other they may be colluding with it. Since it was found that, 'the majority of women strongly resisted the feminist label and were eager to demonstrate their femininity and heterosexuality' (Harris, 1998: 295). Cox and Thompson's (2000) study of female soccer players in New Zealand and Scraton *et al.*'s (1999) study of élite female footballers in Europe highlight similar complexities and paradoxes for players of all levels in their relation to conventional notions of femininity and sexuality.

Young's (1997) preliminary analysis of in-depth interviews with Canadian sports women in largely male-defined activities (rugby, rock-climbing, wrestling, ice-hockey and martial arts) highlights the diversity of responses and meanings given to their experiences by these women. Many women felt much enjoyment in their continued participation but, although weakening constraints in masculine hegemony in sport, this required their continued struggle. One woman emphasised that her sport was athletically demanding and not to be trivialised. 'Anybody who knows anything about wrestling ... knows that girls don't wrestle to be cute. There's nothing cute about it. It is a tough physical and mental sport' (Young, 1997: 299). Many interviewees actively resisted the 'winning-at-all-costs' strategy of excess force and violence and although enjoying the physical and 'aggressive' competitive elements of their sport distanced themselves from 'hegemonic models' of sport such as unethical coaching techniques. Women who challenge male hegemony through entering into 'male' sporting sites experience considerable contradictions. This is highlighted in cultural analyses of sub-cultures of female body-builders and weight-lifters. There is a complex tension over the meaning of female identity through struggles over 'acceptable' representations of the strong female body as located within normalising heterosexual beautifying discourses. Arguably, male/female dichotomising principles are deconstructed by women body-builders: 'The deliberately muscular woman disturbs dominant notions of sex, gender, and sexuality, and any discursive field that includes her risks opening up a site of contest and conflict, anxiety and ambiguity' (Schulz, 1990: 71 cited in Wearing, 1998: 79).

## Conclusion

The insidious nature of the process of masculine hegemony in regaining its control over what it means to be male and female is strongly evident in sports culture. However, cultural hegemony is always vulnerable and must maintain continued vigilance and effort to preserve the *status quo*, particularly in respect of idealised masculinity and limited, inferiorised femininity. Sport and schooling provide sites in which struggles over dominant values and gender ideologies take place and sometimes reformation (transformation) may occur.

On occasions, attempts have been made to promote equality between the sexes in team sports. However, ethnographic research that explored the processes of egalitarianism between women and men in an American co-ed soccer league found that even where participants professed egalitarianism, the co-ed soccer continued both in play and principle to be dominated by males (Henry and Comeaux, 1999).

Nevertheless, different cultural contexts in which sport forms occur may present different characteristic features that may provide opportunities for reconfigurations of gender relations and concepts of masculinity and femininity. Spatial, temporal and environmental aspects are rarely considered in cultural analyses of sport. Cultural and spacial contexts that may give rise to unconventional, alternative sports values and ideologies need exploration. For example '[E]vidence suggests that nature-based sports can not only reaffirm hegemonic masculinities (the 'Rambos') but also, in certain conditions, transform how both masculine bodies and the feminine are defined ... In such contexts, sport can have many of the characteristics ascribed to dominant images of sport (e.g. physical skill, power and exertion). However, a key difference is that co-operation with, and sensitivity to, the environment is valued instead of aggression and competition' (Humberstone, 1998: 387).

Emphasis upon difference and diversity calls upon analyses that acknowledge not only the system of meanings and webs of power operating through organisations and institutions in sport, but also the inter-connections of constraints and opportunities of 'ethnicity', race, class, disability, sexuality and so forth, as well as sex. Poststructuralist insights further emphasise the significance of agency in the construction of various forms of femininities and masculinities and in resistance to prevailing gender regimes. Drawing upon Foucault's (1984) notion of 'heterotopias', Wearing (1998: 147) argues that, 'Leisure spaces (heterotopias) for women provide spaces for rewriting the script of what it is to be a woman, beyond definitions provided by powerful males and the discourses propagated as truth in contemporary societies'. These spaces, she argues, provide opportunities to challenge the binary notion of woman as 'other' to and inferior to men. Further, leisure spaces may provide spaces for 'repeated performative' practices that constitute multiple subjectivities in which men and women can move beyond limitations of 'cultural gender stereotypes' and in which interactions between men and women may create mutual respect and alternative ways of being and acting both apart and together. It is possible that such leisure spaces might be constituted within particular forms of sport.

## Notes

1 Post-colonial perspectives are missing from much sport analyses, particularly when linked with issues around gender. But see Wearing (1998) which highlights 'Subaltern Studies' and centralises leisure experiences of women marginalised in Eurocentric middle-class theorising. See also hooks (1989).
2 Patriarchy is defined by Hartmann (1981) 'as a set of social relations between men which have [*sic*] a material base and which through hierarchical, established or created interdependence and solidarity among men that enables them to dominate women'. It was central to 1970s analyses of gender differences in power that moved beyond economic causes. The notion has been deconstructed by poststructuralist feminist analyses highlighting the notion of 'other' differences also enmeshed in webs of power such as race, age, ethnicity, sexuality and ability.
3 The significant research approach adopted is largely ethnographic, frequently including life-histories. This is underpinned by an interpretative hermeneutic framework which explores individual and group meanings analysing these taken-for-granted assumptions through critical lenses often locating them in broader social, cultural, organisational and sometimes environmental contexts (see Atkinson and Hammersley, 1998; Denzin, 1997; Fetterman, 1998).
4 For example, Stuart Hall, Angela McRobbie, Paul Willis, etc. See Gelder and Thornton (1997).

5 Bob Connell's (1990; 1995) work is based around life-history interviews with diverse groups of men ranging from the unemployed 'outside' of respectable working class to men involved in the environmental movement where feminism is very strong. His work is crucial to an understanding of the ways in which hegemonic masculinity shapes men's actions and emotions and the dilemmas for men who attempt to resist its persuasiveness and live more egalitarian lifestyles. Nevertheless, Wearing (1998: 98) points out that Connell's emphasis upon heterosexuality as essential in hegemonic masculinity obscures the view that even gay men are empowered by their 'male embodiment through valorization of the phallus and inferiorisation of the female body'.

6 Bricknell's (1999) study highlights the importance of subjectivities (bodies of feelings) in the construction of gender power. Her own full involvement in the offshore racing scene provides for rich descriptive text and sophisticated analyses at levels of emotions, social practices and social structures. As a consequence of the dualistic ideology, i.e. body/mind split, emotions and feelings have been problematic in research. However, such poststructuralist analyses, that attempt deconstruction of hierarchical binary conceptualisations, bring greater understanding of cultural practices that reinforce cultural constraints in gender regimes.

**Reflection questions**

1 Discuss your own school experience of physical education and sport. Was it different for boys and girls? Why?

2 Discuss what you understand by the concepts patriarchy, ideology, hegemony and ideology of motherhood and how they can explain the position of women and men in sport.

3 Discuss the concepts 'hegemonic masculinity' and 'inferiorised femininity' and reflect upon:

 i) your own experiences
 ii) media representations of sporting icons.

 How is 'hegemonic masculinity' and 'inferiorised femininity' reinforced and challenged in (i) and (ii)?

### Tasks

1. In no more than 500 words, write an autobiographical account of the ways in which your own sport and physical education experiences have been shaped by your sex and other characteristics such as race and class.
2. Conduct an open interview with a person of the other sex about their sports and physical education biography. Questions you ask should elicit how the sports experience of your interviewee has been influenced by being either male or female. You might choose to interview someone of a different age and/or ethnic origin. Find out if they have challenged gendered constraints. You should tape-record this interview and transcribe the interview. Ensure confidentiality if the interviewee so wishes and be sensitive in your interviewing.

### Further reading

Clarke, G. and Humberstone, B. (Eds) (1997) *Researching Women and Sport*. London: Macmillan Press.
McKay, J., Messner, M. and Sabo, D. (Eds) (2000) *Men, Masculinities, and Sport*. Thousand Oaks, CA: Sage.
Wearing, B. (1998) *Leisure and Feminist Theory*. London: Sage.

## References

Allin, L. (1998) 'I could hold my own and that was the difference', in Higgins, P. and Humberstone, B. (Eds) *Celebrating Diversity: Learning by Sharing Cultural Differences*. Buckinghamshire: European Institute for Outdoor Adventure and Experiential Learning.

Askew, S. and Ross, C. (1988) *Boys don't Cry: Boys and Sexism in Education*. Milton Keynes: Open University Press.

Atkinson, P. and Hammersley, M. (1998) 'Ethnography and participant observation', in Denzin, N. and Lincoln, Y. (Eds) *Strategies of Qualitative Inquiry*. London: Sage.

Baker-Graham, A. (1999) 'Work with girls and young women', in Higgins, P. and Humberstone, B. (Eds) *Outdoor Education and Experiential Learning in the UK*. Luneburg University, Germany: Verlag Erlebnispadagogik.

Barak, K., Hendrich, M.A. and Albrechtsen, S. (2000) 'Enhancing self-esteem in adolescent girls: a proposed model for adventure education programming', in Humberstone, B. (Ed.) *Her Outdoors. Risk, Challenge and Adventure in Gendered Open Spaces*. LSA Publication, No. 66. Brighton: Leisure Studies Association.

Birrell, S. (1988) Discourse on the gender/sport relationship: from women in sport to gender relations. *Exercise and Sport Science Reviews,* 16, 459–502.

Birrell, S. (1989) Racial relations theories in sport: suggestions for a more critical analysis. *Sociology of Sport,* 6, 212–17.

Bricknell, L. (1999) The trouble with feelings: gender, sexualities, and power in a gender regime of competitive sailing. *Journal of Sport and Social Issues,* 23, 2, 421–38.

Bryson, L. (1987) Sport and the maintenance of masculine hegemony. *Women's Studies International Forum,* 10, 4, 349–60.

Bryson, L. (1990) 'Challenges to male hegemony in sport', in Messner, M. and Sabo, D. (Eds) *Sport, Men and the Gender Order: Critical Feminist Perspectives.* Champaign, IL: Human Kinetics.

Burt, R. (1994) 'Representations of masculinity in contemporary theatre dance', in Brackenridge, C. (Ed.) *Body Matters: Leisure Images and Lifestyles.* LSA Publication, No. 47. Eastbourne: Leisure Studies Association.

Carrigan, T., Connell, B. and Lee, J. (1985) Towards a new sociology of masculinity. *Theory and Society,* 5, 14, 551–604.

Clarke, G. (1995) Homophobia and heterosexism in physical education. Can we move into a new era? Paper presented at the Physical Education Association Annual conference: Moving into a New Era. Twickenham, England.

Clarke, G. (1997) 'Playing a part: the lives of lesbian physical education teachers', in Clarke, G. and Humberstone, B. (Eds) (1997) *Researching Women and Sport.* London: Macmillan Press.

Clarke, G. and Humberstone, B. (Eds) (1997a) *Researching Women and Sport.* London: Macmillan Press.

Clarke, G. and Humberstone, B. (Eds) (1997b) *Managing a Women's Sport Organisation: Interpreting Biographies Researching Women and Sport.* London: Macmillan Press.

Clarke, J. and Critcher, C. (1985) *The Devil makes Work: Leisure in Capitalist Britain.* London: Macmillan.

Cockburn, C. (1999) The trouble with girls: A study of teenage girls' magazines to sport and physical education. *The British Journal of Physical Education,* 30, 3, 11–15.

Cohen, J. and Manion, T. (1981) *Perspectives on Classrooms and Schools.* London: Holt, Rinehart & Winton.

Connell, R.W. (1990) 'An iron man: the body and some contradictions of hegemonic masculinity', in Messner, M. and Sabo, D. (Eds) *Sport, Men and the Gender Order; Critical Feminist Perspectives.* Champaign, IL: Human Kinetics.

Connell, R.W. (1995) *Masculinities.* Berkeley, CA: University of California Press.

Connell, R. *et al.* (1982) *Making the Difference, School, Families and Social Division.* London: Allen.

Connolly, P. (1998) *Racism, Gender Identities and Young Children.* London: Macmillan.

Cox, B. and Thompson, S. (2000) Multiple bodies. Sportswomen, soccer and sexuality. *International Review for the Sociology of Sport,* 35, 1, 5–20.

Deem, R. (1986) *All Work and No Play.* Milton Keynes: Open University Press.

Delemont, S. (1980) *Sex Roles and the School.* London: Methuen.

Dempsey, K. (1990) Women's leisure: men's leisure. *Australian and New Zealand Journal of Sociology,* 25, 1, 27–45.

Denzin, N. (1997) *Interpretive Ethnography.* London: Sage.

Evans, J. (1989) Swinging from the crossbar: equality and opportunity in the physical education curriculum. *British Journal of Physical Education,* 20, 2, 84–87.

Evans, J., Davies, B. and Penney, D. (1996) Teachers, teaching and the social construction of gender relations. *Sport, Education and Society*, 1, 2, 165–184.

Fetterman, D. (1998) *Ethnography Step by Step*. London: Sage.

Flintoff, A. (1993) 'Gender, physical education and initial teacher education', in Evans, J. (Ed.) *Equality, Education and Physical Education.* London: Falmer Press.

Foucault, M. (1984) 'Space, knowledge and power', in Rabinow, P. (Ed.) *The Foucault Reader.* Harmondsworth: Penguin.

Gelder, K. and Thornton, S. (1997) *The Subcultures Reader.* London: Routledge.

Gramsci, A. (1985) *Prison Notebooks: Selections.* New York: International Publishers.

Green, E., Hebron, S. and Woodward, D. (1990) *Women's Leisure, What Leisure?* London: Macmillan.

Griffin, C. (1985) *Typical girls: Young Women from School to the Job Market.* London: Routledge and Kegan Paul.

Griffin, P. (1990) 'Addressing homophobia in PE: responsibilities for teachers and researchers', in Messner, M. and Sabo, D. (Eds) *Sport, Men and the Gender Order: Critical Feminist Perspectives.* Champaign, IL: Human Kinetics.

Hall, M.A. (1996) *Feminism and Sporting Bodies: Essays in Theory and Practice.* Leeds: Human Kinetics.

Hall, M.A. (1997) Women's sport and feminist praxis: bridging the theory/practice gap. *Women in Sport and Physical Activity Journal*, 6, 2, 272–287.

Harding, S. (1986) *The Science Question in Feminism.* Milton Keynes: Open University Press.

Hargreaves, J. (1994) *Sporting Females.* London: Routledge Press.

Harris, J. (1996) 'Defending like women': an interpretive sociological study of female collegiate football players. Unpublished PhD thesis. Brunel University.

Hartmann, H. (1981) 'The unhappy marriage of Marxism and feminism: towards a more progressive union', in Sargent, L. (Ed.) *Women in Revolution.* London: Pluto Press.

Henry, J.M. and Comeaux, H.P. (1999) Gender egalitarianism in coed sport. A case study of American soccer. *International Review for the Sociology of Sport,* 34, 3, 277–290.

Hooks, B. (1989) *Feminist Theory: from Margin to Center.* Boston, MA: South End Press.

Humberstone, B. (1986) 'Learning for a change', in Evans, J. (Ed.) *Physical Education, Sport and Schooling: Studies in the Sociology of Physical Education.* Lewes: Falmer Press.

Humberstone, B (1990) 'Warriors or wimps?: creating alternative forms of physical education', in Messner, M. and Sabo, D. (Eds) *Sport, Men and the Gender Order: Critical Feminist Perspectives.* Champaign, IL: Human Kinetics.

Humberstone, B. (1993) 'Equality, physical education and outdoor education-ideological struggles and transformative structures?', in Evans, J. (Ed.) *Equality, Education and Physical Education.* London: Falmer Press.

Humberstone, B. (1998) Re-creation and connections in and with nature: synthesising ecological and feminist discourses. *International Review for the Sociology of Sport,* 33, 4, 381–392.

Humberstone, B. (2000) Introduction, in Humberstone, B. (Ed.) *Her Outdoors. Risk, Challenge and Adventure in Gendered Open Spaces.* LSA Publication, No. 66. Brighton: Leisure Studies Association.

Krane, V. (1996) Lesbians in sport: towards acknowledgement, understanding and theory. *Journal of Sport and Exercise Psychology,* 18, 13, 237–247.

McArdle, D. (1999) Sex discrimination in physical education employment – levelling the playing field. *The British Journal of Physical Education,* 30,3, 16–18.

McLennan, G. (1995) *The Power of Ideology in Block 4 Power and Politics, Society and Social Science: A Foundation Course.* Milton Keynes: The Open University.

Mennesson, C. (2000) 'Hard' women and 'soft' women: the social construction of identities among female boxers. *International Review for the Sociology of Sport*, 35, 1, 21–48.

Messner, M. (1992) *Power at Play: Sports and the Problem of Masculinity.* Boston: Beacon Press.

Messner, M. (1998) 'Boyhood, organised sport, and the construction of masculinities', in Kimmel, M. and Messner, M. (Eds) *Men's Lives.* Needham Heights, MA: Allyn & Bacon.

Messner, M. and Sabo, D. (Eds) (1990) *Sport, Men and the Gender Order.* Champaign, IL: Human Kinetics.

Miles, R. (1989) *The Women's History of the World.* London: Paladin.

Murphy, P., Williams, J. and Dunning, E. (1990) *Football on Trial.* London: Routledge.

Oakley. A. (1972) (2nd ed. 1985) *Sex, Gender and Society.* Aldershot: Gower.

Renolds, E. (1997) 'All they've got on their brains is football': sport, masculinity and the gendered practices of playground relations. *Sport, Education and Society,* 2, 1: 5–23.

Rowe, D. (1995) *Popular Cultures: Rock Music, Sport and the Politics of Pleasure.* London: Sage.

Scraton, S. (1992) *Shaping Up to Womanhood: Gender and Girls' Physical Education.* Milton Keynes: Open University Press.

Scraton, S. (1993) 'Education, coeducation and physical education in secondary schooling', in Evans, J. (Ed.) *Equality, Education and Physical Education.* London: Falmer Press.

Scraton, S., Fasting, K., Pfister, G. and Bunuel, A. (1999) It's still a man's game? The experience of top-level women footballers in England, Germany, Norway and Spain. *International Review for the Sociology of Sport,* 34, 2, 99–111.

Skelton, C. (2000) A passion for football: dominant masculinities and primary schooling. *Sport, Education and Society,* 5, 1, 5–18.

Spratt, G., McCormack, J. and Collins, D. (1998) 'The discovery project', in Higgins, P. and Humberstone, B. (Eds) *Celebrating Diversity: Learning by Sharing Cultural Differences.* Buckinghamshire: European Institute for Outdoor Adventure and Experiential Learning.

Talbot, M. (1988) 'Their own worst enemy? Women and leisure provision', in Wimbush, E. and Talbot, M. (Eds) *Relative Freedoms: Women and Leisure.* Milton Keynes: Open University Press.

Talbot, M. (1997) Holistic approaches to the place of sport in women's lives. *Women in Sport and Physical Activity Journal,* 6, 2, 72–87.

Thompson, S.M. (1999) *Mother's Taxi: Sport and Women's Labor.* Albany: State University of New York Press.

Wearing, B. (1990) Beyond the ideology of motherhood; leisure as resistance. *Australian and New Zealand Journal of Sociology*, 26, 1, 36–58.

Wearing, B. (1998) *Leisure and Feminist Theory*. London: Sage.

Weathers, H. (4 June 1998) Girlie gear sarong for sexy David. But does it work for women? *The Mirror*, 3.

Whitaker, T. (4 June 1998) Beckham has got his Posh frock on. *The Sun*, 1.

Whitehead, N. and Hendry, L.B. (1976) *Teaching PE in England: Description and Analysis*. London: Lepus.

Williams, A. (1989) 'Girls and boys come out to play (but mainly boys) – gender and physical education', in Williams, A. (Ed.) *Issues in Physical Education for the Primary Years*. London: Falmer Press.

Williams, R. (1981) *Culture*. London: Fontana.

Williams, R. (1988) *Keywords: A Vocabulary of Culture and Society*. London: Fontana.

Wimbush, E. (1988) 'Mothers meeting', in Wimbush, E. and Talbot, M. (Eds) *Relative Freedoms: Women and Leisure*. Milton Keynes: Open University Press.

Wright, J. (1997) The construction of gendered contexts in single sex and coeducational physical education lessons. *Sport, Education and Society*, 2, 1, 55–72.

Wright, J. (1999) Changing gendered practices in physical education: working with teachers. *European Physical Education Review*, 5, 3, 181–197.

Wright, J. and Clarke, G. (1999) Sport, the media and the construction of compulsory heterosexuality: a case study of women's rugby union. *International Review for the Sociology of Sport*, 34, 3, 227–244.

Young, K. (1997) Women, sport and physicality: preliminary findings from a Canadian study. *International Review for the Sociology of Sport*, 32, 3, 297–306.

Yule, J. (1998) 'Sub-cultural strategies in patriarchal leisure professional cultures', in Aitchison, C. and Jordan, F. (Eds) *Gender, Space and Identity*. LSA Publication, No. 63. Eastbourne: Leisure Studies Association.

Zaman, H. (1997) 'Islam, well-being and physical activity: perceptions of Muslim young women', in Clarke, G. and Humberstone, B. (Eds) *Researching Women and Sport*. London: Macmillan Press.

# 5 The social construction of the body in physical education and sport

*David Kirk*

## Introduction

Bodies come in various shapes, sizes and colours. Some bodies are healthy, others are sick. Some bodies perform better than others in activities such as sports. Some bodies are disabled. We experience our bodies in ways that provide constant reminders that being human is to be embodied. We feel strong, comfortable, poorly, agitated, nervous. We experience other bodies as attractive, ugly, sexy, fat. Bodies are everywhere. They are integral to our experiences of being human. This means that we know a lot about bodies simply from living in and with them.

Physical educators and sport scientists know bodies in this everyday, intuitive way. But this way of knowing bodies rarely intrudes on their professional work. Because the performance of bodies is so central to sport, exercise and physical recreation, physical educators and sport scientists also seek to know bodies from a professional perspective.

From this professional perspective, physical educators have since at least the eighteenth century viewed the body as 'an object of exact calculation' (Turner, 1984) whose performative capacities can be measured, analysed and improved. Early forms of physical training in schools from the 1880s to the 1940s were based on various systems of rational gymnastics, known in the USA as 'calisthenics'. These forms of physical training promoted the idea of the body as an object of exact calculation.

After the Second World War, developments in the use of science to understand performance in sport further promoted this view. New fields of knowledge emerged during the 1940s and 1950s, such as biomechanics, exercise and sport physiology, and skill acquisition. This new scientific research soon began to assist sports people to improve their performances by providing a scientific base to their training and competition. Since the 1940s, this scientific perspective on the body has become increasingly successful in terms of enhancing performance in sport, and very powerful in terms of shaping physical educators' thinking about the body.

The professional perspective provides a very different view of the body from the everyday intuitive understanding we develop through experience. Increasing prominence of bodies in popular culture and advertising, increasing concerns for body-related issues such as health and fitness, and illnesses such as coronary heart disease, AIDS and cancer have raised people's awareness of their intuitive understanding of bodies. This trend in turn has prompted many scholars in physical education and sport studies to question whether the objective, scientific view of the body is sufficient or appropriate for the work teachers and coaches do.

In the 1980s, Richard Tinning (1985) alerted physical educators to a concern that we may be contributing to a 'cult of slenderness' without realising it. More recently, Andrew Sparkes (1999) used narrative methods to explore teachers' and athletes' experiences of their bodies. Kathleen Armour (1999) argued that a new rationale for physical education in schools should be body-focused. Chris Hickey *et al.*, (1998) and Michael Gard and Robert Meyenn (2000) among others have used a focus on the body as a means of exploring aspects of sport, masculinity and sexuality. Jan Wright (2000) proposed that physical educators need to look to forms of movement other than sport to find alternative perspectives on the body and physical activity.

These publications represent only a small proportion of the scholarly work in physical education and sport that is centred on a sociological perspective on the body as a means of criticising and developing the traditional, objective perspective. The social construction of the body is a core concept that runs through all of this research and writing by sociologists of physical education and sport. The purpose of this chapter is to introduce this concept. The chapter also seeks to show how the processes of schooling and education play a part in socially constructing bodies. The chapter concludes with a discussion of the implications of this sociological perspective on bodies for practices in physical education and sport.

## Naturalistic and constructionist views of the body

It isn't just physical educators and sport scientists who have overlooked the social construction of bodies. Until recently, scholars in sociology, history and philosophy have also neglected the human body (Turner, 1984). Many social researchers have acknowledged the individual within society. But relatively few have extended their analyses to include the part bodies play in producing and reproducing social practices. Part of the reason for this neglect has been the success of the biological and physical sciences in providing explanations of the structure and function of the body. We tend to take for granted that bodies are flesh, blood and bones. The relevance of biophysical explanations of the body seems self-evident. The success of biophysical science has contributed to a naturalistic view of the body, a view that sees the body as a biological and physical phenomenon.

On the occasions when social scientists have turned their attention to the body, their theories have tended to reflect this naturalistic view (Shilling, 1993). This view has lead, for example, to claims that differences in sport performance between females and males can be explained solely in terms of biological factors such as strength ('men are stronger') and psychological factors such as motivation ('men are more aggressive'). Similar arguments are made to explain racial differences in sport performance (McKay, 1991). Researchers who agree with a naturalistic view of the body assume that biological differences explain variations in behaviour. In other words, differences in sex, colour, size and other physical attributes of bodies are seen to be the cause of how people behave and what they believe.

Another problem with the naturalistic view is that it is too deterministic. An example of determinism would be where a social behaviour, such as being 'masculine', is thought to be dependent on and determined by biological factors such as muscularity and physical size.

This naturalistic view of the body has been challenged recently. Researchers have argued that people's understanding of their bodies is developed by the society they live in. They claim that bodies are social at the same time as they are biological and physical.

A view of the body as socially constructed suggests that biology does not determine social behaviour. In the case of masculinity, constructionists would point out that there are different forms of masculinity and different behaviours are associated with being masculine. It may be the case that some groups in society consider a large, muscular physique to be an essential quality of masculinity. But many men who are neither physically large nor muscular nevertheless are considered to be masculine.

From a constructionist point of view, bodies are important to understanding how and why people as individuals and groups behave in the ways they do. The body transmits messages. Sometimes this process is called 'body language'. Bodies also receive messages from others, such as for example the appropriate ways for males to dress. Social and biological factors interact in all of these cases and examples. A naturalistic view of the body stresses only one side of the process, and presents social behaviour as 'naturally' connected to biology. However, as our everyday intuitive knowledge of our bodies suggests, bodies exist in culture and nature simultaneously.

## The body in culture/nature

Given the dominance in western cultures of naturalistic views of the body, the concept of the body in culture is potentially a difficult one to grasp. The bodies of accident victims, transplant patients and others undergoing cosmetic surgery are literally and physically reconstructed every day by surgeons. Such commonplace practices make it relatively easy to think analogously of the body as a machine. Like machines, bodies have components that can, up to a point, be taken apart and reassembled. The workings of the body can in similar fashion to other machine-like objects be scrutinised and malfunctions diagnosed and remedied. Mary Shelley's monster, literally constructed by Dr Frankenstein, is the classical working out of the body-as-machine idea. So familiar are these ways of thinking about the body that to some of us the ideas of the social construction of the body and of the body in culture may seem to be nonsense.

A good way to begin to break down this barrier to understanding the notion of the body in culture is to consider the values attributed to different body shapes. At the level of conscious, thoughtful reflection, most people acknowledge that it is unfair and probably inaccurate to judge a person's worth on the basis of their physical appearance. Yet, as Joanne Finkelstein (1991) points out, the notion that character is reflected in appearance is widespread and is a powerful force in our daily interactions with others. She argues that:

> To accept, in the twentieth century, that character is summarized in our bodies, that personality and individuality are a function of our appearance and physical prowess, confronts us, to some extent, as an unlikely article of faith. When we consider the popularity of practices such as cosmetic surgery, strenuous exercise and dieting, which transform our body shape and appearance and which are frequently undertaken on the belief that our sense of self will be more assured when our appearance is different, then we are forced to consider that a continuity of thought with that of the physiognomists (of the nineteenth century) may be being expressed
>
> (7)

Physical appearance is not only widely utilised as a means of summing up a person's character. Body shapes more generally have over time come to act as symbols, signifying particular social values. At the present time in Britain and elsewhere, slender and muscular bodies are generally looked upon favourably. They are considered to signify health, capability, self-control and sexual attractiveness. Some people, however, may regard too much muscle as revolting. An example is body-building, where the self-absorbed attention paid to the body is thought to signify narcissism. Fatness, especially extreme obesity, is also regarded with revulsion. An obese body in western societies often symbolises slothfulness, poor health, greed and lack of self-control.

In other words, flesh-and-blood bodies take on particular meanings. Like a script, bodies tell a story about the person they embody. The physical appearance of bodies conveys ideas and values. Like scripts, bodies are read. Each of us in the course of our everyday lives interprets the signs they emit.

Body shape is just one example of the many ways in which the body is in culture and nature simultaneously. Skin colour and facial features are characteristics of bodies that also, at the same time as they are biological facts, have cultural significance. Particular ways of walking, carriage and comportment, all manner of bodily movements are interpreted and made sense of in everyday situations. Much of the time, the signs bodies emit are neither consciously communicated nor consciously interpreted. Making sense of the body is part of routine, taken-for-granted social behaviour.

It is important that we do not think of this distinction, that the body is in culture and nature simultaneously, as a binary, as opposite poles. Just as it would seem incredible to consider that we might exist without our bodies, so it is difficult to imagine our bodies as merely biological entities that cannot be read or interpreted. One important site in which we read or interpret the social significance of bodies is the media.

## Media representations of the body

Open just about any magazine or turn on the television and you are confronted regularly with bodies on display, usually in clothing that shows off the model's body shape to best effect. Much of the time, these images of bodies appear in advertisements as a means of selling a product. Sometimes, the body that appears on the television screen and the product being sold have some obvious connection, as in the advertisements for sports clothing or shoes.

However, sometimes there is no obvious connection between the image and the product. The bodies in these cases are used to attract our attention to the advertisement. They also link the values associated with particular body shapes to the product. An example might be the image of a fit and muscular athlete in an advertisement for an insurance company. In this case, the advertisers may be trying to link to the insurance company the values we associate with a fit, successful, powerful and talented body.

Something happens to bodies when they appear in this form, as a means of selling a product. All the social values that are connected with various shapes and sizes of bodies as a matter of course in everyday life get mixed up together and then repackaged, or reconstructed, in order to sell the product. It is this process, of making new associations between bodies and social values, that can be referred to as representation.

In consumer societies, our sense of ourselves in relation to society is only possible through the continuous activity of making choices and decisions. Researchers argue that we are compelled into active self-formation by a lack of fixed traditional roles. The acts of acquiring, consuming and throwing away are at the centre of a complex process of self-formation. Advertising is crucially placed to give substance to this process, since it stimulates desire and offers apparent alternative personae and lifestyles from which to choose.

The material the media supplies is not passively absorbed. Each of us actively appropriates this material to make sense of ourselves and our place in the social world. The media also manufactures our hopes and expectations of the future and provides a means of expressing our experiences. Media in consumer culture plays a crucial role in the formation of our self-identities. Visual representations of the body offer important resources in the process of self-formation. Advertising in particular not only establishes bodily norms, it also stimulates desire around these norms for the ways of life the body is being used to signify.

Advertisements do ideological work at a submerged or implicit level through the association and linking of otherwise unrelated ideas (Kirk, 1992). Advertisements create structures of meaning and they achieve this through their more obvious function to sell products. Advertisements reassemble or reconstruct already existing pieces or chains of information. These chains are comprised of a series of already meaningful elements that are attached to other already meaningful elements to create a new chain of meaning.

It is possible for each of us to interpret an advertisement differently. However, if the advertisement is to be effective at selling products, then it must be interpreted in a particular way. The image is a puzzle that needs to be decoded before it can be understood. The creators of advertisements attempt to reduce the possibility of a reader misunderstanding their intentions by targeting the advertisement at a specific group of readers. Moreover, for advertisements to work, it is important that they are not believed literally. For instance, you don't have to believe that 'Persil Washes Whiter' or that 'Coke Is The Real Thing!'. Advertisements work instead at the level researchers call the signifier, at the meeting point of associations of already established chains of meaning.

Framing refers to what is selected for inclusion in an advertisement and what is left out. Advertisements are put together in this calculated way in order to target particular groups of people who are potential customers for the product. Advertising can have such a powerful influence on our body image because advertisers target specific groups of people by including in the advertisement information, ideas and images they know will be recognised by that group of people.

Media representations of bodies are, in a sense, reconstructing bodies by repackaging the associations that are made between bodies and values in our everyday lives. Researchers who support a naturalistic view of the body argue that this makes these constructions 'artificial'. Social constructionists say that the media is just one site among others in which bodies are socially constructed, and that the ideas about bodies that are prominent in society are the outcomes of the interaction of many sites. Along with the media, another key site for constructing and making sense of bodies is education and schooling.

## Schooling bodies

Even though bodies are now receiving closer scrutiny from sociologists, schools as sites of constructing and constituting the body have tended to be overlooked. School sport and physical education in particular present themselves as key topics of interest in this regard, but these topics generally continue to remain on the margins of sociology's main agendas. This is in some respects surprising, given the prominence of media sport and the exercise industry in contemporary British society. On the other hand, perhaps this omission is not after all so hard to understand when we consider the intellectualist tradition in western societies that regards physical education as less important than other school subjects (Armour, 1999). Educational processes are, however, central to the process of socially constructing and constituting the body.

Marcel Mauss (1973) provides a clear illustration of the importance of educational practices in constructing the meanings of various 'techniques of the body'. On the basis of anthropological evidence, Mauss argued that the body is not a fixed biological category. Instead bodies are shaped by everyday practices that we assume are the same across cultures. However, this is not the case. Mauss shows how 'basic' activities such as sleeping, resting and caring for bodies differ from society to society. These differences are particularly marked in movement, and include different postures and gaits in walking and running, and different ways of dancing, jumping, climbing, descending, swimming and applying forceful movement. Mauss comments that:

> In all of these elements of the art of using the human body, the facts of education were dominant. The notion of education could be superimposed on that of imitation. For there are particular children with very strong imitative faculties, others with very weak ones, but all of them go through the same education ... What takes place is a prestigious imitation. The child, the adult, imitates actions which have succeeded and which he [*sic*] has seen successfully performed by people in whom he has confidence and who have authority over him.
>
> (73)

Mauss's use of the term education extends beyond formally organised learning experiences in schools. His analysis of the techniques of the body demonstrates that our repertoires of movements, ranging from everyday and commonplace movements to specialised and complex movements, are learned activities. As such, they belong as much to the category of culture as nature. Mauss draws our attention to the extent to which the learning of bodily practices is woven into the fabric of everyday life in all societies. He demonstrates the essentially social character of this process of imitative learning. Mauss also shows that techniques of the body differ within societies as well as across societies. Moreover, different forms of movement and bodily practices characterise different stages of life and so need to be viewed developmentally.

Chris Shilling (1991) has stressed Mauss's point about differences within cultures in relation to contemporary western societies like Britain, arguing that the body and the 'physical capital' invested in it play key roles in the production of social inequalities. He is particularly concerned to point out the class and gender dimensions of these inequalities. Different social groups make different investments in the body, depending on their need to work to secure the fundamental resources of life such as shelter, food and security. Shilling describes the relationship between social groups and their access to resources as their 'distance from necessity'.

According to Shilling, those who are less distant from necessity tend to see the body as a means to an end, as an instrument for securing the fundamental resources for survival. Manual labour, the use of the body itself as a means of securing resources, is an example of this form of physical capital; prostitution is another. Those who have a greater distance from necessity are less likely to engage in overtly manual labour and so tend to see the body as an end in itself. Consequently, they are more prone to engage in bodily practices that emphasise physical pleasure and the non-necessity of physical activity.

Shilling suggests that physical capital can be converted into economic and social gain, but social class limits the range of opportunities available for such conversion. For instance, he points out that 'children from (the dominant) classes tend to engage in socially élite sporting activities which stress manners and deportment and hence facilitate the future acquisition of social and cultural capital' (Shilling, 1991: 656). Shilling points out that incorporating consideration of gendered bodies within and across social classes can significantly strengthen this analysis of physical culture. In the case of producing both classed and gendered bodies, he suggests that educational processes play a key role. He points out that biology is not given and that physical capital is acquired through a process of constant work, since:

> The initial gender identities given to biologically male and female bodies contradict their physiological development. So, ten year old girls are defined as 'weak' and 'fragile' even though their bodies are usually larger than their male counterparts.
>
> (665)

It is largely through formal and informal educational processes that normative values surrounding the body are sustained. Schools are important sites in which these processes are worked through and institutionalised. Physical education and sport constitute specialised sets of practices within this site that make a crucial contribution to the social construction and normalisation of the body. Just as important are the links between formal educational institutions and other sites in which the body is schooled.

Schooling in this respect has both constraining and facilitating aspects. As Mauss and Shilling point out, bodies are disciplined in ways that conform to prevailing cultural norms. But this disciplining process is also enabling, since it facilitates the achievement of acceptable social interaction. Michel Foucault (1977) suggests that a dual process is unfolding here in which docility-utility is a key purpose. Foucault (1977: 25) comments that 'discipline produces subjected and practised bodies, docile bodies. Discipline increases the forces of the body (in economic terms of utility) and diminishes the same forces (in political terms of obedience)'.

Bodies in consumer societies need to be regulated in order to be useful to the process of economic productivity. Mere subjugation of the body would be useless in this context. It is here that the practices of schooling the body emerge as key components of contemporary social order, practices through which bodies are shaped and energies channelled but also controlled according to social, political, cultural and economic requirements. It is through this process of schooling, broadly conceived, that the techniques of the body are acquired, techniques that characterise particular societies and the social order of these societies.

Foucault's analysis of the regulation of the body in relation to time and space is an especially useful approach to considering the part sport plays in this process.

## Sport as a site for constructing bodies

Sport is a good example of the social construction of bodies since it is so obviously concerned with mastering physical skills that allow individuals to perform in prescribed ways. All sports do this explicitly, since all sports make demands on performers with regard to techniques, knowledge of rules and strategic understanding. We can apply Foucault's concepts of corporeal regulation in time and space to team games as a means of illustrating the part sport plays in constructing bodies.

Team games are an example of what Foucault (1977: 26) called disciplinary technology. According to Foucault, disciplinary technologies are practices that are intended both to constrain and enable bodies and to normalise and regulate their conduct. Game theorists have noted that games are rule-bound activities. It is the rules that provide games with their characteristic forms. These rules define the objective of the game, the kinds of movements players might perform, and the ways in which they can conduct themselves in relation to other players. Within the context of these rules, players and coaches devise techniques and strategies that may assist them to win the game.

In most games, space is organised explicitly, from the drawing of boundary lines that contain the playing area to markings within the playing area that permit or prohibit actions or players entering or occupying the defined space. Time is also organised explicitly, from the drawing of a temporal boundary that defines when play is to begin and end to the timing of particular actions. These time boundaries mark the borders between what some writers have viewed as the unreality of behaviour conducted according to the rules of the game, and the reality of everyday life.

Players who learn to play a game well submit themselves to the regulation of their bodies in time and space. The repetitive work that is required to achieve some degree of mastery of the techniques of games creates movement patterns that, once learned, tend to stay with the player, and may even influence and at times interfere with other movements, such as a squash player's difficulties with a tennis shot. It is even possible, indeed not uncommon, for highly-practised techniques and strategies of movement to become dominant characteristics of a person's movements outside the game.

The design of equipment, playing surfaces and other technological developments further prescribe how bodies might move, and the kind of bodies that might participate in games. Team games require particular forms of social relations between players on the same side and on opposing sides. In light of these techniques for regulating bodies through precise manipulations of space and time, it is not surprising that social commentators and educators found in team games a rich source of prescriptions for human conduct beyond the games themselves.

## Implications for physical education and sport

This chapter began with the observation that we know a lot about bodies intuitively. As professionals concerned with the performance of bodies in physical education and sport settings, this understanding has often been ignored or marginalised in favour of a scientific perspective on the body. Knowledge of biomechanics, physiology and skill acquisition has had a significant impact on the improvement of performance in sport. At the same time, scholars in physical education have noted that this scientific perspective objectifies the body. Some have gone further to suggest that a solely scientific understanding of the body may not provide the most appropriate base for teaching and coaching in physical education and sport.

A sociological perspective on the body reveals that the body is in culture and nature simultaneously. From this perspective, we can see that educational processes in physical education and sport are important contributors to the social construction of bodies. Schooling bodies through physical activities was described as a regulative process that both enables and constrains bodies. A sociological perspective on the body does not seek to displace the naturalistic perspective, though it does criticise the idea that a biophysical way of knowing is the only appropriate component of the professional perspective of physical educators and sport scientists. A sociological perspective also acknowledges the importance and legitimacy of our everyday intuitive knowledge of bodies and seeks to inform and extend this understanding.

So what might be the implications for a view of the body as socially as well as biologically constructed? There are at least three inter-related implications we can consider here.

### *Deconstructing myths*

One of the powerful uses of biophysical knowledge has been to help people better understand the biological and physical sources of health and well-being. In the process, science has deconstructed myths that are misleading or unhelpful such as the old-fashioned idea that regular exercise can prevent individuals catching a cold. A sociological perspective can in a similar way deconstruct cultural myths about the body. For example, school physical education has a key role to play in empowering young people with the skills and knowledge to deconstruct dangerous or misleading media representations of bodies, such as the idea that a slender body is necessarily healthy, attractive or even attainable for all people. In the process, physical education can assist young people to learn that diverse forms of embodiment are normal and acceptable, including ways of being masculine and feminine.

### *Providing alternative forms of physical education*

When it is accepted and understood that the body is in culture and nature simultaneously, it is easier to conceive of alternative forms of physical education. Sport-based physical education has been the dominant form of the subject in British schools since the end of the Second World War. The naturalistic view of the body has encouraged this development since it is relatively easy to improve sports performance through the application to training and competition of biophysical knowledge. But this perspective does not allow us to ask questions about the appropriateness or otherwise of physical contact and violence in sport or of the personal experience and social symbolism of pain and injury (Sparkes, 1998; Gard and Meyenn, 2000). A view of the body as socially constructed does provide a means of asking such questions. It also facilitates the exploration of alternatives to sport-based physical education, such as the Feldenkrais approach to movement (Wright, 2000) or the Alexander technique (Tinning, 1998).

### *Informing embodied experience*

Biophysical and sociological knowledge can inform embodied experience. Since we each possess intuitive knowledge of bodies, this may be a useful starting point for physical education. For physical educators to tap this knowledge, they need first of all a professional perspective that acknowledges the existence and legitimacy of experiential knowledge. A view of the body solely as 'an object of exact calculation' is unlikely to be helpful in this respect. Instead, physical educators need to use person-centred pedagogies that personalise and integrate knowledge for learners. A learner's view of the world needs to be understood if it is to be informed (Oliver and Lalik, 2000).

## Conclusion

The purpose of this chapter was to introduce the idea that bodies are socially constructed. It was emphasised that this does not imply that the biology of bodies is unimportant. Rather, the point was made that the body is in nature and culture simultaneously. A constructionist view of the body is interested in the relationship between nature and culture in constructing bodies. The chapter also set out to show how the media and the process of schooling play key roles in socially constructing bodies. In the case of the media, this is done through linking body types, shape and sizes to particular social values, such as the idea that a slender, muscular body is healthy. In the case of schooling, a whole range of practices is employed to shape bodies, such as the discipline required of children to sit still for a lengthy period of time at school desks.

In both cases, there are important implications for physical educators of the idea that bodies are socially constructed. The media regularly highlights bodies in sport and exercise settings to sell products. And in schools, physical education and sport form specialised practices for schooling and thereby socially constructing bodies. It was suggested that physical educators should develop the notion that bodies are socially constructed to assist young people to deconstruct sometimes harmful cultural myths about body shape, size and competence and to help them better understand their own physical selves. The idea of the social construction of bodies might also provide physical educators with some clues and some inspiration for developing new forms of their subject to meet emerging needs in new and changing times.

## Reflection questions

1 What does the phrase 'schooling bodies' mean and how is physical education implicated in this process?
2 How might a focus on the social construction of bodies provide a basis for developing alternative forms of physical education?
3 What does Finkelstein mean by the phrase that 'character is immanent in appearance'? What are the implications of this phrase for our understanding of embodiment?

## Tasks

1 In a group, discuss and then describe what you think is an ideal body and identify who or what has influenced your views. Note the major characteristics of your descriptions. Then discuss, describe and note the main features of the ideal body for participating in the following sports:

- rugby union prop forward
- netball goal attack
- football wing-back
- downhill skier
- weightlifter
- golfer
- artistic gymnast.

Does it matter whether the sports performers listed are male or female? Add your own favourite sport to this list if you wish. Then discuss the similarities and differences you have identified for these sports. In a paragraph, write down what your results tell us about the social construction of bodies.

2 Collect some photographs of men and women playing sport between the late 1800s and today. Discuss in a small group the changes to their clothing. Look especially at the emergence of different kinds of clothing and accessories. What are the changing social values that are reflected in these changes?

## Further reading

Kirk, D. (1998) *Schooling Bodies: School Practice and Public Discourse, 1880–1950*. Leicester: Leicester University Press.
Oliver, K. and Lalik, R. (2000) *Bodily Knowledge: Learning about Equity and Justice with Adolescent Girls*. New York: Peter Lang Publishing.
Shilling, C. (1993) *The Body in Social Theory*. London: Sage.

## References

Armour, K.M. (1999) The case for a body-focus in education and physical education. *Sport, Education and Society*, 4, 1, 5–16.

Finkelstein, J. (1991) *The Fashioned Self.* Cambridge: Polity Press.

Foucault, M. (1977) *Discipline and Punishment: The Birth of the Prison.* London: Penguin.

Gard, M. and Meyenn, R. (2000) Boys, bodies, pleasure and pain: interrogating contact sports in schools. *Sport, Education and Society*, 5, 1, 19–34.

Hickey, C., Fitzclarence, L. and Matthews, R. (Eds) (1998) *Where the Boys Are: Masculinity, Sport and Education.* Geelong: Deakin Center for Education and Change.

Kirk, D. (1992) Physical education, discourse and ideology: bringing the hidden curriculum into view. *Quest*, 44, 35–56.

Mauss, M. (1973) Techniques of the body (trans. B. Brewster). *Economy and Society*, 2, 70–87.

McKay, J. (1991) *No Pain, No Gain. Sport in Australian Culture.* Sydney: Prentice Hall.

Oliver, K. and Lalik, R. (2000) *Bodily Knowledge: Learning about Equity and Justice with Adolescent Girls.* New York: Peter Lang Publishing.

Shilling, C. (1991) Educating the body: physical capital and the production of social inequalities. *Sociology*, 25, 4, 653–672.

Shilling, C. (1993) *The Body in Social Theory*. London: Sage.

Sparkes, A.C. (1998) Athletic identity: an Achilles heel to the survival of the self. *Qualitative Health Research,* 8, 5, 644–664.

Sparkes, A.C. (1999) Exploring body narratives. *Sport, Education and Society*, 4, 1, 17–30.

Tinning, R. (1985) Physical education and the cult of slenderness. *ACHPER National Journal,* 107, 10–13.

Tinning, R. (1998) Slipped disc(ourses): whatever happened to back health and physical education curriculum and practice? *ACHPER Healthy Lifestyles Journal*, 45, 3, 16–19.

Turner, B.S. (1984) *The Body in Society.* Oxford: Blackwell.

Wright, J. (2000) Bodies, meanings and movement: a comparison of the language of a physical education lesson and a Feldenkrais movement class. *Sport, Education and Society*, 5. 1, 35–50.

# 6 Race, ethnicity and sport

*Bob Chappell*

## Introduction

Discussions about race and ethnicity are confusing unless terms are defined. As Polley (1998: 136) quite rightly says 'it is worth thinking critically about the terminology and ideology involved'. Coakley (1998: 249) defines race as 'a category of people regarded as socially distinct because they share genetically transmitted traits believed to be important in the group or society'. Further, Coakley maintains that when people talk about 'races' they assume the existence of a classification system used to categorise all the people of the world into distinct groups on the basis of certain biological traits or dispositions present at birth. Groups such as Asians, Australian Aborigines, American Indians, Whites and Blacks are some of the most popular distinctive groups. It must be realised, however, that many people cannot be neatly pigeon-holed into these categories. For example, Daley Thompson, a double Olympic gold medalist in the decathlon is the son of a black Nigerian father and a white Scottish mother. When approached for an interview for a book entitled *Black Sportsmen* by Ernest Cashmore (1982) Thompson declined to be interviewed as he did not perceive himself to be black. A person's own perception of themself is crucial in this regard (Polley, 1998).

Polley reminds us that:

> academic discourse has moved away from the notion of 'race' – the purity of genetics and biology that is needed to classify humans as belonging to one racial group or another is simply unrealistic, and it would be impossible to set up dividing lines between racial groups that would be meaningful or satisfactory to all analysts'.
>
> (136)

In place of race as a category, researchers within the social sciences have began to use the term ethnicity. According to Coakley (1998: 250) ethnicity refers to 'the cultural heritage of a particular group'. So ethnicity refers to common features other than biological features. These features might include language, religion, interests and family structure. An ethnic group is a socially distinct group because they share the same way of life associated with a common cultural background.

Ethnicity, therefore is not based on genetically determined physical traits such as skin colour, hair type, eye shape, and lip thickness but on a common cultural background. However the terms 'race' and 'ethnicity' are frequently used interchangably. The terminology and ideology of race is still popular within the press, in employment, schools and in general conversation. The most notable sign of difference is skin colour, far more obvious than cultural differences, and consequently race remains a part of everyday common-sense ideology (Polley, 1998).

## The social process as a theoretical framework

There has been an ongoing debate in order to explain the emergence of African, African-American and African-Caribbean athletes as spectacular stars at international sports events. The modern world is awash with images of black athletes. The physical talents of black people and the media-generated images which sustain them encourage the idea that blacks are biologically different, and more specifically that black athletes are superior to white athletes. The images of black athletes on television, and in newspapers and magazines, sustain the traditional view of blacks having physical attributes which allow them to excel at sport. In this context 'sport functions as a principal medium in which racial folklore flourishes' (Hoberman, 1997: xv).

Many scientists have attempted to explain the physical abilities and achievements of athletes in racial terms. A series of articles in *Sports Illustrated* in 1971 entitled 'The Black Athlete: A Shameful Story' by Martin Kane highlighted these explanations. Kane said that, there was a body of scientific opinion which suggested physical differences in the races might well have enhanced the physical potential of black athletes in certain events.

In attempting to highlight participation and performance along racial lines some scientists suggested that black athletes had an innate ability to play certain sports; they had larger bodies, thicker bones, longer arms and legs, shorter trunks and narrower hips. The black athlete was also attributed with quicker automatic movements compared with white athletes and could relax under pressure. But theories of racial athletic aptitude consisted of unsubstantiated scientific reasoning and unscientific thinking about racial differences. Hoberman (1997) explained in great detail the near impossibility of demonstrating racial differences under the best of scientific circumstances. Much of the evidence presented by scientists was anecdotal. Bad sampling techniques were used, there were no control groups, the measurements were ambiguous, and the researchers had suspect motivation. Hence, ideas about black athletic superiority belong to more comprehensive racial folklore which holds that black people are harder, physically stronger and biologically more robust than other people.

More recent research challenges the biological explanation of the superiority of black athletes, and would identify socio-cultural and socio-economic factors that have channelled a disproportionate number of black people into a limited number of sports. In short, the majority of sociologists would argue for a cultural rather than a biological interpretation of relative success. In this context Eitzen and Tessendorf (1978: 109) said:

> We do not know whether African-American athletes possess physical traits superior to those of whites or not. Even if it were proved that African-Americans do have genetic advantages over whites, we believe that genetic differences are likely to be less important than social reasons for African-American dominance.
>
> (109)

Hence, the explanation of the pre-eminence of African, African-American and African-Caribbean athletes is social, and is not based on the physical superiority of one group of people over another. The black athlete does not necessarily have greater physical attributes. The environmental factors of culture, custom, education and the availability of role models are more important than the factor of race. By arguing for a cultural rather than biological interpretation of relative success Leonard (1998) maintains that 'the fact that performance differentials exist does not mean that blacks are inherently superior but rather that the role models are available for blacks, and closed occupational doors in other areas have prompted them to channel themselves into sports' (230).

## Race, sport and ethnicity in the United States

The history of black involvement in sport in the US is very interesting. Initial success was with boxing, which has continued, and as jockeys, in which there is now no black involvement. According to Ashe (1993) during the nineteenth century, black slaves looked after the horses in the stables, and did other menial tasks. The white landowners owned the horses; the trainers of the horses were also white, and this owner/worker relationship represented the power discrepancy marked by all levels of social relations in the US during that period.

Black jockeys initially dominated racing to such an extent that in 1875, fourteen of the fifteen jockeys in the Kentucky Derby, the premier flat race of the country, were black. Isaac Murphy, a black jockey, won the Kentucky Derby three times in the late 1800s (Leonard, 1998). Of the following twenty-seven Kentucky Derbies, fourteen were won by black jockeys. As a result of their success black riders could earn as much as $30,000 per year, an extremely high salary during that period.

Evidently the Jockey Club, the overall governing body of the sport in the US, whose members were white, resented the success of black jockeys. They introduced a system of licensing for jockeys. As black jockeys had to be re-licensed, the white members of the Jockey Club systematically reduced the number of black jockeys. By the end of the nineteenth century their numbers had decreased, and the domination of horse racing by black jockeys disappeared.

According to Leonard (1998), boxing was one of the first sports in which black people excelled. He records that a black American, Tom Molyneux, was the

National Heavyweight champion in 1800. More specifically, Weinburg and Arond (1952) illustrated the involvement of certain ethnic groups in a study of professional boxing in the US. Between 1909 and 1948 a number of ethnic minority groups dominated boxing. These involved Irish, German, Italian and more recently black boxers. Recruitment into boxing was from certain ethnic groups who were usually associated with low socio-economic backgrounds. Weinburg and Arond believed that because of the aggressive nature of the sport, the boxers were accorded high status in their ethnic group, and used boxing as a means of social mobility.

Jack Johnson was the first black boxer to become known worldwide when he became the Heavyweight Champion of the World by defeating the white Canadian, Tommy Burns in 1908. This enraged the white boxing authorities especially as Johnson became a celebrity amongst the black population. In 1910 Johnson fought the 'great white hope' Jim Jeffries in a 'symbolic' confrontation (Ashe, 1993), and defeated him. In the same year, Johnson was sent to prison for one year for contravening the 'Man Act', a little-used law, which referred to the transportation of women across state boundaries for immoral earnings. The white authorities could not tolerate his success and sought to prevent him from boxing. Racism towards boxers during this period was related to the broader structural dimensions of inequality and power discrepancies between blacks and whites which existed at that time.

Discrimination against black sportspeople occurred in the same way as it did in other social institutions in the US. According to McPherson (1976), black athletes were excluded from most professional sports until the 'colour bar' was broken by Jackie Robinson in 1947. From the early 1900s until 1947 racism was prevalent in most professional sports just as it was in most other social institutions. In 1947 Jackie Robinson, a baseball player, became the first black professional baseball player in the previously 'all-white' league. He acted as a pioneer for other black sportspeople to become professionals in baseball, American football and basketball. In basketball, three players played in the National Basketball Association (NBA) in 1950. In 1966 Bill Russell became the first black person to become a coach when he was appointed head coach of the Boston Celtics. In 1971 Wayne Embry became the first black person to become a general manager of a NBA team (Milwaukee Bucks).

Since becoming involved in professional sport in the US, black sportspeople have achieved a remarkably prominent position in major sports. Statistics indicate that between 1956 to 1995 there has been a percentage increase in black players from 14 per cent to 65 per cent in American Football; in baseball there has been a percentage increase in black players from 9 per cent to 16 per cent, and in basketball a percentage increase from 20 per cent to 80 per cent during the same period (Eitzen and Yetman, 1982; Yetman and Berghorn, 1993; Leonard, 1998).

As black people comprise 12 per cent (Leonard, 1998) of the total population of the US, there is a disproportionate percentage of black athletes involved in some professional sports, though they are still largely excluded from others. Black athletes are prominent in athletics, boxing and basketball which are relatively cheap to play. These sports may be played in limited areas with a mimimum of equipment, and are also accessible through schools and clubs set in working-class areas where most black Americans live (Polley, 1998). Conversely, a number of sports such as golf, swimming, tennis and equestrian sports have been connected to the middle and upper classes. These sports have remained predominately white. This imbalance indicates that black successes in certain sports are due to social class as well as ethnicity. For Small (1994) black people are not supreme in sport. They are good at a tiny selection of sports and their success can be explained by a complex combination of opportunities, motivation, economics and role models.

In basketball, for example, integration accelerated after the 'Jackie Robinson Affair' in 1947. In 1948 less than 10 per cent of the collegiate squads were integrated, but by 1980, 90 per cent of the teams were integrated. There was an increase in the number of black players being recruited to colleges and universities so that during the period 1966–75 there was a breakdown in the previously segregated teams especially in the south of the US (Berghorn *et al.*, 1988). By 1975, black players comprised 33.4 per cent of the nations collegiate players which was a remarkably high figure as black people only constituted 10.4 per cent of the student population at that time.

The change in the professional game of basketball was even more pronounced. In 1995, 80 per cent of the players in the NBA were black. Therefore, it would appear that many of the barriers which had previously excluded participation had been eliminated. Now black players were over-represented on college and professional basketball teams relative to their distribution within the total population. Despite this involvement by black players in basketball, authors such as Loy and McElvogue (1970), McPherson, Curtis and Loy (1989) and Margolis and Piliavin (1999) maintained that racial segregation in sport did occur, and this segregation was related to positions of centrality.

According to Grusky (1963) cited in Maguire (1991: 258), 'centrality' was seen to designate how 'close a member is to the centre of the group's interaction, how frequently that member interacts to a greater or lesser range with other team-mates, and the degree to which other team members must co-ordinate tasks and other activities with other members'. For Loy and McElvogue (1970), the key element of centrality is leadership and the degree of responsibility for the game outcome. Central positions are those positions where there is a great amount of interaction with other team-mates, and in which decisions regarding the nature of the game are made. Conversely, non-central positions are those in which there is little interaction with team-mates and in which few decisions regarding the nature of the game are made. So, in basketball, the guard (playmaker) and the centre (a pivotal central position) are central positions, and forwards are perceived to be non-central positions. In baseball, the pitcher and catcher might be perceived as central positions. In American Football the quarter-back is perceived as a central position.

A feature of North American sport, including basketball is that black players have been traditionally over-represented in non-central positions (forwards), and under-represented in central positions (guard and centre), whereas for white players this situation is reversed. This allocation of playing position by race is an interesting issue and was initially studied by American sociologists in American football, basketball and baseball. Initially, scientists felt that black sportspeople had certain physical advantages which ensured that given the opportunity to play, they were outstanding at certain sports such as basketball and American football. Within sports, due to racial discrimination and racial stereotyping, black players were deemed to be more suited to play certain positions in a team.

This over-representation of black players in certain positions in sports is known as 'stacking'. Eitzen and Yetman (1982) define stacking as, 'minority group member assigned to specific positions and excluded from competing for others' (156). More specifically, stacking in basketball relates to over-representation of black players as forwards and their under-representation as guards and centres. In baseball African-Americans are over-represented among the three outfield positions and under-represented in the infield and at catcher; Latino players are over-represented in the middle infield positions, and white players are over-represented in the most central position of catcher and other infield positions. In American football, whites are over-represented at quarterback, centre, guard, linebacker and kicker. African-Americans most frequently play in the positions of defensive back, running back and receiver (Margolis and Piliavin, 1999).

Stacking in North American sports may be due to racial stereotyping by coaches. Coaches may perceive that different positions require certain physical and mental attributes, and stereotypically attribute those charactersistics to members of different racial/ethnic groups. However, in basketball since the 1970s, black players are as likely to play in the guard and centre position, thus suggesting that racial discrimination has decreased in basketball. Research by Berghorn *et al.* (1988) determined that in men's collegiate basketball 35 per cent of centres were black and 65 per cent were white. Eitzen and Furst (1989) maintain that the greater number of white players in the centre position is due to height being the most important factor when playing this position, and amongst the population there are more whites with height advantage – 'whites are eight times more likely than blacks to be at the upper end of the height continuum from which centres are selected (because blacks comprise only 14 per cent of the population)' (47).

## Coaches and managerial positions

Of increasing interest to sociologists in the US is the lack of black people in coaching and management positions. In this respect Berghorn *et al.* (1988) maintained that:

> although the percentage of black players in each of the three most prominent American professional team sports of basketball, baseball and American football greatly exceeds their percentage of the total population, there is ample evidence to say that few opportunities are available to them in managerial or entrepreneurial roles.
>
> (107)

In 1979, for example, despite black players comprising two-thirds of all professional basketball players, only two out of the twenty-two head NBA coaches were black. However, black people were increasingly found on the coaching staffs of collegiate basketball teams, although specific statistics in support of this assertion are contradictory. What is clear is that in relation to the number of black players, there is a very considerable under-representation of black managers and coaches in sport. By 1966, in professional American football there were three black head coaches and four black general managers. However, an increasing number of assistant coaches (23 per cent) were black. In basketball, a sport dominated by black players, 20 per cent of head NBA coaches were black in the 1995/96 season. More recently, however there has been an appreciable increase in the number of black coaches in collegiate basketball. This may be due to black protests in colleges and universities over equality issues prompting the authorities to appoint black coaches and managers.

Black assistant coaches may be appointed in order to give emotional support to the players, most of whom are black. The head coach determines tactics and strategies in preparation for games and during games, so is accorded a more responsible position. As a large percentage of players are black, a black assistant coach is beneficial in recruiting by being able to relate to the player and family. This may be another example of racial stereotyping in that black assistant coaches are seen to be giving emotional support to the players, most of whom are black. Conversely, the white head coaches are perceived as calm, intelligent and good planners. This implies that different races have different attributes, and that racial stereotyping occurs.

Research by Yetman and Berghorn (1993) support the claim that there is an increasing number of black head coaches. Some of these are coaching at the most successful universities, and a very high percentage of universities had black assistant coaches in 1990. For Yetman and Berghorn (1993: 303), 'men's collegiate basketball has achieved a level of management integration unparalleled in any other sport'. Clearly, collegiate basketball has been far more progressive in terms of appointing black coaches, but the numbers appointed do not approach the very high rates of participation by black players. This suggests that discrimination still exists. Eitzen and Yetman (1982) felt that the relative paucity of black coaches was the result of two forms of racism – overt racism whereby owners of clubs ignore black coaches because they feel they are incompetent, and subtle racism whereby black coaches are not considered because as players they did not play in leadership positions, and therefore cannot accept positions of leadership as coaches.

However, it could be suggested that those in positions of power in collegiate basketball, that is athletic directors, who are responsible for employing coaches and the owners of professional sports teams, may continue discriminatory practices. In both professional and collegiate sport, coaching and management positions are under the control of those who have the power of determining those positions. Hence, a limited number of black coaches has been appointed. According to Coakley (1998) only 7 per cent of the coaches in the NBA were black in 1992, even though 75 per cent of the players were black. In the National Football League (NFL) only 7 per cent of the head coaches were black, even though 62 per cent of the players were black. In universities the proportion of black head coaches is nowhere near the proportion of black participants especially in American football, basketball and athletics (track and field). All coaching positions are available to both black and white coaches, but athletic directors and others in some cases do not fill those positions with black people.

## Race, ethnicity and sport in Britain

Casual observations suggest that black African-Caribbeans have been extremely successful in certain sports in Britain. Indeed, 50 per cent of the British athletics team is black; the England basketball team of 1999 playing in the European Championships only had two white players in the squad of twelve; and a great percentage of British boxing champions is black. Further, black sportspeople are achieving great success in soccer, rugby, karate, table tennis and cricket.

In Britain second generation black sportspeople rose to prominence in the late 1970s and the early 1980s achieving success initially in boxing, and later in athletics and soccer. Sport has had a significant role to play in the gradual process of allowing black immigrants to earn some form of respect and acceptance from white society. Black people's involvement in sport continued to intensify in the 1990s, and in the sports in which they competed they achieved considerable success. The emergence of black sportspeople in a number of sports has provided individual social mobility. Some of these have become stars in the media and in other areas of society. For example, soccer players John Barnes and Ian Wright have developed careers in advertising; athlete Daley Thompson and soccer player Garth Crooks have careers in presenting sports programmes including the 1996 Olympic games; soccer player, John Fashanu and rugby player, Jeremy Guscott presented the popular television programme 'The Gladiators', and Garth Crooks and Brendon Batson work for the Professional Football Association. Sports in which black people have little involvement include swimming, golf and racket sports, sports in which facilities and finance are important. Sports played in private clubs such as golf or equestrian, and sports requiring expensive equipment and facilities are popular among high-income and high-status groups. Traditionally, black people have lived in working-class areas in Britain and have been attrracted to football, boxing, basketball and athletics. These sports can be played in limited areas with the minimum of equipment. This suggests that black participation is due to social class as well as ethnicity. Black women have achieved success in athletics and more recently netball and basketball, but there is little opportunity to play professional sport in Britain (Polley, 1998).

The 1994 Census indicated that African-Caribbeans comprised 1.6 per cent of the total population in Britain (Owen, 1994), yet they now comprise 50 per cent of the Great Britain Athletics Team, and 11.5 per cent of professional footballers in the Football League during the 1989/90 season (Maguire, 1991b). Ethnicity did not emerge as an area for analysis by British academics until the late 1970s when a significant number of black British sportspeople achieved success nationally and internationally. They included Viv Anderson and Cyrille Regis in football; Tom Conteh, Maurice Hope in boxing; Tessa Sanderson and Daley Thompson in athletics, and Clive Sullivan in rugby league. During the 1970s a number of athletic events such as the 100 metres, 200 metres and long jump became dominated by black athletes. Interestingly the British record holder for the long jump is still the white athlete Lynn Davies; the record holder for the triple jump is the white athlete Jonathon Edwards, and the record holder for the high jump is the white athlete Steve Smith. Athletics has been identified as a sport in which black men and women are able to excel. Success by Linford Christie, John Regis, Tessa Sanderson, Colin Jackson, Mark Richardson and others has indicated that black athletes were disproportionately over-represented relative to the size of the British black population.

In boxing prior to 1948 non-white boxers were prevented from boxing for a British title. In 1948 the British Boxing Board of Control (BBBC) removed the colour bar that had prevented non-whites from challenging for titles. According to Cashmore (1982) this change was to accommodate Dick Turpin and then Randolf Turpin who won the world middleweight title in 1951. By the late 1970s there was an increasing number of black boxers emerging so that there was an over-representation of black British champions. Among the most successful were Lloyd Honeyghan, Maurice Hope, John Conteh and Frank Bruno. In the world rankings, 90 per cent of world champions in all weights were black in 1995 (Polley, 1998).

The main research conducted on race and sport in Britain was by Cashmore (1982) who attempted to explain this apparent over-representation of blacks in sport. Initially, Cashmore (1982: 42) focused on the research by Kane (1971) in the US which highlighted the supposed physical superiority of black athletes stating that the 'natural ability angle is appealing in its simplicity and comprehensiveness'. Cashmore also pointed to similar racial stereotyping on the part of sports coaches in Britain. However, eventually Kane's research was rejected due to its pretensions to scientific validity and its racist undertones.

Cashmore (1982) felt that considering the high number of black children who aspire to excellence in sport it was not surprising that a large percentage excel. But equally a large percentage fail. However, one needs to ask why so many African-Caribbeans wish to excel in sport. Cashmore speaks with emotion when he says, 'the reasons for success do not lie in the rather obscure realms of anatomy, physiology or psychology. Sportsmen [*sic*] are not born they are made through social processes' (45).

The most serious systematic study of racial composition of sports teams in Britain was conducted by Maguire (1991b) in soccer, and Weddurburn (1989) in Rugby Union. Both researchers attempted to use quantitative and qualitative research to determine the involvement of African-Caribbean males in sport. They accepted the fact that existing American research provided useful lines of enquiry, but it needed to be combined with the experiences of racism in British society. Most American research used quantitative research, but the authors felt that a combination of quantitative and qualitative might provide more insights.

By examining the racial composition of all players in the Football League for the seasons 1985/6 and 1989/90, Maguire (1991b) concluded that stacking (the disproportionate concentration of ethnic minorities, particularly black players, in certain team positions which deny them access to other team roles) exists. In soccer, Maguire determined that there was a disproportionate number of black players in wide positions, such as full-back, wide mid-field positions and wide forward positions, and a distinct lack of black players as goalkeepers, centre back, centre of mid-field and centre forward. These central positions are considered by the Federation Internationale de Football Association (FIFA, 1974) as the 'backbone' of competence, and correspond to the concept of centrality utilised in American research. Maguire concluded that this disproportionate distribution of black players in certain positions was mainly due to stereotyping by managers and coaches in that they considered black players had certain attributes such as speed which is required in wide positions. Alternatively, managers and coaches thought that white players had cognitive attributes such as decision-making, which are required in central positions. These perceived black attributes are based on physical qualities, whereas the perceived white attributes are based on mental qualities.

In relation to 'stacking' and positions of centrality, Maguire gives little attention to the concept of 'role modelling' in which young players, wishing to emulate certain outstanding players, restrict themselves to playing in certain limited positions. As one of the first successful black players, Clyde Best, was a forward it is not surprising there has been a large over-representation of young players wishing to emulate him. Conversely, as there have been few outstanding black goalkeepers, it is not surprising that there are few professional black goalkeepers.

Young black players have professional forwards, wide mid-field players and full backs to emulate as role models, but fewer central players and goalkeepers. This over-representation of black players in certain positions in soccer is mainly due to racial stereotyping in the first instance by managers, coaches and teachers who consider that black players have certain physical attributes which are required in wide positions, whereas white players have other attributes which are required in central positions. More recent research in the 1994/95 English professional soccer season by Norris and Jones (1998) reconfirmed that black players were disproportionately represented in certain positions, and that centrality was related to stacking.

In Rugby Union, Weddurburn (1989) demonstrated that in the top three divisions of the National League only 2 per cent of the players were black, yet 61 per cent of those players were wingers. Weddurburn (himself a winger and black) determined that the coaches felt that the qualities required in those positions in which there was an over-representation of black players were speed and strength. For positions in which there were no black players, coaches felt that the players needed cognitive qualities in order to make decisions and judgements about the game. In short, rugby coaches were of the opinion that black players were fast and strong, and could not play in positions demanding quick thought and decision-making. From the evidence reported by Maguire (1991b) in soccer and

Weddurburn (1989) in Rugby Union, some coaches racially stereotype players in relation to the qualities required to play certain positions.

In Rugby League the first black player in the British league was Lucien Banks over 80 years ago. Since then there have been others, and historic representation contributes to the illusion of an absence of racism in the sport. Clive Sullivan was the first black sportsperson to captain a British national side. He led the British Rugby League team to victory in the 1972 World Cup in France. However, Long and Spracken (1996) concluded from a one season study in September 1994 that there was a clear indication of 'stacking' in rugby league. Seventy-five per cent of black players played as backs, and 65 per cent of these played on the wing.

Chappell, Jones and Burden (1996) investigated racial trends in terms of participation and integration in the highest levels of English professional basketball. They used a longitudinal approach by examining the racial composition of the English National Basketball League during the period 1977–94. The research indicated that there was a significant increase in the number of black players in the league between 1977–94 in all the positions of guard, forward and centre. The percentage of black guards (a position of centrality) rose from 12.5 per cent in 1977 to 63 per cent in 1994; the percentage of black forwards (a non-central position) rose from 12.2 per cent in 1977 to 55.6 per cent in 1994, and the percentage of black centres (a central position) rose from 18.2 per cent in 1977 to 66.7 per cent in 1994. Therefore, it appeared that there was an equal distribution of black players in all three positions. Thus evidence to support the contention of stacking in basketball in Britain in the seasons studied was not provided. Subsequently, the authors concluded that black basketball players have not been subjected to positional assignment on the basis of racial stereotypes. This contrasts with earlier American findings.

Research by Chappell and Karageorghis (2000) on race, ethnicity and gender in British basketball indicated that there was an over-representation of black females in the forward position, thus indicating that stacking was occurring. There was also an over-representation of white coaches in the First Division of the English National Women's league during the 1996/97 season.

Malcolm (1997) examined racial stereotyping in relation to cricket. More specifically he studied the relationship between race and playing role, the phenomenon he stated was previously termed 'stacking'. He suggested that participation roles in cricket were 'heavily influenced by, and highly influenced upon, patterns of 'racial' stereotyping more generally' (2). The data used by Malcolm showed that compared to their respective proportions in the population as a whole, British African-Caribbeans are over-represented among first-class cricketers in Britain. More specifically they are over-represented as fast bowlers, a role requiring speed, strength and aggression, and under-represented as batsmen, a role requiring tactical awareness and thought. In conclusion it could be stated that stereotyping occurs in cricket in that British African-Caribbeans are stereotyped as weak at batting, but good fast bowlers.

Black athletes are over-represented in boxing, athletics, football and basketball, and under-represented in other sports. These are sports in which finance and facilities are less important. Further, the attributes required to play these sports are the physical attributes of speed and strength. Thus it might be suggested that participation in these sports actually reproduces crude stereotypes of black people in society at large. That so many black athletes succeed must be read as a sign of perceived limited opportunities in other walks of life. This encourages many African-Caribbean youths to concentrate on sport rather than other meaningful endeavours and careers involving different attributes.

## Sport and Asian culture in Britain

Of the total population in Britain in 1991, 840,000 (1.5 per cent) were Indian, 477,000 (0.9 per cent) Pakistani, and 163,000 (0.3 per cent) Bangladeshi (Skellington, 1996).

Sports participation research in Britain shows that Asians have lower participation rates than for other groups, especially for women (Sports Council, 1993), and that in general women's participation is less than that of males (Sports Council, 1994). People of Asian descent are under-represented in most sports in Britain except for hockey, cricket, and badminton (Kew, 1997). These findings, along with the methodologies and ideologies of the authors are criticised by Raval (1989) who claims that 'they use common-sense stereotypical assumptions to attribute parental constraint, religion and culture as root causes for lack of participation' (239).

It is important to refrain from regarding South Asians as a homogeneous group, as such a generalisation ignores the ethno-cultural diversities that exist within the group. The diversity of people collectively labelled as 'South Asian', include Indian, Pakistani, Bangladeshis and East African (mainly Kenyan) (Kew, 1997). However, the length of this section dictates that generalisations have to be made. This is a necessity and should not be interpreted as a lack of awareness of the diversity of South Asians. In this section the term Asian is used as a generic term to describe all people of South Asian decent. Fleming (1991) quite rightly maintains that the significance and function of sport in Asian cultures is not adequately understood. This may be due in part to a pre-occupation with African-Caribbean sports participation, as they have a greater visibility within sport. Indeed, the presence of other ethnic minorities in sport such as Irish, Poles and Chinese have not been researched in the same way as that of African-Caribbeans. The sporting history of South Asian immigrants in Britain has also not been researched in great detail, thus reinforcing the stereotype that 'Asians are more interested in studies than in sport' (Polley, 1998: 136).

Typically Asians are perceived as weak and fragile, too frail for contact sports such as rugby, lacking in stamina and poorly coordinated. Many teachers view Asians as not being very good at physical education, and therefore unlikely to succeed at sport. According to Fleming (1991: 52) 'school sport reinforces and perpetuates stereotypes, and others based on physiological and anatomical prejudices remain unchallenged'. An outcome of this negative stereotyping is that whereas African-Caribbeans are channelled into sport, Asians are channelled away from sport. International success has been achieved by some Asian sportspeople in cricket, hockey and squash, but less so in other high profile sports such as soccer. It has been suggested that for many Asian parents in Britain sport is not a serious activity to be recommended and encouraged for young Asians. This apparent lack of parental support for participation in soccer, for example, is remarked on by some soccer coaches (Burdsey, 1998). Coaches maintain that Asian parents are less supportive of their soccer playing children than other groups. Certainly, some players feel that their parents are less supportive, but it is difficult to generalise as other Asian parents are just as supportive as those of other ethnic groups, particularly second and third generation British Asians.

Some coaches believe that many Asian parents do not actively encourage involvement in sport due to a culture in which success in academic subjects is perceived to be very important. As a consequence participation in sport may not be given a high priority. For Cashmore (1982) in Asian culture, education is a highly-valued commodity, whereas a career in sport is seen as being precarious and short term.

For Asians, involvement in some sports such as professional football is synonymous with racism and violence. Consequently, some parents are reluctant to allow their children to become involved in football. Racism is still prevalent in professional football. An alleged decrease in racist chanting, and an increase in African-Caribbean players and overseas players cannot cover up the existence of racist attitudes at all levels of football. Racism is rife in amateur football (verbal and physical), but also in a covert institutionalised form by the reluctance of some leagues to accept Asian teams (Burdsey, 1998).

Perhaps due to racism in professional and amateur football, many Asian players are choosing to play the 5-a-side rather than the 11-a-side game. This may be due to 5-a-side being played in a smaller, safer environment in which Asian players can play in a more comfortable, racist-free game. The lack of Asian professional football players may be due to many Asians playing the 5-a-side game which restricts the development of the full range of skills required for the professional game. It is unlikely that professional coaches would wish to recruit Asian players if they continue to play in such restricted environments. Conversely, some Asian players believe clubs are racist, and will not send coaches to watch and recruit them. This view has been reiterated in a number of documentary television programmes highlighting talented Asian football players who have not been given the opportunity to play professionally.

The absence of Asian role models in sport reinforces the view held by some Asian parents that sport is not a serious activity for young Asians. Role models are important in encouraging young people to be involved. The lack of Asian role models might hinder young Asians wishing to become professional football players, although contemporary evidence suggests that many are striving to play professionally. Whereas Asian players and club coaches acknowledge that the lack of role models is a major factor influencing the absence of Asian footballers, an Asian footballer cannot become a role model unless the player is of the standard required. If not of the required standard, poor performances would have a detrimental effect, and would reinforce racial stereotypes. It might also mean that Asian players become victims of their own myths by believing that they lack ability. Thus there is a need for a number of Asian professional players rather than an individual, not only to make a larger impact, but also to share the inevitable exposure and abuse.

Research findings suggest attitudes and behaviours regarding Asians participating in sport are starting to change, but unfortunately stereotypes and preconceptions still remain. For example, Brian Close, the chairman of Yorkshire County Cricket Club, maintains that despite there being numerous Asian cricketers in Yorkshire, none are good enough to play for the county. In order to play cricket for Yorkshire, tradition formerly dictated that a player must be born in the county. Yet, although some Asian cricketers are Yorkshire born and bred, Brian Close when interviewed on BBC television for a documentary entitled 'The Race Game' insisted on calling them 'foreigners'. Stereotypes based on scientific racism have been a particular problem affecting Asian participation. Football coaches have cited religion and diet as contributing factors mitigating against participation in soccer. One only need to look at the qualifications for recent World Cup finals by Islamic nations Saudi Arabia and Iran to appreciate that their religion does not prevent them playing football. A number of coaches in Britain appear to believe that all Asian religions contribute to one uniform culture, when the differences between them are often more significant than the similarities. Myths such as 'Asians are too frail for contact sports', and 'Asians can only play hockey' appear to be diminishing, but need to be countered if participation rates are to increase (Burdsey, 1998).

There is a widespread view of South Asian females being passive and not interested in participating in sport. For example, Lovell (1992) maintains that they are often perceived as passive and frail, and these images can restrict involvement of South Asian women in sport. Carroll and Hollinshead (1993) proposed that there are four main factors which restrict South Asian women from participating in physical education in schools. First, for devout Muslim females, participation in 'purdah' (the Islamic term used to describe the state of being covered from head to toe) presents problems with some activities. Second, showering presents problems – not the act of showering itself, but its communality. Exposure of their bodies produces strong feelings of shame/guilt for many Muslim females. Third, the month-long festival Ramadan, in which Muslims must fast between dawn and dusk, results in them becoming very tired, and strenuous physical activity can cause discomfort and be distressing. During Ramadan water is not allowed to enter the mouth between sunrise and sunset, so difficulties arise in swimming. Finally, participation in extracurricular activities is limited as considerable restrictions are placed on some Muslim girls by parents with particular concerns regarding daughters travelling alone or developing social relationships with boys.

It would be a distortion to suggest that South Asian women have no involvement in sport. There is a significant presence of South Asian women in badminton, squash, dance and aerobics/keep fit classes. Interestingly, racket sports and dance are seen as 'traditional' Asian pursuits. Participation in aerobics, however, can be perceived as an example of the westernisation of South Asian women, as aerobics aims to develop the ideal female westernised physique. Participation is popular when projects are organised by other Asian women.

Fleming (1991) claims that participation in sport by South Asians is élitist and male dominated, and therefore it is not surprising that for South Asians in Britain it is mainly a male preserve. This male domination of South Asian sport has meant that participation by females has been restricted. Women have been obliged to take a subsidiary role and work their social agenda around men's leisure activities (Bains and Johal, 1998). Lovell (1992) highlights the pressure exerted on South Asian women to conform to traditional values of womanhood, with the result that leisure time is often committed to home-based responsibilities. Consequently, the restrictions placed on South Asian women have resulted in sport simply not forming a central part of their general leisure time. The under-representation of South Asian women in British sport is partly the result of the patriarchal nature of Asian family structures, and the internalisation of gender-specific roles and values which are historically rooted within the Asian culture. Sport is associated with masculinity, in which men are encouraged to participate, and women although not prohibited are neither expected nor encouraged to do so.

However, there is more recent evidence to suggest that South Asian women are becoming involved in the traditionally white, male world of football. In Leicester, for example, Hema Chauhan, the Sports Development Officer, has developed a solid infrastructure of female football in the city. She has also lobbied the Football Association to introduce national and regional development officers for the women's game (Bains and Johal, 1998). There are now twenty teams in the Leicester Girls' Football League of which five are predominantly Asian. Further, the importance of promising female players such as Punjabi-Indian Jaspreet Gahia as role models cannot be understated. The points raised have implications for those initiating sports policy. It is vital that sports providers do not simply attempt to impose sport onto Asian women. It is essential to examine more closely the reasons behind the lack of interest by detaching ourselves from our own cultural assumptions as to what constitutes 'normal' leisure activities.

## Conclusion

In conclusion it is necessary to remind ourselves that the term 'race' assumes the existence of a classification system used to categorise people into distinctive groups on the basis of certain biological traits. Alternatively, ethnicity refers to the cultural heritage of a particular group, such as language or religion. However, in general conversation the terms 'race' and 'ethnicity' are used interchangeably. The racial composition of sportspeople has been a popular topic of academic research especially in the US. This research confirms that black athletes are over-represented in American football, baseball and basketball when compared to the total black population. In these sports blacks are also over-represented in certain positions (stacking). This over-representation is mainly the result of racial stereotyping by teachers and coaches who perceive that black athletes have certain attributes which are suited to those positions. These attributes are usually the physical attributes of speed and strength. Positions in which decision-making is important are usually occupied by white players. In Britain similar over-representation in sport occurs. Black sportspeople are over-represented in boxing, soccer, basketball and certain track and field events. The reasons for this over-representation are related to the lack of opportunity to participate in all sports, and limited opportunities in other non-sports related endeavours. Sports participation research in Britain shows that Asians have lower participant rates than for other ethnic groups. This is particularly the case for Asian women. Stereotypical views suggest that Asians are perceived as weak and fragile, too frail for contact sports, lack stamina and are poorly coordinated. If advances are to be made, and sports participation increase among ethnic minority groups, dominant ideologies must be challenged. This can only happen if those responsible for sports strategies become critically aware of the issues.

### Note

I am indebted to my colleague, Daniel Burdsley, for his help in the preparation of this paper.

### Reflection questions

1. How do you account for the success of African-Caribbean males in sport in Britain?
2. Discuss the predominance of black athletes in peripheral positions in certain sports and their participation in a limited number of sports.
3. Discuss the contention that participation rates in sport vary across ethnic groups and between genders within ethnic groups.

### Tasks

1. Watch one sports programme and make a note of the commentator's use of language when referring to the ethnicity of the participants.
2. Examine a specific team sport, and note the positions of the players in terms of their ethnicity.

## Further reading

Carrington, B. and McDonald, I. (2001) *Racism and British Sport*. London: Routledge.
Hoberman, J. (1997) *Darwin's Athletes: How Sport has Damaged Black America and Preserved the Myth of Race*. New York: Mariner Books.
Jarvie, G. (Ed.) (1991) *Sport, Racism and Ethnicity*. London: Falmer Press.

## References

Ashe, A. (1993) *The Race Game*. BBC2.

Bains, J. and Johal, S. (1998) *Corner Flags and Corner Shops: The Asian Football Experience*, 194–202. London: Victor Gollancz.

Berghorn, F.J., Yetman, N.R. and Hanna, W.E. (1988) Racial participation and integration in men's and women's intercollegiate basketball: continuity and change, 1958–1985. *Sociology of Sport Journal*, 5, 107–124.

Burdsey, D. (1998) Who needs Cantona when we've got Jas Juttla? An investigation into the absence of Asian players in British professional football. Dissertation, Birmingham University.

Carroll, B. and Hollinshead, G. (1993) 'Equal opportunities: race and gender physical education: a case study', in Evans, J. (Ed.) *Equality, Education and Physical Education,* 154–169. London: Falmer Press.

Cashmore, E. (1982) *Black Sportsmen*. London: Routledge & Kegan Paul.

Cashmore, E. (1990) *Making Sense of Sports*. London: Routledge.

Chappell, R. and Karageorghis, C. (2000) Race, ethnicity and gender in British basketball. Paper presented for publication in *Women in Sport and Physical Activity*.

Chappell, R., Jones, R.L. and Burden A.M. (1996) Racial participation and integration in English professional basketball, 1977–1994. *Sociology of Sport Journal,* 13, 300–310.

Coakley, J. (1998) *Sport in Society: Issues and Controversies*. London: Mosby.

Eitzen, D. and Furst, D. (1989) Racial bias in women's collegiate volleyball. *Journal of Sport and Social Fitness*, 13, 46–51.

Eitzen, D. and Tessendorf, I. (1978) Racial segregation by position in sports: the special case of basketball. *Review of Sport and Leisure*, 2, 109–128.

Eitzen, D. and Yetman, N. (1982) 'Racial dynamics in American sports: continuity and change', in Parkin, R. (Ed.) *Social Approaches to Sport,* 156–180. London: Associated University Press.

F.I.F.A. (1974) World Cup Technical Committee Report. London: FIFA.

Fleming, S. (1991) 'Sport, schooling and Asian male youth culture', in Jarvie, G. (Ed.) *Sport, Racism and Ethnicity,* 30–58. London: Falmer Press.

Grusky, O. (1963) The effects of formal structure on managerial recruitment: a study of basketball organisation. *Sociometry*, 26, 345–353.

Hoberman, J. (1997) *Darwin's Athletes*. New York: Houghton Mifflin.

Kane, M. (18 January 1971) An assessment of black is best. *Sports Illustrated.*

Kew, F. (1997) *Sport: Social Problems and Issues.* Oxford: Butterworth-Heinemann.

Leonard II, W.M. (1998) *A Sociological Perspective of Sport.* London: Allyn and Bacon.

Long, J. and Spracken, K. (1996) Positional play: racial stereotyping in Rugby League. *Bulletin of Physical Education*, 32, 18–22.

Lovell, T. (1992) 'Sport, racism and young women', in Jarvie, G. (Ed.) *Sport, Racism and Ethnicity*, 58–74. London: Falmer Press.

Loy, J.W. and McElvogue, J.F. (1970) Racial segregation in American sport. *International Review of Sport Sociology*, 5, 5–23.

Maguire, J.A. (1991a) Race and position assignment in English soccer: a preliminary analysis of ethnicity and sport in Britain. *Sociology of Sport Journal*, 5, 257–269.

Maguire, J.A. (1991b) 'Sport, racism and British society: a sociological study of England's élite male Afro-Caribbean soccer and Rugby Union players', in Jarvie, G. (Ed.) *Sport, Racism and Ethnicity*, 94–123. London: Falmer Press.

Malcolm, D. (1997) Stacking in cricket: a figurational sociological reappraisal of centrability. *Sociology of Sport Journal*, 14, 263–282.

Margolis, B. and Piliavin, J.A. (1999) 'Stacking' in major league basketball: a multivariate analysis. *Sociology of Sport Journal*, 16, 1, 16–34.

McPherson, B., Curtis, J. and Loy, J. (1989) *Social Significance of Sport.* Champaign, IL: Human Kinetics.

McPherson, B. (1976) 'Minority group involvement in sport: the black athlete', in Yiannakis, A. (Ed.) *Sports Sociology: Contemporary Theories*, 153–156. New York: Kendall Hunt.

Norris, J. and Jones, R.L. (1998) Towards a clearer definition and application of the centrality hypothesis in English professional association football. *Journal of Sport Behaviour*, 21, 181–195.

Owen, D. (1994) Spatial variations in ethnic group populations in Great Britain. *Population Trends*, 78. London: Office of Population Census and Surveys.

Polley, M. (1998) *Moving the Goalposts: A History of Sport and Society since 1945.* London: Routledge.

Raval, S. (1989) Gender, leisure and sport: a case study of young people of South Asian descent – a response. *Leisure Studies*, 8, 237–240.

Skellington, R. (1996) *'Race' in Britain Today.* London: Sage.

Small, S. (1994) *Racialised Barriers: The Black Experience in the United States and England in the 1980s*. London, UK: Routledge.

Sports Council (1993) *Sport in the Nineties: New Horizon*, 31. London: Sports Council.

Sports Council (1994) *Black and Ethnic Minorities in Sport: Policy and Objectives*,15. London: Sports Council.

Wedderburn, M. (1989) You're black, you're quick, you're on the wing: a sociological analysis of the experience of England's élite, black rugby players. MSc postgraduate project, Loughborough University.

Weinburg, S. and Arond, H. (1952) The occupational culture of the boxer American. *Journal of Sociology*, 57, 460–469.

Yetman, N. and Berghorn, F. (1993) Racial participation and integration in intercollegiate basketball: a longitudinal perspective. *Sociology of Sport Journal*, 10, 301–304.

# 7 Equality, equity and inclusion in physical education and school sport

*Dawn Penney*

## Introduction

In recent years, sport organisations in the UK and internationally have increasingly been called upon to address 'equal opportunities issues' and specifically to consider the degree to which they have recognised and provided for the needs of all individuals in communities. As we will see in this chapter, initiatives forthcoming from governments and sporting bodies have approached and interpreted the notion of 'equal opportunities' in various ways. In physical education, equal opportunities has similarly become established as 'an issue' to be addressed by policy-makers and practitioners alike. In England and Wales the development of a National Curriculum was heralded as a significant step towards, if not a guarantee of, equal opportunities in education. The introduction of the National Curriculum established that it was a statutory requirement for all state (i.e. government funded) schools to provide all children with a broad and balanced curriculum that would include physical education (see DES, 1989). However, there was open recognition that the implementation of the National Curriculum for Physical Education (NCPE) would see children in different schools experiencing a different range of activities, taught in different ways. The curriculum, teaching and learning in physical education would certainly not be the same in all schools, nor for all children in any school. The extent to which the introduction of the NCPE would facilitate or precipitate advances in physical education in relation to the matters of equality and equity remained to be seen, as statutory requirements were interpreted and implemented in various ways in schools throughout England and Wales.

Reflection on the ways in which equality, equal opportunity and equity have been approached in contexts of physical education is undoubtedly timely. The most recent revision of the National Curriculum in England (that established new requirements to take effect from September 2000 for the curriculum in key stages 1, 2 and 3, and September 2001 for the key stage 4 curriculum)[1] featured a new explicit emphasis for schools and teachers within them to ensure that their practices are 'inclusive', prompting us to consider how inclusive the provision of physical education and sport is, but perhaps more importantly, how inclusive it can be in the future. But before we can make any judgements or predictions in relation to these concerns, we need to address the far from simple matter of what we mean by 'inclusion' in contexts of physical education and sport, and of how talk of 'inclusion' and 'inclusive practices' relates to concerns for greater 'equality' and/or 'equity'. These are terms that are often interchanged without a distinction in meaning being either acknowledged or explained. Arguably they are terms that are frequently misused and misunderstood. This chapter will emphasise that equality, equity and inclusion are not easily defined, that their meaning is contestable and that consequently there is a need to pursue the understandings that underpin their use in particular contexts. In addition, we will see that when addressing issues of equality, equity and inclusion we cannot restrict our inquiries to the 'immediate' contexts of physical education and school sport. Rather, these contexts need to be recognised as being in a dynamic relationship with wider social, cultural, political and economic contexts. The ways in which equality and equity are expressed in physical education and school sport is unavoidably influenced by, but also plays a critical role in shaping, the interests, values and expectations of individuals and societies. Any genuine concern for promoting greater inclusivity and equity in physical education and school sport needs to address this dynamic relationship and furthermore, explore the potential that it presents for developments in physical education and sport to challenge inequities in society. This chapter will therefore consider characteristics of wider sporting, social and political contexts that impact upon the provision of physical education and sport in schools, and explore the ways in which initiatives in school contexts serve either to reinforce, or play a role in prompting, changes in these wider contexts. To begin with, however, the focus is upon terminology and the perceptions, understandings and issues that are variously associated with 'equality', 'equity' and 'inclusion' in physical education and school sport.

## Equality, equity and inclusion

I have indicated that these terms are often interchanged and that understandings of them will vary. However, in important respects, they are concerned with 'the same things' and it may be useful to address some points of commonality before seeking clarification of differences in meanings. Invariably, concerns to address equality, equity and/or inclusion can be associated with two things: difference; and fairness or justice. Although these are matters of common concern, a key issue in understanding the distinctions between the various terms is the particular ways in which notions of difference and justice are understood and approached in initiatives relating to the provision and development of physical education and sport.

### *Equality, access and opportunity*

Concerns to see greater equality in physical education and sport have often been a response to recognition that different people do not have the same opportunities to experience, enjoy and develop their ability in sport and that certain factors, such as the location of facilities, the prices charged for entry and activities and the scheduling of activities, act to exclude certain people from involvement in sport. Characteristics of provision and characteristics associated with the potential participants have been identified as 'barriers', meaning that for certain individuals and/or groups of individuals, access is effectively denied.

In the context of physical education school facilities vary and variations are likely to be reflected in the range of activities provided. The availability of particular facilities thus plays a part in shaping who has access to particular activities in physical education and school sport. But the provision of facilities does not ensure that all pupils will be able to access the activities on offer. We need to pursue who the facilities and the activities provided are really available to and the ways in which differences between individuals will influence their ability to access 'opportunities'. We can note, for example, that pupils living in rural areas are often disadvantaged in terms of their ability to access and enjoy extracurricula physical education and school sport. If pupils are reliant upon school bus services to get home, it is likely that they will be unable to stay after school for activities. They may also find it difficult to reach sport facilities that exist in their nearest town. Similarly, family circumstances may prevent some children participating in these activities. Some children have to look after younger brothers or sisters after school and thus again, may not be in a position to take up the opportunities provided for them to be involved in school sport. In short, children are not all equally positioned to participate in physical education and sport, and social and economic issues can play a key role in shaping who has access to activities.

Having recognised these issues we can pose the question of whether the situations observed are fair or just. Is it right or fair that some people, by virtue of where they live, of how wealthy they are, of whether or not they can afford to own and run a car, have very different access to sport? Should more be done to extend access to more people? In recent years there has been growing awareness of variations in the opportunities that different people have to participate in sport as a result of firstly, their personal circumstances, and secondly, the location and other characteristics (such as scheduling or pricing) of provision. Throughout the 1980s and 1990s many policy-makers and providers in the UK acknowledged the different circumstances (and particularly resources) of different population groups, and established that things could and should be done to extend sporting opportunities to more people, and particularly, to those identified as disadvantaged groups. Thus, women, young people, disabled people, the over-fifties and members of ethnic groups have all, at various times, featured as 'target groups' in sport policies and initiatives that have sought to address issues of access under the umbrella of 'equal opportunities'. Developments have increasingly acknowledged that if we are to extend participation then there is a need for providers to respond to the different needs and interests of various groups. In particular, we have seen a growing recognition that different arrangements are needed if sporting provision is to appeal to and be accessible to particular groups. For example, many leisure centres now include specific sessions for women only, having acknowledged that many women feel more comfortable in a single sex context and may be more inclined to participate if activities are provided on this basis.

To some extent, therefore, we have seen policy-makers and providers acknowledging that differences between individuals are significant in relation to their concerns for sport to be accessible to and enjoyed by more people. However, arguably, attention has focused on only certain differences, and in particular, pragmatic matters that influence people's ability to access forms of physical activity that are dominant in our society. Issues such as the cost of participation, or transport to facilities, or the timing of sessions have been amongst matters frequently addressed. Essentially the interest has been in extending access to particular opportunities. There has been little to indicate an appreciation that what different people recognise and value as 'an opportunity' will vary. The discussion that follows seeks to highlight some of the gaps or silences in many debates concerning issues of equal opportunity and equality in physical education and sport, and consider some of the implications for future developments of the different concepualisations outlined. My starting point is to take a closer look at what have been regarded as 'equal opportunities issues' in contexts of physical education, and the developments initiated in response to identified issues.

### *Activities, outcomes and opportunities*

One of the longstanding characteristics of physical education in England and Wales is its gendered pattern of organisation. Many schools have retained situations in which the provision of physical education for girls is the responsibility of female staff, while that for boys is the responsibility of male staff. In some schools different activities are included in the curriculum for girls as compared to that for boys. Even if physical education provided in curriculum time is not structured and organised in this way, the vast majority of extracurricula provision is organised on a single-sex basis (see for example, Penney and Harris, 1997; Bass and Cale, 1999). The introduction of the National Curriculum prompted renewed questioning of whether such differences are fair, just and/or can be justified on educational grounds. Is it fair that, for example, boys' experiences of games typically involves them participating and becoming skilled in the sports of soccer and rugby, while girls are more likely to experience netball and hockey? The learning experiences and opportunities in the area of games are invariably different for girls and boys. There is not equal access to particular activities.

On the one hand we need to contemplate whether a call for 'equal opportunities' demands a change to such arrangements. However, we also need to consider whether provision of the same range of activities for both boys and girls is an essential characteristic of 'equal opportunity' in physical education. During the past decade debates in some schools will have focused upon how the 'same curriculum' could be provided for all pupils. For some physical education departments, this has led to questions about pupil groupings and particularly whether single-sex and/or mixed-sex groupings should be adopted in the interests of 'equal opportunities' in physical education. Dilemmas regarding groupings have usefully served to highlight the shortcomings of simplistic conceptualisations of 'access' and 'opportunity' and that 'access to the curriculum is not synonymous with access to learning' (Williams, 1993: 128). Moves to mixed-sex groupings have frequently given rise to reports of boys dominating mixed-group games settings, with the grouping arrangement therefore regarded as having a detrimental effect on girls' enjoyment of and progression in physical education (see for example, Scraton, 1993). In such circumstances, we can see very clearly that the experience of an activity or lesson, and thus the opportunity provided, is not the same for all pupils. Nor are gender issues the only matters influencing the experiences and learning of pupils in mixed-group settings. As I discuss further below, gender issues may well be important and it is critical to address their influence, but we all have multiple identities and furthermore, are also potentially subject to 'multiple forms of oppression and discrimination' (Cole and Hill, 1999: 3). Cole and Hill point out that 'teachers, student teachers and others [including pupils themselves] may, usually unwittingly, also demean, discriminate against, label and stereotype in all sorts of ways' (3).

Irrespective of whether or not mixed or single-sex grouping is employed, there is no guarantee that all pupils are being given access to the same quality of experience or the same potential advancement in their learning in physical education. In single-sex settings just as in mixed settings, some pupils may dominate lessons. In neither setting can we be assured that lessons will feature activities that enable all pupils to develop their skills in, and knowledge and understanding of, the subject. Ability is a key variable shaping (creating for some and inhibiting for others) pupils' experiences in physical education and school sport and their potential to access the opportunities on offer. In the curriculum context recognition of this variable has been at the heart of efforts to develop differentiation in physical education teaching, and specifically, moves to structure activities and design learning experiences in ways that will mean that teaching accommodates and provides for pupils' varying levels of skill development. However, differentiation has also frequently been identified as an area of weakness in physical education teaching and it remains an issue demanding attention.

So how do developments such as these relate to our interests in pursuing the matters of equality, equity and inclusion? Addressing differentiation signals a recognition that some pupils may effectively be excluded from some or all of the aspects of learning that a physical education lesson is designed to facilitate, and that individual differences between pupils, particularly in relation to prior learning and levels of skills, knowledge and understanding, are important matters to address in curriculum planning. Arguably differentiation is very much about inclusion, driven by the desire to create learning environments and learning experiences that are inclusive of all pupils with often very diverse levels of ability. As teachers taking a new group of all pupils will be particularly aware, by virtue of their different (and often notably gendered) backgrounds and past experiences in and of sport, pupils are positioned very differently when they come to physical education (Evans *et al.*, 1987; Williams, 1993). Addressing these differences is clearly critical if teachers are to succeed in facilitating learning and enjoyment for all in contexts of physical education and school sport.

We also need to note that it is not the task of the teacher to attempt to eradicate these differences. A key point to recall here is that differentiation is designed to provide different pupils with access to different learning opportunities. As Talbot (1993) has observed, if we view equality in terms of 'equal outcomes' we are in danger of reducing attainment to the lowest common denominator. In these respects physical education is no different to any other subject. The aim in differentiation should be to address the ways in which the curriculum and teaching can ensure that all pupils are enabled access to the skills, knowledge and understanding that is appropriate to their different levels of learning and different learning potentials. This task is far from easy, particularly in the current very pressured contexts of teaching. However, it is arguably one of the most important challenges for teachers concerned to develop inclusive physical education curricula.

Gender and ability are just two of a growing list of 'issues' that teachers have been prompted to address in the interests of equal opportunities in education and physical education. The list (encompassing gender, class, age, race, ethnicity, religion, disability and sexuality) has reflected recognition of the many dimensions to 'difference' between individuals and an appreciation of the potential impact that various differences may have on participation in physical education and sport. Research has drawn attention to the ways in which individuals may variously be disadvantaged as a consequence of being perceived as in some way 'different from the norm' (see for example Benn, 2000; Wright, 1996). It has also sought to raise awareness of the complexities of difference and in particular, the diversities within identified groups. It has highlighted the need to avoid simplistic categorisations if we are to avoid creating new and as potentially damaging stereotypical images and understandings as those that we are seeking to challenge and/or avoid. Arguably physical education and sport still have a long way to go before they can be regarded as embracing the insights that research has provided in relation to, for example, sexuality or ethnicity, or the identified need to explore and respond to differences within identified groups as much as those between them. In part, researchers themselves have to take some of the blame here. In frequently focusing upon a single 'issue' researchers may be inhibiting the development of understandings, policies and initiatives that privilege the individual with their inherent multiple identities. There is a strong case for more work that seeks to transcend the potentially misleading and damaging divisions between equality issues that still appear to be portrayed as notably distinct.

In now moving towards a focus upon equity in physical education and sport, I am concerned to pursue whether or not this recognition of and focus upon an increasing number of 'issues' can be seen as a sound foundation from which to consider questions of inclusion in physical education and sport. Specifically I point to the need to consider the particular ways in which policy-makers, teachers in schools and others involved in the provision of sport are viewing the differences between individuals that they have recognised; what differences they are in fact recognising, and what differences they may be overlooking in their responses.

These matters are central to a related concern, of whether or not the actions taken in contexts of physical education and school sport are serving to reinforce and reproduce, or by contrast challenge, prejudices and inequalities in wider society.

In relation to this latter point, research focusing on gender issues has usefully highlighted the potential shortcomings of well-intentioned developments. Scraton (1993) has drawn attention to the tendency for extension of access to constitute an extension of access to traditionally male activities, with physical education thereby reinforcing the dominant and privileged status of these activities in wider society; and for mixed-group settings to reinforce gendered power relations, with 'boys reproducing their dominant role and girls learning their subordination' (Scraton, 1993: 145). Talbot (1993) has similarly highlighted the tendencies for '"me-too feminism", in which boys' activities are used as the norm … and boys' performances always regarded as the norm or benchmark against which girls' performances should be measured' (83). Other work has usefully reminded us that it is not only gender identities and relations that physical education has the scope to reproduce or challenge. Shilling (1993) for example, rightly identifies our tendency to overlook the powerful ways in which physical education bestows different values not only on different activities, but also on different bodies, such that certain bodily forms (inscribed with but also judged in the light of, multiple identities) come to be accepted and celebrated within but also beyond arenas of physical education and sport, while others remain marginalised or openly rejected in these arenas. Shilling also draws attention to some of the key assumptions that may underpin many initiatives that have arisen under the banner of 'equal opportunities' in physical education and sport; that participation (and I would add, more specifically the pursuit of élite performance) in sport, 'is a "good thing" which can yield similar benefits to all sections of society' (56). As Shilling explains 'This assumption fails to explore how sports may carry different meanings and unequal benefits and risks for their participants' (56). While Shilling associates these differences with social-class background, there is clearly a need to recognise that it is not only social class that has an impact in these terms. Carroll and Hollinshead's (1993) and Benn's (2000) work has drawn attention to the ways in which race and religion result in participants being positioned in particular ways in contexts of physical education and has usefully demonstrated the dynamic interplay between matters of race, religion and gender, reminding us of the need for analyses to embrace the multiplicities of individual identities, not all of which can be expanded upon here. There is certainly a need to pursue in greater depth the various differences that have been explored in research in physical education, but we also need to direct attention towards some underpinning matters that have relevance 'across the board' in relation to equal opportunities 'issues' in physical education and sport. The next section therefore returns to these generic concerns.

## From equality to equity: viewing difference differently

It is useful to reflect on some of the issues discussed above from a personal perspective. How do you view other young people in the UK today and particularly those with apparently fewer opportunities than yourself to participate in physical education and sport? How do you view those who are less proficient in sport than yourself? Quite possibly, you see such individuals as 'lacking' in some way and thus view the differences between them and yourself in 'deficit' terms. This is typically how differences between individuals and/or different groups of individuals have been framed in discussions relating to the matters of equality and equal opportunities in physical education and sport. Differences in patterns of participation and in provision are viewed as signalling gaps or shortfalls that represent 'a problem'. As explained, target-group initiatives have invariably regarded some individuals as disadvantaged compared to others and have reflected the view that efforts (and resources) should therefore be directed towards redressing imbalances in the provision for different groups in society. There are two dimensions that I want to consider here. On the one hand we need to look at the way in which the existing situation and particularly the identified differences are being viewed. On the other, we need to explore what is being proposed as an appropriate response to the situation. The two matters are inextricably linked, but it is important to recognise that there are two issues. Essentially, we need to be concerned with what is considered 'the problem' and what are then deemed to be suitable courses of action in arenas of physical education and sport.

To reflect on the former, the label of 'deficiency' and identification of deficiency as a problem is important. In assigning this label and defining deficiency as a problem, we are making a judgement on particular grounds. It is a judgement made on the basis of particular social and cultural values, with the assumption that these values are and/or should be shared by all. Thus initiatives designed to extend access to and opportunities in activities need to be recognised as being instigated from a position of social and cultural dominance. Typically, they are destined to promote patterns of behaviour that will reinforce this dominance. Invariably there is a failure to acknowledge that the activities and behaviours that we may regard as appropriate, desirable and/or worthy of public recognition are not necessarily viewed in the same light in other social or cultural contexts. There is also an accompanying failure to recognise that there may be much that we can learn from other societies and cultures and the values and behaviours that they privilege. Values and practices dominant in other societies and cultures may serve to reveal new ways of thinking about our lives, lifestyles and sport and physical education within these, and as such provide important insights for future developments in physical education and sport. Bale and Sang's (1996) account of the development and transition in *Kenyan Running* provides vivid insights into the different values and practices that have characterised and defined the sport in different historical and cultural contexts and the way in which particular, modern and western values have progressively redefined the sport and its inherent 'movement culture'. They explain that 'The athletic body, as well as the cultural landscape, had changed. The relatively unrestricted and free movement of the pre-colonial period had been replaced by the corset of running as racing with its starting and finishing lines and its geometrically arranged lane marking' (98–99). Bale and Sang (1996) thus direct us to the potential for sport and physical education to take different forms to those we regard as the norm, but also remind us of the dominance of particular forms of sport in the modern world. They comment that 'Although sport does not have to be as serious as it currently seems to be, it is difficult to resist the pressures which are made explicit in the Olympic code – higher, stronger, faster – with its emphasis on centimetre, gram and second. In our modern society there are no prizes for slow running, there are no prizes for style, and results are often regarded as being more important than performance' (21) and reflect that 'Success in sport can only be achieved in most of the modern world by a particular kind of sporting culture' (17).

When we recognise that the price of international recognition for Kenyan running has been the disappearance of other body and movement cultures, the increased profile of Kenya and Kenyan athletes in international sporting contexts takes on a different perspective. Gaining acclaim in international sporting arenas has demanded the acceptance of the superiority of certain practices, sporting and cultural identities over and above others; and the consequent sacrifice or rejection of practices and identities that were previously highly valued.

Pursuing equity in sport and physical education is fundamentally about valuing the differences so vividly reflected in Bale and Sang's account of the 'development' of Kenyan running. Having a commitment to equity demands that we do not merely recognise or respect individual and cultural differences, but instead, see them as a resource. Evans and Davies (1993) explain '… the issue must not be whether differences can be dissolved … but how they can be celebrated in ways which negate prejudice and stereotyping and at the same time respect individual cultural identity' (19). Thus, from an equity perspective, no one set of values or behaviours should be regarded as superior to others, or as 'the norm' against which others are measured or judged. There is recognition that behaviours and values always need to be located, temporally and culturally, that at different times, in different places and cultures, different behaviours and values will be regarded as normal and desirable, and that there is richness to be gained from diversity. Recognition of these issues is particularly important when we consider inclusion or inclusivity in contexts of physical education and sport, and specifically, what sorts of development will signal progress towards greater inclusion in these contexts.

## Equality, equity and inclusion – policies and practices in physical education and sport

In seeking to illustrate the implications of different understandings and conceptualisations of 'equal opportunities' in relation to what may then be regarded as a means of achieving greater inclusion, it is useful to again focus upon extracurricula physical education. In England and Wales this has often been identified as a context that is accessible to and directed towards the interests of relatively few pupils. Various studies have highlighted that the focus of attention is invariably a schools' representation and achievement in formal competitions with other schools (see for example, Bass and Cale, 1999; Mason, 1995; Penney and Harris, 1997; Sports Council for Wales, 1995). Extracurricula activities typically comprise matches and practices for those pupils selected for school teams. If we consider what would signal a move towards greater inclusivity in provision, we can begin to see that there is the scope not merely for various suggestions as 'solutions', but also for different views in relation to what is regarded as the shortcoming or problem. The current situation could be seen as signalling an absence of sufficient numbers of school teams and/or leagues for more teams to play in. Running a second or third team could be regarded as a notable step towards extending opportunity to more pupils and thus addressing concerns that some pupils may be excluded if they are not selected for the first team.

But is the development of more teams 'the answer'? It is an answer that assumes a particular problem and furthermore, particular needs and interests for all pupils. Organising more school teams assumes that the representative team structure and/or coached practice sessions that focus on skill development will be suitable for all pupils and that all pupils desire these sorts of sporting experience. What is not acknowledged is that some pupils may not have aspirations to participate in this structure, or feel comfortable doing so. Where are the opportunities to participate informally, for fun with friends of varied abilities? Why is it that participation in a formal structure is viewed differently from (and invariably, as superior to) casual participation? Why is it that participation in certain sports or activities is valued over and above others? In confronting these matters we come back to the dominance of particular values and behaviours associated with them, and see that contexts of physical education and sport are inevitably influenced by and invariably reflect the values that are dominant in wider society. We can not escape the fact that 'gold standard' is what matters for most people. It is what is celebrated by the media and public and it is what many pupils and their parents expect and assume that physical education and school sport will be directed towards.

If we now regard current patterns of extracurricula provision from an equity perspective, very different issues arise. As Evans and Davies (1993) have explained, having a commitment to equity demands that we do not merely recognise differences between pupils but rather, seek to celebrate their individual identities in and through physical education and school sport. Extending participation, from this perspective, has different implications and involves a different view of 'what the problem is'. It demands that we develop provision that is sufficiently varied so as to provide a context in which different identities and interests may be expressed and celebrated. This means being open to the introduction of new forms of physical education and sport that reflect different interests and values to those that we are most familiar with and have come to regard as those that it is 'only natural' to adopt. It may involve extending the range of activities on offer and/or ensuring that provision is not solely directed towards the pursuit of

Olympic ideals. There needs to be both the scope and encouragement for 'other' values and interests to be pursued in and via physical education and sport, not least of which are fun and friendship. These benefits of participation are surely deserving of greater attention and status in schools.

Initiating practices that challenge established norms and expectations is far from easy and there are barriers to such developments both within and beyond the arenas of physical education and school sport. As Talbot (1993) states 'To recognise homophobia in the classroom is one thing; to offer alternatives which are seen as possible and relevant by boys and male colleagues is quite another' (85). This serves to remind us that it is not only our own perceptions and expectations of and for physical education that we have to consider. Parents, our immediate colleagues, senior managers in schools, pupils and individuals in policy-making arenas all have particular visions of what physical education as a subject is essentially 'about', what typical lessons can therefore be expected to 'look like' and what children should learn. In addition, however, Talbot (1993) prompts us to acknowledge the 'active and positive' characteristics of situations that for her, distinguish provision of opportunity from provision of access; 'freedom *from* constraint confers access, while freedom to *do* as one wishes confers opportunity' (85, my emphasis). For Cole and Hill (1999) the issues go further and, specifically, need to be seen in relation to the matters of social structures and social mobility. This they regard as the key to distinguishing 'between equal opportunities on the one hand, and equality on the other' (1). They explain:

> Equal opportunities policies, in schools and elsewhere, seek to enhance social mobility within structures which are essentially unequal. In other words, they seek meritocracy, where people rise (or fall) on merit, but to grossly unequal levels or strata in society: unequal in terms of income, wealth, lifestyle, life-chances and power.
>
> (1)

They continue:

> Egalitarian policies (policies to promote equality) ... seek to go further. Firstly egalitarians are committed to a transformed economy, and a more socially just society, where wealth and ownership are shared far more equally, and where citizens ... exercise democratic controls over their lives and over the structures of the societies of which they are part and to which they contribute.
>
> (2)

Cole and Hill thus prompt us to address the ways in which developments in physical education relate to (reinforce and/or challenge) inequalities in sporting structures and the need for us to recognise and seek to challenge inequalities beyond schools. In the discussion that follows I focus attention on contemporary policy developments relating to physical education in England and Wales. I specifically consider the extent to which, and the ways in which, these developments can be regarded as prompting moves towards greater equity and inclusion in contemporary physical education and sport, and how the developments relate to wider sporting and social contexts (with their inherent inequalities). As indicated above, such inquiry demands that we consider the values recognised in and promoted by developments, explore which individuals are likely to feel able to access the opportunities provided in physical education and school sport, and consider the opportunities that experiences in physical education and sport create 'for whom' in wider society. Quite deliberately the discussion is not confined to a description and analysis of 'what is' but also aims to address the 'yet to be realised potential' inherent in contemporary contexts of physical education and school sport. My interest is in considering the ways in which the actions of schools and teachers within them may, in the future, present stronger challenges to longstanding inequities in physical education, school sport and wider sporting and social contexts. However, I also emphasise the importance, when pointing to such potential, to retain connections with the realities of contemporary contexts, and thus to acknowledge clear barriers to the development of sustainable challenges to identified inequities.

## Physical education: an entitlement for all children

The National Curriculum established a 'broad and balanced curriculum' as a statutory entitlement for all pupils in all state schools in England and Wales, but as noted, it was always acknowledged that the statutory entitlement would not, and could not, be the same in all schools. The development of the National Curriculum for Physical Education can therefore be seen as signaling some commitment to equality – but a limited commitment, compromised by pragmatic and economic agendas and constraints. Although the 'flexibility' inherent in requirements may have repeatedly been claimed to reflect a desire to respect the professionalism of teachers, it was also clearly associated with the recognition that implementation was set to occur in very varied school contexts, and furthermore, needed to be possible in these varied contexts. The statutory requirements did not, therefore, seek to prescribe the detail of school curricula, nor the ways in which teachers should teach. It was accepted that there would be differences in the opportunities and experiences arising in different schools, but also, for different pupils within any one school. Decisions taken by teachers in schools would play a critical role in determining the degree to which the National Curriculum catered for the diverse needs and interests of pupils.

However, it is also important to note that although the entitlement curriculum was destined to be different in different schools, it would nevertheless be a particular entitlement. The development of the NCPE was shaped not only by economic concerns, but also by the dominance of a particular ideological stance in relation to what the focus of attention in physical education should be. As Penney and Evans (1999) have emphasised, its structure and requirements privileged certain knowledge over and above other knowledge and were certainly not neutral or value free. Penney and Evans (1997; 1999) have discussed the dominance of particular discourses within the official texts of the NCPE, the marginalisation and/or exclusion of others, and the political pressures and influences underpinning these characteristics of the texts. They contend that in the way in which the NCPE is structured, in the specific requirements relating to the activities to be included in the curriculum and in the different value thereby accorded to some experiences as compared to others, the NCPE can be seen as reinforcing the privileged position of discourses of élite performance and interests in 'traditional' team games. In these respects the NCPE can be seen to mirror and serve to perpetuate the dominance in wider society of particular sports and a particular focus in relation to participation in sport. Far from pointing towards the egalitarian interests that Cole and Hill (1999) have stressed signify an interest in equality, the NCPE has openly privileged restorationist interests that seem destined to reinforce rather than challenge social inequalities. Furthermore, as Penney and Evans have also emphasised, the NCPE was clearly shaped with this perpetuation in mind (Penney and Evans, 1999).

The dominance of restorationist discourses in the development of the NCPE is an important issue in relation to concerns to establish physical education as a subject that expresses and promotes equity. However, this should not detract from recognition of the positive contribution that the development of the NCPE has made to the pursuit of equity in physical education, nor exploration of the potential to establish practices within the framework of the NCPE that represent important steps towards greater equity. Early NCPE documents were notable for their emphasis on the need to recognise the distinction between access and opportunity in contexts of physical education (see Talbot 1993), prompting the development of more complex conceptualisations of 'equal opportunities' in physical education. Perhaps more significantly, it has always been emphasised that the National Curriculum is merely a framework for curricula, leaving schools and teachers within them with important decisions to make. These decisions have included the specific activities to be incorporated in physical education, the time to be devoted to each, grouping arrangements and the teaching approaches to be employed. Thus, although the government's texts may have lacked much in the way of a positive lead for teachers to develop curricula that express a commitment to challenge matters such as racism, sexism and homophobia in physical education, school sport and wider society, absences in the text can provide openings for such action. In the implementation of the NCPE there is important scope for individual teachers to raise the profile of equity. Clarke and Nutt (1999) have pointed to some of the ways in which teachers can be proactive in this respect, suggesting for example, that games such as korfball or tchoukball and modified versions of games such as rugby may provide positive learning experiences for more pupils (both girls and boys) regardless of ability, and explaining the ways in which different grouping arrangements can actively challenge conventional role expectations. Via such initiatives we may see the implementation of the NCPE prompting greater equity not merely within, but also beyond arenas of physical education and school sport.

Regrettably, the type of developments that Clarke and Nutt (1999) outline may well be more the exception than the norm in schools in England and Wales. The potential inherent in the NCPE for the development of notably 'new' or 'different' curricula and teaching approaches that consciously challenge stereotypical views and practices in physical education and sport seems to have largely remained a matter of 'potential'. Bedward and Williams (2000) recently reflected that 'It would seem that the introduction of the National Curriculum physical education constituted a missed opportunity to revise out-dated practices of gender-differentiated physical education' (115). Penney and Evans (2000) have stressed, however, that the opportunity should not yet be deemed 'missed', saying that with yet another revision to the statutory requirements, we once again '...stand on the edge of opportunity, either of progressive development, or surface level change' (28). In the final section of the chapter I therefore focus on this latest revision to the NCPE. Specifically, I address the new expectations and demands that accompany the new agendas and new language that features in the latest documentation issued to schools in England, and explore the implications of the government's stated commitment to the development of a National Curriculum that is 'inclusive'. I again stress the need (particularly when considering the responses that may be forthcoming in implementation of the new requirements) to address the dynamic between developments in physical education and school sport and interests and agendas relating to wider sporting and political arenas.

### *From entitlement to inclusion: The 'new' National Curriculum for Physical Education*

The revision of the National Curriculum in 2000 brought new discourses to the fore of government texts, specifically, of inclusion in education and physical education. In the forward to the revised NCPE the Secretary of State for Education and Employment emphasised that:

> An entitlement to learning must be an entitlement for all pupils. This National Curriculum includes for the first time a detailed, overarching statement on inclusion which makes clear the principles schools must follow in their teaching right across the curriculum, to ensure that all pupils have the chance to succeed, whatever their individual needs and the potential barriers to their learning may be.
>
> (DfEE/QCA, 1999: 3)

In all subject areas teachers are now required to plan and teach the National Curriculum with 'due regard' to three principles for inclusion:

- Setting suitable learning challenges;
- Responding to pupils' diverse learning needs; and
- Overcoming barriers to learning and assessment for individuals and groups of pupils.

(DfEE/QCA, 1999: 28)

We have yet to see the ways in which these principles will be developed in practice in physical education and can therefore do no more than hypothesise about the understandings and conceptualisations of equality and/or equity that will inform and be apparent in responses. In some respects the text seems in danger of directing teachers towards a limited focus on access to curricula that have predefined learning outcomes. In physical education attention may focus upon different ability levels amongst pupils and the need for learning experiences, teaching approaches and assessment to address these differences. Differentiation is important, but there is also a need for developments that go beyond measures that seek to include more pupils within relatively fixed boundaries to learning. There are prompts in the text for initiatives that challenge established boundaries and specifically, that challenge stereotypical views and encourage pupils to 'appreciate and view positively differences in others, whether arising from race, gender, ability or disability' (DfEE/QCA, 1999: 29).

But while the NCPE now features these discourses of inclusion, it has also retained many long-established and familiar discourses. With the exception of the new requirement that curricula at key stage 4 must address two areas of activity and the freedom of choice as to which areas these are, there is little to prompt a move away from curricula that are dominated by 'traditional' team games. In some respects, the new NCPE can be seen to strengthen the dominance of discourses of élite sports performance in physical education. Elsewhere (see Penney, 2000) I have argued that the statement below, describing 'exceptional performance' in physical education fails to encompass the breadth of learning that many both within and outside the profession claim it facilitates, and that it has the potential to facilitate.

> Pupils consistently use advanced skills, techniques and ideas with precision and fluency. Drawing on what they know of the principles of advanced strategies and tactics or composition, they consistently apply these principles with originality, proficiency and flair in their own and others' work. They evaluate their own and others' work, showing that they understand how skills, strategy and tactics or composition, and fitness relate to and affect the quality and originality of performance. They reach judgements independently about how their own and others' performance could be improved, prioritising aspects for further development. They consistently apply appropriate knowledge and understanding of health and fitness in all aspects of their work.
>
> (DfEE/QCA, 1999: 42)

There is a danger that statements such as this may prompt a narrow focus upon improved performance in specific sports and in so doing, mean that physical education recognises and provides for the skills and interests of only a minority of pupils. Extending the range of skills, knowledge and understanding that are incorporated in descriptions of learning in physical education extends the potential for the subject to be inclusive of the varied educational needs, abilities and interests of all pupils. Notably, at key stage 4 the NCPE now encourages the development of knowledge, skills and understanding that relate to 'other roles' in activity settings, such as coaching or officiating, and develop leadership skills. Developments such as this are critical if the subject can genuinely claim to be 'responding to pupils' diverse learning needs'.

But in contemplating likely responses to the new NCPE requirements and its inherent mix of discourses, we need to reflect upon some of the characteristics of contexts of implementation. Regrettably, many school contexts may be less than supportive, with physical education remaining a low priority in curriculum developments and in-service training provision. Increasingly, the key sources of support for the development of physical education are agencies and organisations associated with sport. This support is invaluable, but in a situation in which the boundaries between physical education, school and junior sport are so blurred, there is certainly no guarantee that attention will focus upon establishing greater equity in provision. The government's strategy for sport, *A Sporting Future for All* (DCMS, 2000) was notable in identifying physical education as having a critical role to play not merely in sport development, but élite sport development. The strategy established the growing number of specialist sports colleges in England, each with links to other secondary and primary schools, as an integral element of the élite sport development network. The provision of opportunities for more children to engage with élite structures is a move to be welcomed. However, such provision needs to be accompanied by parallel developments that offer alternative pathways for those children who may not have either the interest or ability to pursue an élite performance route.

## Conclusion

This chapter has highlighted the complexities inherent in attempting to address matters of equality, equity and inclusion in physical education and school sport. The challenges that these matters pose are considerable and regrettably, the support needed in responding to them may not always be forthcoming, either within or beyond schools. Implementation of the revised National Curriculum for Physical Education can be regarded as once again signalling a notable opportunity for moves towards greater equity in physical education. However, implementation is set to occur at a time when developments both within and beyond physical education mean that there may not be encouragement or support for establishing the egalitarian agendas that I have indicated are critical if developments in physical education are to have impact and meaning in wider sporting and social contexts. Instead, restorationist agendas may well continue to dominate not only 'official policies' relating to physical education and school sport, but also much practice in schools. In relation to concerns to develop greater equity in physical education, the 'flexibility' inherent in the NCPE and the scope that this presents for individual action remains arguably the most critical characteristic and valuable resource for us to pursue.

## Note

1 The requirements for the National Curriculum are expressed in relation to four 'key stages' of education, with key stages 1 and 2 emcompassing the primary years (to age 11) and key stages 3 and 4 encompassing the secondary years of schooling (for ages 11–16 years).

## Reflection questions

1 If we are interested in promoting equity within and beyond physical education, how important is it that the curricula for girls and boys feature the same activities?
2 Are characteristics of teaching, rather than the particular activities, of greater significance in shaping the degree to which physical education expresses and promotes equity and inclusion? How can teachers enhance equity and inclusion via different grouping strategies, teaching approaches, and different forms of assessment?
3 Pupils play an active part in challenging inequities in physical education and sport. Reflect on ways in which you have been marginalised and have marginalised others in contexts of physical education and school sport. Consider the prejudices (relating to who can legitimately participate in sport and whose participation is valued) that may underpin these actions and experiences.

## Tasks

1 Look at the statement for 'exceptional performance' in the National Curriculum for Physical Education. Consider what other skills, knowledge and understanding that we may associate with physical education but that are not obviously identified in the statement. You may find it useful to consider the claims that are made about what learning and qualities physical education develops in children. Examples of these 'claims' can be found at the following internet sites:

- British Association of Advisers and Lecturers in Physical Education
  http://www.baalpe.org/
- The Physical Education Association of the United Kingdom
  http://www.pea.uk.com/
- The National Council for School Sport
  http://www.schoolsport.freeserve.co.uk/

Now develop a new statement for 'exceptional performance' that reflects the wide range of skills, knowledge and understanding that physical education is often associated with.

2 Make suggestions about the ways in which teachers might respond to each of the three principles for inclusion (below) in contexts of physical education in order to promote equity and 'celebrate difference':

- setting suitable learning challenges
- responding to pupils' diverse learning needs
- overcoming potential barriers to learning and assessment for individuals and groups of pupils.

## Further reading

Evans, J. (Ed.) (1993) *Equality, Education and Physical Education.* London: The Falmer Press.

Hill, D. and Cole, M. (Eds) (1999) *Promoting Equality in Secondary Schools.* London: Cassell.

Williams, A. (Ed.) (2000) *Primary School Physical Education. Research into Practice.* London: RoutledgeFalmer.

## References

Bale, J. and Sang, J. (1996) *Kenyan Running. Movement Culture, Geography and Global Change.* London: Frank Cass.

Bass, D. and Cale, L. (1999) Promoting physical activity through the extra-curricular programme. *European Journal of Physical Education*, 4, 45–64.

Bedward, J. and Williams, A. (2000) 'Girls' experience of physical education: voting with their feet?', in Williams, A. (Ed.) *Primary School Physical Education. Research into Practice.* London: RoutledgeFalmer.

Benn, T. (2000) 'Towards inclusion in education and physical education', in Williams, A. (Ed.) *Primary School Physical Education. Research into Practice.* London: Routledge Falmer.

Carroll, B. and Hollingshead, G. (1993) 'Equal opportunities, race and gender in physical education: a case study', in Evans, J. (Ed.) *Equality, Education and Physical Education.* London: Falmer Press.

Clarke, G. and Nutt, G. (1999) 'Physical education', in Hill, D. and Cole, M. (Eds) *Promoting Equality in Secondary Schools.* London: Cassell.

Cole, M. and Hill, D. (1999) 'Equality and secondary education: what are the conceptual issues?', in Hill, D. and Cole, M. (Eds) *Promoting Equality in Secondary Schools.* London: Cassell.

Department for Education (DFE)/Welsh Office (WO) (1995) *Physical Education in the National Curriculum.* London: DFE.

Department for Education and Employment (DfEE)/Qualifications and Curriculum Authority (QCA) (1999) *Physical Education. The National Curriculum for England.* London: HMSO.

Department for Culture, Media and Sport (DCMS) (2000) *A Sporting Future for All.* London: DCMS.

Department of Education and Science (DES) (1989) *National Curriculum – From Policy to Practice.* London: DES.

Evans, J. and Davies, B. (1993) 'Equality, equity and physical education', in Evans, J. (Ed.) *Equality, Education and Physical Education*. London: Falmer Press.

Evans, J., Lopez, S., Duncan, M. and Evans, M. (1987) Some thoughts on the political and pedagogical implications of mixed sex grouping in physical education. *British Educational Research Journal*, 13, 1, 59–71.

Mason, V. (1995) *Young People and Sport in England, 1994.* London: The Sports Council.

Penney, D. (2000) Physical education, sporting excellence and educational excellence. *European Physical Education Review,* 6, 2, 135–150.

Penney, D. and Evans, J. (1997) Naming the game. Discourse and domination in physical education and sport in England and Wales. *European Physical Education Review,* 3, 1, 21–32.

Penney, D. and Evans, J. (1999) *Politics, Policy and Practice in Physical Education.* London: Routledge.

Penney, D. and Evans, J. (2000) 'The National Curriculum for Physical Education: policy, practice and prospects', in Williams, A. (Ed.) *Primary School Physical Education. Research into Practice*. London: RoutledgeFalmer.

Penney, D. and Harris, J. (1997) Extra-curricular physical education: more of the same for the more able? *Sport, Education and Society*, 2, 1, 41–54.

Scraton, S. (1993) 'Equality, coeducation and physical education in secondary schooling', in Evans, J. (Ed.) *Equality, Education and Physical Education.* London: Falmer Press.

Shilling, C. (1993) The body, class and social inequalities,' in Evans, J. (Ed.) *Equality, Education and Physical Education.* London: Falmer Press.

Sports Council for Wales (1995) *The Pattern of Play: Physical Education in Welsh Secondary Schools: 1990–1994.* Cardiff: The Sports Council for Wales.

Talbot, M. (1993) 'A gendered physical education: equality and sexism', in Evans, J. (Ed.) *Equality, Education and Physical Education*. London: Falmer Press.

Williams, A. (1993) 'Who cares about girls? Equality, physical education and the primary school child', in Evans, J. (Ed.) *Equality, Education and Physical Education.* London: Falmer Press.

Wright, J. (1996) Mapping the discourses of physical education: articulating a female tradition. *Journal of Curriculum Studies,* 28, 3, 331–351.

# 8 Socialisation and participation in sport

*Sandra A. Stroot*

## Introduction

Socialisation into sport does not happen in isolation from the rest of society. 'Sport is a social representation of historical, social and cultural forces, and at the same time it affirms, legitimates and reproduces those very same conditions. In other words, sport reproduces social reality and transmits those aspects of culture that convey meanings about the social, political and the economic order of society; about gender, race, and class relations; about the body and physical activity' (Greendorfer and Bruce, 1991: 137).

Eitzen and Sage (1987) described socialisation as the 'process of learning and adapting to a given social system' (77). Socialisation is described by Coakley (2001) as the 'active process of learning and social development, which occurs as we interact with one another and become acquainted with the social world in which we live' (82). The purpose of this chapter is to describe how individuals are socialised into and continue to participate in sport. When examining socialisation and sport, there are two related aspects of the socialisation process: (a) socialisation into sport, which studies the factors that influence the ways children become involved in sport, and (b) socialisation via sport, which examines how involvement in sport has influenced others, including sport participants.

## Socialisation into sport: getting involved

One of the first theories used to guide socialisation research was Bandura's (1977) social learning theory, which falls under a functionalist approach, and emphasises the importance of observing and modelling others. Bandura stated 'Fortunately, most human behavior is learned observationally through modeling: from observing others one forms an idea of how new behaviors are performed, and on later occasions this coded information serves as a guide for action. Because people can learn from example what to do, at least in approximate form, before performing any behavior, they are spared needless errors' (22). 'According to social learning theory, modeling influences produce learning principally through their informative function. During exposure observers acquire mainly symbolic representations of the modeled activities which serve as guides for appropriate performances' (22; 24). These statements indicate that individuals learn to be a part of a group by watching others who demonstrate appropriate behaviours for belonging to the group. The individual must imitate the behaviours in order to be considered an accepted member of this group. Social learning theory explains human behaviour in terms of continuous reciprocal interaction between cognitive (person), behavioural, and environmental influences.

In the socialisation of sport domain, Kenyon and McPherson popularized the social systems approach, based on social learning theory. The social systems approach contains three main elements which contribute to socialisation into sport: significant others, socialising agencies, and personal attributes (Kenyon and McPherson, 1973; Sewell, 1963). Significant others are important persons who influence the attitude and behaviour of the individual, socialisation situations are the socialising agencies or cultures, and personal attributes are the relevant personal characteristics of each individual. Within this model, learning appropriate sport roles results from all three aspects: modelling and behaviours of significant others who influence choice, socialisation situations or agencies, and from the personal abilities of the participant.

### *The nuclear family: the first socialising influence*

When studying the process of socialisation into sport, social learning theory was the framework used to understand how individuals receive messages about their role in the sporting society. The socialisation process begins with the infant, and continues throughout childhood. The first and seemingly most important influence on children's involvement in sport is the family. Parents exercise a great deal of influence on their children's ability to engage in physical activities. For a young child, the family is responsible for making decisions about the type and scope of the child's activities. Parents organise opportunities for very young children to participate in formal and informal physical activities, and provide financial and emotional support to encourage their involvement. In addition, consistent with social learning theory, the child learns about sport participation through observation, imitation, and modelling of parental involvement. Therefore, by having a significant member of the family providing sporting opportunity, support and encouragement, and role modelling in physical activity, children are more likely to participate in sport.

There is overwhelming evidence that the family is a major influence on young children's involvement in sport. In their own study (Greendorfer and Lewko, 1978), and through an extensive review of literature, Lewko and Greendorfer (1978) reported that the family was the primary predictor of sport participation for both boys and girls, and the father was the most significant socialising agent. Snyder and Sprietzer (1973) also found that parents had a significant influence, however the greater influence was by same-sex parents, (e.g. mothers influenced girls and fathers influenced boys). Sage (1980) reinforced the important influence of parents, stating that parents of both male and female athletes tended to be involved in sports, but the parents of male athletes were more involved in a variety of sports. In addition, fathers were shown to be more supportive of their sons than their daughters, whereas minimal difference was found in mothers' support of sons or daughters. In another study by Weiss and Knoppers (1982), collegiate female volleyball players reflected on their own involvement in sport, and reported the family to be responsible for their initial involvement.

It is clear that parental influence is a key factor in children's socialisation and participation in sport. For the initial involvement, the parents control the child's access. The beliefs, attitudes, and values parents place on sporting experiences for themselves and for their children will directly impact the opportunities and experiences of the young child. If the parents are not actively involved, nor intentionally provide sporting experiences for the child, the chance that the child will be exposed to the sporting world at an early age is limited.

Though there is little research on the specific influence of siblings, they also seem to play a role in socialisation into sport. Consistent with social learning theory, Sutton-Smith and Rosenberg (1970) found that younger siblings look to older siblings as role models. We also know that birth order makes a difference, in that second-born siblings are over-represented in sport (De Garay *et al.*, 1974). Though logically it seems that siblings would have an important influence over the process of socialisation in young children, further research is needed to provide evidence of this perspective.

### *Teachers and coaches*

In an early study by Kenyon (1968), it was reported that teachers and coaches were influential in generating interest in sport for both male and female élite athletes in traditional spectator sports such as baseball, basketball, and football (16%), and even more influential in track and field (25%). Higginson (1985) also found that the coach/teacher influence is important for females, especially after the age of 13. The findings in the Kenyon and Higginson studies combined the influence of teachers and coaches, so it was difficult to know whether the teachers or the coaches had the greater influence. Only one study was identified which addressed the specific influence of physical education teachers. Greendorfer and Lewko (1978) reported that physical education teachers were significant socialising agents for boys, but not for girls. Perhaps one of the reasons physical education teachers are not mentioned more often is the limited time children spend in physical education classes.

Coaches are considered a major influence, as coaches are most often respected and admired by their players. Several researchers have identified the importance of the relationship between the players and the coach (Martens, 1987; Seefeldt and Gould, 1980; Smoll and Smith, 1989). As coaches tend to play a central role in the sporting environment, it is important for us to understand the specific impact they may have. Smith and Smoll (1990) identified a significant interaction between the coaches' supportiveness and athletes' self-esteem. Children, especially those with lower self-esteem were responsive to coaches' encouragement and supportive behaviours. If we are trying to build high self-esteem through a sporting context, coaches must be prepared to demonstrate behaviours that will enhance children's feelings of self-worth.

As mentioned previously, much of the early research grounded in a functionalist approach indicated that children became involved in sport though the influence of their nuclear family (parents and siblings). One major criticism of the functionalist approach is the suggestion that socialisation is a 'one-way' process, with the learner passively absorbing the information provided by the person modelling the behaviours, attitudes and norms of the group. This relatively simple one-way process, where the participants' abilities, the environment, and the influence of significant others shapes the socialisation process into sport, suggests we are a product of our society – a 'lump of clay' to be moulded by outside factors.

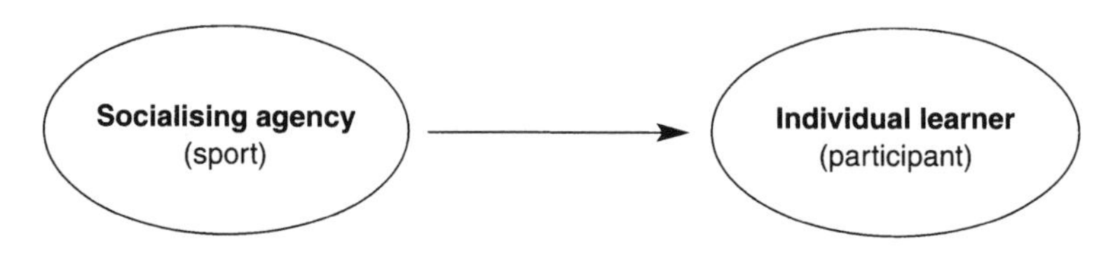


As we look further into the socialisation process, we can see the sport participant has an important role in her or his choice to be involved in sport, especially as the participant gets older and experiences opportunities.

## Continued participation in sport

The socialisation process is a series of multiple experiences and multiple decisions about whether to be involved in sport, and each new experience is filtered through the social and cultural context in which it is situated. After the initial entry into sport, children have gained the experiences necessary to develop perceptions about their own involvement in physical activity. Rather than considering socialisation as a one-way process, as in social learning theory, a two-way interaction offers an opportunity to understand the meaning of sport from the perspective of the participant. Supporting this concept is a widely-recognised theory in sport socialisation, the theory of symbolic interaction. Through social interaction, an individual gathers information about the interactions and symbols used to communicate the important aspects of a culture (or group). The individual filters this new information based upon the past experiences and perspectives she or he brings to the new experience. It is through social interaction with others that the individual interprets experiences and gives meaning to each situation. When people develop shared meanings of a situation, they develop common understandings, which influence the assumptions of how to behave in certain situations. Using the social interaction theory, the experiences and perceptions of the participants are given a greater importance as we try to understand how participants are socialised.

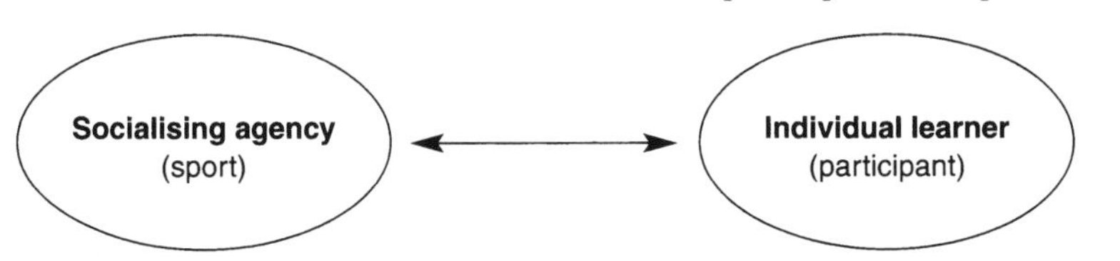


Most of what we know about symbolic interactionism has been gained through qualitative research, or data gathered through interviews and observations with individuals, rather than large-scale questionnaires where data are gathered to show statistical relationships between variables.

As we begin to understand children's continued involvement in sport, it is also helpful to consider the social and psychological domains together; that is, the cultural and social contexts, and how they influence an individual's perceptions of self. By understanding the relationship between these disciplines we gain a greater understanding of the full realm of children's entry into, and continued participation in, sports. Though multiple disciplines may influence a child's perceptions of their experiences in sport, it is through a participant's social interaction in the sporting context, the two-way process described earlier in this chapter, that the participant forms their perspectives about their role in sport. In other words, a person's perception of their role in sport is influenced by significant others, but is formed through an ongoing interaction between the individual living within a society and the social context in which they are interacting.

Eccles (Parsons') Expectancy Model (1983), which incorporates both social and psychological variables, has been used to examine participation in sport (Eccles (Parsons) *et al.*, 1983). Eccles' model foregrounds the concept that parents develop expectations for their children's involvement and achievement in sport based upon their own beliefs and attitudes, the relevant culture, talents, and their own previous experiences in sporting activities (Eccles and Harold, 1991). Eventually, the child will develop her or his own expectations, thereby influencing the choices for involvement and expected achievement in various activities. A person's decision to become involved in sport is as follows: as a person is provided an opportunity to become involved in sport, his or her perceptions are influenced by societal factors (e.g. cultural and gender stereotypes, values and expected behaviours), personal characteristics (e.g. beliefs, aptitudes and talents), and past experiences. Each person's perspectives are influenced by her or his beliefs, shaped by interpretations of past experiences as well as significant other socialisers (parents, peers, teachers, etc.). The participant filters this information, determining whether each new opportunity fits with personal goals, and expectations for success. Positive (incentives) or negative (costs) motivational factors are also influential. All these factors influence the choice for each individual's current or future involvement and achievement in sport.

As discussed on pages 130 and 131, studies examining children's participation in sport suggest that there is a strong positive relationship between parental involvement, interest, and encouragement (Butcher, 1983; Higginson, 1985;

Melcher and Sage, 1978). In two studies, one studying 8–14-year-old swimmers (Woolger and Power, 1988), and another examining 15–18-year-old sport participants, the authors found that the participants' enthusiasm, participation, and enjoyment of the sport were positively related to parental support and participation. Moore *et al.* (1991) found that children of two active parents were six times more likely to be involved in physical activity than children of two parents who were inactive. Brustad (1996) found significant relationships between children's perceptions of their parents' physical activity and their own physical activity; and, contrary to expectations, in this more recent study there were no gender differences for parent encouragement of involvement in physical activity. It may be that the changes in modern society are influencing parents' views, which encourage both sons' and daughters' participation. Obviously parent involvement and support remain an important influence as children continue to participate in sport.

As children get older, others begin to have a greater influence than the family. Interesting studies by Horn and Hasbrook (1986; 1987) and Horn and Weiss (1991) provide evidence of developmental change as the 8-year-old child relies on adults for sources of information to assess physical competence, however between the ages of 10 and 14, the child shifts to peer sources for the same information. At the latter ages, children and adolescents also compare their own physical competence against their peers, and make judgements about how they 'measure up' against their peers. As peers become more important, children and adolescents begin to value their perceptions, and use peers' input to help form their own perceptions of their physical competence. It is through this comparison, while interacting within a social context, that children assess their own strengths and limitations compared to those of their peers.

It seems that physical competence is very important to children and adolescents, as it is one of the major criteria contributing to children's social acceptance by their peers. We previously mentioned that at around the age of 10, children begin to identify peers as their primary source of information and evaluative feedback rather than their parents. Not only do children judge their own competence by their peers' responses, but their peers judge them as well. Peers become the measure of social acceptance, and the social acceptance is greatly influenced by the child's ability to participate successfully in the activities that are valued by their peers (Asher, 1983). In other words, in order for children to gain acceptance into a group they must be competent in the areas that are valued by the group.

We have learned that peer acceptance for children and adolescence is enhanced by their ability in sport (Adler *et al.*, 1992). Duda (1981) reported that peer recognition and self-worth are influenced by competence in the physical domain. Therefore, if physical competency is valued by children, one of the primary ways that children can become a part of a group is to be perceived as physically competent. Chase and Dummer (1992) provided information indicating that children and adolescents highly value competence and achievement in sport, and children who are competent have higher self-concepts and are able to develop positive social relationships with other children. Several researchers have reported that boys as young as six years old have recognised that achievement in sports contributes toward their popularity with others (Buchanan *et al.*, 1976; Eccles and Harold, 1991; Stein *et al.*, 1971). Similarly, Weiss and Duncan (1992) stated that children who had higher levels of peer acceptance in a summer camp program were those children who were physically more competent.

We know that physical competence and social acceptance are both important to a child's feelings of self-worth and to a child's ability to be a part of a group. As participants move from childhood into adolescence, Klint and Weiss (1987) tested Harter's (1982) competence motivation theory by examining the relationship between competence perceptions and motives for participation in sport. Harter supports the concept that a participant's perception of competence will act as a motivator for continued involvement in sport. The findings from the Klint and Weiss study supported this notion, when they found that athletes who scored high in perceived physical competence rated physical skill development as a more important reason for participating than the athletes who had low perceived physical competence. Interestingly, athletes who had high perceptions of their social competence were motivated to participate in physical activity because of social affiliations, such as team atmosphere or friends' participation. Therefore, categories where athletes perceive themselves to be most competent are the categories which will act as motivators for continued participation in an activity. Those who perceive themselves to be high in the physical domain will be motivated by opportunities for physical performance; those who perceive themselves to be high in the social domain will be motivated by opportunities for social affiliation.

## Sporting identity and commitment to sport

For children to want to continue participation in an activity, they must enjoy the experience. Gould (1987) studied attrition in children's sport, and found both personal and situational reasons for withdrawal. Some of these reasons were lack of playing time, lack of fun, boredom, and over-emphasis on competition. Negative examples provided here seem to impact younger players more than older players, however the major reasons children want to participate is to socialise with their peers, have fun and learn skills. If these factors are not in place, children and adolescents drop out of sport programmes. Interestingly, by the time a child reaches adolescence, a minimal amount of time is spent in sport-related activities (Kirshnit *et al.*, 1989; Rekers *et al.*, 1988). This is an area needing further research to achieve a better understanding of the reasons behind this trend.

Both school and community opportunities are available for children and adolescents to continue sport participation. Where they participate may depend upon the sport they choose and the context in which they live. In the US, most of the team sport activities are primarily rooted in school-based programmes, whereas, sports like gymnastics have both schools, communities and private clubs to support their participation. In some European communities many sport programmes for adolescents are primarily based in the community sports clubs.

As children and adolescents continue to participate in sport, one of the socialising agencies becomes the sporting culture itself. In the US, learning to participate in sport is considered educational, and as it is a function of the schools to educate the 'whole child', physical education is a part of almost every school curriculum. Athletics (sports) is seen as a central part of the school. One way for the community to identify with their schools is through the athletic (sports) programmes. In high school settings, adolescents are often identified according to the high school they attend, and the mascot representing the school – e.g. 'You are from North High School. You must be a Tiger!' In this situation, the school becomes a social agency, and in order to belong, the students identify with the school; therefore, a part of the students' identity is linked to the school which they attend. As athletics (sports) is such a large part of most high schools in the US, successful athletes, especially males, hold a high status in the school. If the students wish to be identified as an athlete, they must be accepted and recognised by others as athletes. As we mentioned earlier, athletes who are highly competent in their sport are seen by others as the more popular students in the schools.

Donnelly and Young (1999) described four phases of becoming accepted into a sport culture:

1 becoming knowledgeable about the sport
2 spending time and becoming associated with the people who participate in the sport
3 learning about the expectations and behaviours of other participants, and
4 being accepted into the group by other participants.

Most children who continue their sport participation into their adolescence have developed a commitment to participation, which includes continued practice and participation in game situations. As they continue to practise, they continue to become more competent. At this time, they are described by others, and describe themselves as athletes, or more specifically, describe themselves according to their chosen sport or by the position they have chosen to play (e.g. basketball player, or point guard). Once players identify with a certain sport, the culture of the sport may begin to influence the person. Players may begin to wear a certain style or brand of athletic shoes, or specific types of clothes which identify the people within the sporting culture in which they belong, and particular behaviours associated with the sport. This is a way of displaying their connection with the sport, and publicly showing their identity. As players continue to become more competent they will reach more competitive levels of sport involvement, thereby prolonging and strengthening their identities as athletes.

There has been a long-held belief that involvement in sport would provide a positive influence on the participants. Contrasting findings have been found when researching this assumption, however, Curtis *et al.* (1999) stated that there are more positive consequences (physical, psychological, sociological, and cultural), and few negative consequences 'except where the involvement is excessively frequent, too rigorous, or overly competitive' (349). Research findings are clear, however, that adult participation in physical activity is directly related to early involvement as children in physical activity and to early experiences in school-related physical activity (Curtis *et al.*, 1999; Howell and McKenzie, 1987; Kelly, 1980; Malina, 1996; Powell and Dysinger, 1987).

## Influence of social factors on participants' involvement in sport

The first sentence in this chapter refers to the fact that socialisation into sport does not happen in isolation from the rest of society. There are many groups of people in our society who have unequal access to many opportunities. This type of discrimination also occurs in the sporting context, and though the current literature base has addressed some of these issues in greater depth than others, it is important to continue the discussion.

### *Gender*

Because of stereotypical assumptions that boys are supposed to be more active than girls, and that sporting activities are more appropriate for boys than girls, socialisation into sport, influenced by our larger society, is often gender-based and the process involved differs for boys and girls. Lewko and Greendorfer (1978) indicated that play styles, game and toy selection, and gender labelling of physical activities did exist for boys and girls in society, with boys benefiting from more opportunities and more encouragement to participate in physical activity.

Though peer acceptance is equally important for all children and adolescents, there are again differences in the role physical competence plays for males and females. In fact, early research showed that sports and games were the most important factors young boys used to compare their social standing with their peers (Veroff, 1969). Again, in 1981, Duda reported that boys and girls found it very important to be successful in sports, but that it was more important for boys to succeed in a sporting context than for girls. In 1976, Eitzen found that physical competence was the most important status criterion for adolescent males. It seems as though differing opportunities exist for boys and girls, and that peers have an important influence on an individual's perceptions of competence and success in sport. Both these factors have a direct influence on boys' and girls' continued participation in sport, clearly providing an uneven social context, which disadvantages the girls. (For more information, please refer to Chapter 4.)

### *Social class*

Social class is another factor to consider when we examine opportunities in sport. Obviously the child whose family has a limited income will have fewer opportunities to join 'the club' to play tennis and golf, go surfing in the ocean, go snow skiing in the mountains or water skiing behind the new boat. These types of activities are open only to those who have the money to access the sites and the necessary equipment. People with less money are limited to publicly-funded facilities, or to those requiring only limited equipment and small participation fees. I remember a discussion in my own sociology of sport class, where my group began to associate the size of the ball used in a sport to the social class of people who would participate in that particular sport. We used the following examples:

Lower social class (less money – larger ball)
  Basketball
  Bowling
Higher social class (more money – smaller ball)
  Tennis
  Golf

Though this analogy falls apart if given much scrutiny, I still remember that it acted as a catalyst for the members of my group to examine in more depth the differing opportunities for children's involvement in sport based upon the amount of money available.

The United States Census Bureau (2000) offers information on participation patterns of people representing a range of income levels during the year 1999. Table 2 provides a summary of the top fifteen activities for people with incomes under $15,000 and over $75,000.

*Table 2* Participation in physical activity for persons with household incomes over $75,000 and under $15,000

| *Top 15 activities for persons with household income under $15,000* | *Percentage of participants* | *Top 15 activities for persons with household income over $75,000* | *Percentage of participants* |
|---|---|---|---|
| Exercise walking | 28.9% | Exercise walking | 34.4% |
| Swimming | 15.2% | Swimming | 30.4% |
| Fishing – fresh water | 12.8% | Exercising with equipment | 28.3% |
| Camping | 11.9% | Bicycle riding | 22.1% |
| Bicycle riding | 11.4% | Golf | 19.6% |
| Exercising with equipment | 10.8% | Camping | 18.1% |
| Bowling | 10.7% | Work out at club | 17.6% |
| Billiards | 9.9% | Bowling | 16.9% |
| Basketball | 7.8% | Roller skating / inline | 14.6% |
| Dart throwing | 7.6% | Hiking | 14.2% |
| Hiking | 6.9% | Fishing – fresh water | 14.0% |
| Aerobic exercising | 6.2% | Basketball | 13.9% |
| Running/jogging | 6.2% | Aerobic exercising | 13.8% |
| Work out at club | 5.8% | Boating – motorboating | 13.8% |
| Hunting with firearms | 5.2% | Billiards | 13.0% |

Source: US Census Bureau, 2000

Though many of the activities are the same, those mentioned only by participants with a household income under $15,000 were dart throwing, hunting with firearms and running/jogging. There is some cost for firearms, but generally, the three activities listed above are of minimal cost. Physical activities only mentioned by participants with the higher income include golf and motorboating. Obviously golf and motorboating require more income than many of the other activities on both lists. Another way to examine these data is to look at the percentages of people who are able to participate in the activities. For example, though both groups participate in 'exercising with equipment', 28.3 per cent of those with the higher income participate, as compared to 10.8 per cent of people with the lower income. In addition, there is no discussion of the types of 'equipment' used for these activities.

Based on the US Census Bureau data, it is also possible to examine the difference in participation within specific activities. When examining Table 3, ten activities are listed which show the most marked difference between people whose household income is over $75,000 and under $15,000, with more participants representing the higher income level.

As we look at Table 3, we can see that 17.5 per cent more people with higher incomes exercised with equipment than people with lower incomes. Though both groups participate in some similar activities, there are bigger differences in those activities where the cost is greater (e.g. golf, club, boating), thereby offering access to these activities to those with more money.

*Table 3* Per cent difference in participation in physical activities for persons with household incomes over $75,000 and under $15,000

| *Physical activity* | *Above $75,000* | *Below $15,000* | *Per cent difference* |
|---|---|---|---|
| Exercising with equipment | 28.3% | 10.8% | 17.5% |
| Golf | 19.6% | 3.1% | 16.5% |
| Swimming | 30.4% | 15.2% | 15.2% |
| Work out at club | 17.6% | 5.8% | 11.8% |
| Bicycle riding | 22.1% | 11.4% | 10.7% |
| Roller skating / inline | 14.6% | 5.2% | 9.4% |
| Boating – motorboating | 13.8% | 4.6% | 9.2% |
| Aerobic exercising | 13.8% | 6.2% | 7.6% |
| Hiking | 14.2% | 6.9% | 7.3% |
| Skiing – alpine/downhill | 7.7% | 0.7% | 7.0% |

Source: US Census Bureau, 2000

As we look at the more popular team sports in Table 4, there are fewer participants, but there is a smaller difference between the groups. This may be that team sports are offered through community recreation programmes, and many people have access to the community facilities. However, even in activities where the cost

*Table 4* Per cent difference in participation in popular team sports for persons with household incomes over $75,000 and under $15,000

| *Physical activity* | *Above $75,000* | *Below $15,000* | *Per cent difference* |
|---|---|---|---|
| Basketball | 13.9% | 7.8% | 6.1% |
| Soccer | 8.3% | 3.4% | 4.9% |
| Baseball | 7.4% | 4.7% | 2.7% |
| Softball | 6.5% | 4.4% | 2.1% |
| Football – touch | 4.2% | 2.8% | 1.4% |
| Volleyball | 5.2% | 4.3% | 0.9% |
| Football – tackle | 2.1% | 2.7% | –0.6% |

Source: US Census Bureau, 2000

is less (e.g. basketball), and access is more open, those with a higher income participate at a greater percentage than those with a lower income. One rationale for this difference might be that those with more money have more leisure time to participate in physical activities. Many people with limited income are working at two jobs to support themselves and their families, and have less time for leisure activity.

Given these data, it is again clear that children have differing opportunities to participate in physical activities, based upon income levels of their parents. These discriminatory opportunities go well beyond participation, also affecting people's ability to become spectators. The rising prices of tickets for college or professional sporting events virtually eliminate opportunities for the poor to see the 'big games'. And as the price of tickets varies, the middle-class spectators are relegated to the seats in the rafters, as these are the only seats they can afford, while the more affluent sports fans are in the expensive luxury boxes or executive seats. (For more information, please refer to Chapter 7.)

### *Race and ethnicity*

Other important societal factors which affect participation in sporting events are the influences of race and ethnicity in our society. We may want to distinguish between these terms: race refers to groups of people characterised by physical or biological traits, whereas ethnicity refers to groups of people characterised by their cultural heritage and traditions. It does become a confusing issue, as the differing races may have a unique ethnic culture as well. It is clear, however, that people falling within various racial and ethnic groups have differing opportunities to become involved in sport.

There are very distinct participation patterns of athletes belonging to various racial groups. If we focus on élite levels of basketball, football or track, it is likely that we will find relatively large percentages of African-Americans participating in these sports. If we study baseball or soccer, we will find larger numbers of Latino players, as well as African-Americans and Caucasians. However, when we begin to look at snow skiing, ice hockey or golf, the participants are predominantly Caucasian, with few representatives of other racial groups. Lapchick and Mathews (2000) provided percentage data on four ethnic groups of players (African-American, Caucasian, Latino and Other) from five professional leagues: National Football League (NFL), the National Basketball League (NBA), the National Hockey League (NHL), Major League Baseball (MLB) and Major League Soccer (MLS). African-Americans were dominant in both the NFL and the NBA with 65 per cent and 77 per cent respectively. The second most commonly represented group in these two leagues was Caucasian with 33 per cent and 23 per cent respectively. The MLB was more evenly divided with African-Americans having 15 per cent, Caucasians 59 per cent and Latinos 28 per cent. Soccer, the MLS, also had sizeable minority groups; African-Americans 16 per cent, Caucasians 62 per cent, Latinos 21 per cent and Other 1 per cent. By contrast, Caucasians were almost the sole group represented in the NHL with 98 per cent. These data mirror the patterns we see in children's choices and opportunities for involvment in sport. As there is no physical reason why African-American athletes cannot learn to play ice hockey, we again examine the social factors that may influence these patterns.

When we explore some of the reasons for the various participation patterns, several issues emerge. In some cases, geographic location may influence opportunities for participation. It is much easier for a child who lives in the northern part of the country to learn to ice skate and play ice hockey than a child who lives in a southern climate. Similarly a child who lives by the ocean will have a greater chance to learn to surf. However geographical differences do not explain the greater variance in sporting opportunities for children in the same geographical areas. Take golf for example; it is much more likely that a Caucasian child will have parents who play golf, and are therefore able to provide access and opportunities in the sport, and along with siblings and peers act as a support network, encouraging their child's participation. Most of the people who play golf must be affluent enough to suscribe to a club, or at least to pay green-fees in a public club on a regular basis, thereby limiting this sport to parents and children who have some financial stability. Though it may seem unreal to some of us, it is still true that a few private golf courses in the US have limited access for women – only women whose husbands belong to the club can play on the course; and some private clubs still do not allow African-Americans to play on the course at all.

If we try to understand how individuals receive messages about their role in the sporting society, we begin to think about the opportunities provided for initial involvement in sport, and role models that might help children believe they can participate in a specific sporting activity. First, we continue to look at early opportunities for children to learn to play golf. If access to golf is more readily available to Caucasian, affluent males, then children whose parents are less affluent, children of people of colour, and even children of single mothers have fewer opportunities to learn to play golf. In addition, many parents of poorer children and children of colour did not learn to play golf themselves, so they do not provide such a role model for their children.

When we focus on African-American children in this scenario, we see that as these young boys and girls get a bit older they watch golf on television, and may begin to think about playing. Remember, children learn about their possibilities for sport involvement in a social context, interpreting their perceptions of success according to access, encouragement and support from significant people in their lives. These children are also of the age at which they begin to compare competencies and future opportunities with others in order to make judgements about their future involvement. As their parents did not have easy access to golfing opportunities, such children were unable to develop skills in golf, may not feel competent enough to participate and may not see people like themselves acting as role models. The children therefore assume that golf is for the 'rich, white folks', not for them. They do not visualise golf as a viable choice and they begin to look for another sporting activity in which they have some experience, success and support, and where they see successful role models with whom they can identify. These African-American boys and girls may look toward football, basketball or track and field, thereby perpetuating the pattern we spoke of earlier.

We do know, however, that popular sports figures such as Tiger Woods can provide a positive role model for future African-American golfers. Other factors limiting access still act as barriers to initial and continued participation in some sports but nonetheless, golf, tennis and gymnastics have become much more popular for African-American boys and girls since Tiger Woods (golf), the Williams sisters (tennis), and Dominique Dawes (gymnastics) have become so successful and so visible in their respective sports. These élite athletes are able to provide important role models for children. (For more information, please refer to Chapter 6.)

## Conclusion

We started this chapter by using Greendorfer and Bruce's (1991) description of sport within society, then described socialisation as the 'process of learning and adapting to a given social system' (Eitzen and Sage, 1987: 77) or the 'active process of learning and social development, which occurs as we interact with one another and become acquainted with the social world in which we live' (82). As the process of socialisation into sport happens within the larger society, the same issues faced in society are often reflected in the sporting context.

Bandura's social learning theory has been used to describe how sport participants learn to be an accepted member of their group. One of the major socialising forces for children's entry into sport is the nuclear family, especially the parents. Teachers and coaches are also influential in the initial socialisation. However, as children get older, peers become a more important influence than the family. Around the age of 10, children also begin to compare themselves against others, and physical competence becomes an important criterion for these comparisons. Children who are more competent in physical skills tend to be more popular with their peers than children who are not. The children's perception of themselves can be influenced by others' reactions to their abilities. Through the reciprocal interaction between the children and other influential socialising factors, children begin to develop self-perceptions about their competence. Based upon this social comparison, if children are confident in their abilities, they are more likely to pursue future involvement in sport. If children continue participation in sport, their competencies increase, and they begin to identify themselves with their particular sport. They may become involved in community or school teams, and as their involvement becomes visible, others identify them with the chosen sport as well. The participant may become known as 'a basketball player' or 'a shortstop', as her or his identity becomes known.

Differing social factors can greatly influence a child's access to sport. Those factors such as gender, socio-economic status, race, and ethnicity can enhance or inhibit opportunities for sport participation. Just as in other aspects of the larger society, a person's involvement in sport is based upon their experiences in a social context, and the meaning that these experiences have for each individual. Unless some type of intervention occurs, children are likely to have opportunities to participate in similar physical activities as their parents, thereby perpetuating unequal access for girls and boys from different socio-economic and racial or ethnic groups.

**Reflection questions**

1. Describe Bandura's social learning theory and the theory of interaction. Compare and contrast the two theories.
2. Describe major factors influencing the initial involvement in sport/physical activity and factors influencing the ongoing participation in sport/physical activity.
3. Describe how the following social factors influence children's opportunities for involvement in sport: gender, social class, and race/ethnicity. Do you believe this practice is discriminatory? If so, how? If not, why not?

**Tasks**

1. Interview your childhood guardian(s) to find as much information as you can about your own initial involvement in sport. Enhance that information with your own memories, and write your sport autobiography. How does your story compare or contrast with the information provided in the chapter?
2. Choose ten participants to interview – five who are currently involved in physical activity, and five who are not currently involved in physical activity. After you gather the information, summarise your findings so you can compare and contrast the two groups.

Ask each of your participants the following questions, and then add any you think are important:

a Demographic questions:
- How many brothers and sisters do you have? Older? Younger?
- What was your family's socio-economic background when you were growing up?
- What is your racial and/or ethnic background?

b Do you remember your initial involvement in sport/physical activity? If so, can you describe your first memories?

c Do you consider yourself competent in sport/physical activity? On what do you base this perception?

d Can you provide a brief history of your involvement in sport/physical activity?

e Why did you choose to be involved in sport/physical activity at this time? OR Can you describe why you chose not to be involved?

## Further reading

Coakley, J. (2001) *Sport in Society: Issues and Controversies*. New York: McGraw Hill Companies.
Eitzen, D.S. and Sage, G.H. (1997) *Sociology of North American Sport*. Chicago: Brown & Benchmark.
Smoll, F.L. and Smoll, R.E. (1996) *Children and Youth in Sport: A Biopsychosocial Perspective*. Chicago: Brown & Benchmark.

## References

Adler, P.A., Kless, S.J. and Adler, P. (1992) Socialization into gender roles: popularity among elementary school boys and girls. *Sociology of Education*, 65, 169–187.

Asher, S.R. (1983) Social competence and peer status: recent advances and future directions. *Child Development*, 54, 1427–1434.

Bandura, A (1977) *Social Learning Theory*. Englewood Cliffs, NJ: Prentice-Hall.

Brustad, R.J. (1996) Attraction to physical activity in urban schoolchildren: parental socialization and gender influences. *Research Quarterly for Exercise and Sport*, 76, 3, 316–323.

Buchanan, G.T., Blankenbaker, J. and Cotton, D. (1976) Academic and athletic ability as popularity factors in elementary school children. *Research Quarterly*, 47, 320–325.

Butcher, J. (1983) Socialisation of adolescent girls into physical activity. *Adolescence*, 18, 73–766.

Chase, M.A. and Dummer, G.M. (1992) The role of sports as a social status determinant for children. *Research Quarterly for Exercise and Sport*, 63, 418–424.

Coakley, J. (2001) *Sport in Society: Issues and Controversies.* New York, NY: McGraw-Hill Higher Education.

Curtis, J., McTeer, W. and White, P. (1999) Exploring effects of school sport experiences on sport participation in later life. *Sociology of Sport Journal*, 16, 4, 348–365.

De Garay, A., Levine, L. and Carter, J.E.L. (Eds) (1974) *Genetic and Anthropological Studies of Olympic Athletes.* New York: Academic Press.

Donnelly, P. and Young, K. (1999) 'Rock climbers and rugby players: identity construction and confirmation', in Coakley, J. and Donnelly, P. (Eds) *Inside Sports*, 67–76. London: Routledge.

Duda, J.L. (1981) A cross-cultural analysis of achievement motivation in sport and the classroom. Unpublished doctoral dissertation, University of Illinois.

Eccles, J.S. and Harold, R.D. (1991) Gender differences in sport involvement: applying the Eccles expectancy-value model. *Journal of Applied Sport Psychology*, 3, 7–35.

Eccles (Parsons), J., Adler, T.F., Futterman, R., Goff, S.B., Kaczala, C.M., Meece, J.L. and Midgley, C. (1983) 'Expectations, values and academic behaviors', in Spence, T.J. (Ed.) *Achievement and Achievement Motivation.* San Francisco: W.H. Freeman.

Eitzen, D.S. and Sage, G.H. (1997) *Sociology of North American Sport.* Chicago: Brown and Benchmark.

Gould, D. (1987) 'Understanding attrition in children's sport', in Gould, D. and Weiss, M.R. (Eds) *Advances in Pediatric Sport Sciences*, 2, 66–67. Champaign, IL: Human Kinetics.

Greendorfer, S. and Bruce, T. (1991) Rejuvenating sport socialization research. *Journal of Sport and Social Issues*, 15, 2, 129–144.

Greendorfer, S. and Lewko, J.H. (1978) Role of family members in sport socialization of children. *Research Quarterly,* 49, 2, 146–152.

Harter, S. (1982). The perceived competence scale for children. *Child Development*, 53, 87–97.

Higginson, D.C. (1985) The influence of socializing agents in the female sport-participation process. *Adolescence*, 20, 73–82.

Horn, T.S. and Hasbrook, C.A. (1986) 'Informational components influencing children's perceptions of their physical competence', in Weiss, M.R. and Gould, D. (Eds) *Sport for Children and Youth,* 81–88. Champaign, IL: Human Kinetics.

Horn, T.S. and Hasbrook, C.A. (1987) Psychological characteristics and the criteria children use for self-evaluation. *Journal of Sport Psychology,* 9, 208–221.

Horn, T.S. and Weiss, M.R. (1991) A developmental analysis of children's self-ability judgments in the physical domain. *Pediatric Exercise Science,* 3, 310–326.

Howell, F. and McKenzie, J. (1987) High school athletics and adult sport-leisure activity: gender variations across the lifecycle. *Sociology of Sport Journal*, 4, 329–346.

Kelly, J. (1980) 'Leisure and sport participation', in Smith, D. and Macaulay, J. (Eds) *Participation in Social and Political Activities,* 170–176. San Francisco: Jossey-Bass.

Kenyon, G.S. (1968) A conceptual model for characterizing physical activity. *Research Quarterly*, 39, 1, 96–105.

Kenyon, G.S. and McPherson, B.D. (1973) 'Becoming involved in physical activity and sport: a process of socialization', in Rarick, G.I. (Ed.) *Physical Activity: Human Growth and Development,* 304–333. Orlando, FL: Academic Press.

Kirshnit, C.E., Ham, M. and Richards, M.H. (1989) The sporting life: athletic activities during early adolescence. *Journal of Youth and Adolescence*, 18, 6, 601–615.

Klint, K.A. and Weiss, M.R. (1987) Perceived competence and motives for participating in youth sports: a test of Harter's competence motivation theory. *Journal of Sport Psychology,* 9, 1, 55–65.

Lapchick, R.E. and Mathews, K. (2000) *Racial and Gender Report Card* (for 1998). Boston: Center for the Study of Sport in Society (Northeastern University).

Lewko, J.H. and Greendorfer, S.L. (1978) 'Family influence and sex differences in children's socialization into sport: a review', in Landers, D.M. and Christina, R.W. (Eds) *Psychology of Motor Behavior and Sport*, 434–447. Champaign, IL: Human Kinetics.

Malina, R.M. (1996) Tracking of physical activity and physical fitness across the lifespan. *Research Quarterly for Exercise and Sport*, 67 (Suppl. 3), 48–57.

Martens, R. (1987) *Coaches' Guide to Sport Psychology.* Champaign, IL: Human Kinetics.

Melcher, N. and Sage, G.H. (1978) Relationship between parental attitudes toward physical activity and the attitudes and motor competence of their daughters. *International Review of Sports Sociology*, 13, 75–88.

Moore, L.L., Lombardi, D.A., White, M.J., Cambell, J.L., Oliveria, S.A. and Ellison, R.C. (1991) Influence of parents' physical activity levels on activity levels of young children. *Journal of Pediatrics,* 118, 215–219.

Powell, K.E. and Dysinger, W. (1987) Childhood participation in organized school sports and physical education as precursors of adult physical activity. *American Journal of Preventative Medicine*, 3, 276–281.

Rekers, G.A., Sanders, J.A., Rasbury, W.C., Strauss, C.C. and Morey, S.M. (1988). Differentiation of adolescent activity participation. *Journal of Genetic Psychology*, 150, 3, 323–335.

Sage, G.H. (1980) Parental influence and socialization into sport for male and female intercollegiate athletes. *Journal of Sport and Social Issues,* 4, 2, 1–13.

Seefeldt, V. and Gould, D. (1980) *Physical and psychological effects of athletic competition on children and youth.* Washington, DC: ERIC Clearinghouse on Teacher Education.

Sewell, W.H. (1963) Some recent developments in socialization theory and research. *The Annals of the American Academy of Political Science*, 349 (September), 163–181.

Smith, R.E. and Smoll, F.L. (1990) Self-esteem and children's reactions to youth sport coaching behaviors: a field study of self-enhancement processes. *Developmental Psychology,* 26, 987–993.

Smoll, F.L. and Smith, R.E. (1989) Leadership behaviors in sport: a theoretical model and research paradigm. *Journal of Applied Social Psychology,* 19, 1522–1551.

Snyder, E.E. and Spreitzer, D. (1973) Family influence and involvement in sports. *Research Quarterly,* 44, 249–255.

Stein, A.H., Pohly, S. and Mueller, E. (1971) The influence of masculine, feminine, and neutral tasks on children's achievement behavior, expectancies of success and attainment values. *Child Development*, 42, 195–208.

Sutton-Smith, B. and Rosenberg, B.G. (1970) *The Sibling.* New York: Hold, Rinehart and Winston.

United States Census Bureau (2000) *Statistical Abstract of the United States*. Author.

Veroff, J. (1969) 'Social comparison and the development of achievement motivation', in Smith, C.P. (Ed.) *Achievement-related Motives in Children*, 46–101. New York: Russell Sage Foundation.

Weis, M.R. and Duncan, S.C. (1992) The relationship between perceived competence and peer acceptance in the context of children's sport participation. *Journal of Sport and Exercise Psychology,* 14, 177–191.

Weis, M.R. and Knoppers, A. (1982) The influence of socializing agents on female collegiate volleyball players. *Journal of Sport Psychology*, 4, 267–279.

Woolger, C. and Power, T.G. (March 1988) Socialization of competitive age girl swimmers. A study of mother and father influences. Paper presented at the Southwestern Society for Research in Human Development, Dallas, Texas.

# 9 The hidden curriculum and the changing nature of teachers' work

*Gareth Nutt and Gill Clarke*

## Introduction

This chapter examines the nature of the hidden curriculum in physical education. Initially our attention is drawn to a reconsideration of what constitutes the hidden curriculum and the means by which it is transmitted; in doing so we focus on the studies of Bain (1990), Kirk (1992) and Fernandez-Balboa (1993). In addition we analyse the significance of this so-called hidden curriculum for the formation of social relationships between teachers and pupils and pupils and pupils. As such we seek to illustrate the pervasive and potentially damaging messages that the hidden curriculum conveys and the complexity of teaching and learning in physical education. In particular we draw attention to the changing nature of teachers' work and specifically the teaching of examinations, and contend that whilst the terrain is shifting we need to be alert to the way that examinations carry a hidden curriculum of their own.

## Revisiting the hidden curriculum

According to Giroux (1983: 43) the hidden curriculum is a powerful medium by which unstated norms, values and beliefs are 'embedded in and transmitted to students through the underlying rules that structure the routines and social relationships in school and classroom life'. Given that much has already been written about the hidden curriculum in physical education we do not intend to rehearse old debates but rather to provide the reader with a brief review of key research by a number of scholars within physical education that is germane to this chapter's focus.

More than a decade ago Bain (1990) provided a critical analysis of the concept of the hidden curriculum. Her analysis comprised of three themes namely, meritocracy, technocentric ideology and the construction of social relations. In her discussion of meritocracy as a form of motor élitism, Bain claims 'that the emphasis on effort rather than achievement in physical education does not challenge the overall meritocratic principles of the school but reinforces the marginal status of the field and the underlying assumptions of mind-body dualism' (28). Technocentric ideology refers to a situation where the 'ends or goals are taken-for-granted and unexamined and attention is focused on the development of increasingly effective and efficient means for achieving the goals' (28–9). In terms of education and specifically physical education we are left with a situation where the body is viewed as a commodity to be schooled and trained. If for example we relate this to health and exercise then it becomes clear how definitions and meanings about what constitutes health remain unexamined. Consistent with the notion of technocratic ideology is the need to subject to critical scrutiny the unprecedented growth of examination physical education – a lacuna in Bain's work, but given the time and context of her research this is unsurprising. Nevertheless, it is necessary to bring the hidden curriculum of examinations into view and this is something that we address later in this chapter. Returning to Bain, her last theme relates to social relations; these she maintains are an important aspect of the hidden curriculum as patterns of interaction 'constitute social practices which may reproduce or challenge existing power relations' (32).

A later paper by Kirk (1992) built on Bain's work and served to highlight the ambiguity of the term hidden curriculum. Whilst providing a useful review of selected studies of the hidden curriculum in physical education Kirk also sought to 'assess its [the hidden curriculum's] potential for helping us better understand physical education as a cultural practice' (35). He makes a convincing case for the need to render the hidden agendas of teaching and learning in physical education more visible. For Kirk two terms help accomplish this: discourse and ideology. In order to make sense of the former we draw on earlier work by one of us on discourse analysis: Clarke (1992) conceptualises discourse widely to include all forms of talking and writing. It follows that this is about the power of the whole communication process. Kirk (1992) in seeking to explain his conception of ideology draws on earlier work by Hall to argue the case for the descriptor ideology to be reserved for 'those cases where the linking of one discourse with others takes on the appearance of a necessary relationship, where this is in fact unwarranted, and where the outcome of such arbitrary linking has social and political consequences' (43). Kirk helps to clarify this by stating that 'we might say that discourse does *ideological work* when particular elements of discourse are linked together in ways that suggest necessary, rather than contingent relationships' (44). Thus, we can begin to see how beliefs about the slender body and stereotyped notions of masculinity and femininity become naturalised, unquestioned and taken for granted as regimes of truth to be followed and promoted unquestionably. In applying these concepts it is possible to appreciate how the hidden curriculum, that is the norms, values and ways of behaving that pupils are exposed to (both consciously and unconsciously) serve to legitimate stereotyped gendered and racialised subject positions which impact on teachers' and pupils' identities in damaging ways.

Fernandez-Balboa (1993) expands on some of Kirk's contentions to focus specifically on the socio-cultural characteristics of the hidden curriculum. He makes a powerful case for the need to question and transform the practices of physical education so as to contribute to a more just and equal society. Fernandez-Balboa reveals how the practices of physical education contribute to the inculcation of particular sets of values which frame thinking not only about the world but also about ourselves and others. This leads to the maintenance of the *status quo* and a situation whereby unequal power structures and social inequalities remain undisturbed. The real challenge he claims is 'to go beyond a mere acknowledging of the present conditions of ... physical education ... to make a conscious effort to change our oppressive beliefs and behavioural patterns' (249). It is to this challenge we now turn by addressing hegemonic ideologies of femininity and masculinity and heterosexism and homophobia with physical education. By doing so we reveal how the hidden curriculum continues to operate within the domain of physical education.

## The process of schooling and the transmission of the hidden curriculum: ideologies of masculinity and femininity

Schools and physical education departments are not neutral sites operating in social and political vacuums, rather, as argued previously they are imbued with dominant values and ideologies that do much to reflect and maintain the *status quo.* It has been well documented how sport was developed by men for men, indeed, it has been said that the gender of sport, and we would add physical education, is male (Whannel, 1983). Traditionally, sport and physical education has been regarded as an arena for boys to learn how to be 'real' (heterosexual) men (see Jennifer Hargreaves, 1994). It is (heterosexual) men who by and large have had the power to define what counts as legitimate, acceptable sporting behaviour and display. The culture of physical education is deeply rooted in hegemonic ideologies of masculinity and femininity. Further, it is evident that this feminine/heterosexual culture is at odds particularly with that of girls and young women (Scraton, 1987, 1992, 1993). Over ten years ago Scraton (1987) pointed out that:

> School PE fails to provide 'meaningful experiences' for many young adolescent women because it appears at odds with the culture of femininity. Their resistances which are complex and not always consistent, relate to what they perceive as on offer from PE:
>
> a the development of muscle
> b sweat
> c communal showers/changing facilities
> d 'childish', asexual PE kit
> e low status activities.
>
> It is acceptable for the 'tomboy' in junior or lower secondary school to participate in and enjoy these activities but not so acceptable to adult femininity. (180)

What is on offer acts as a vehicle for the transmission of a not so hidden curriculum insofar as powerful messages are conveyed about what is acceptable practice and behaviour for girls (and boys) within the domain of physical education.

The National Curriculum for Physical Education (NCPE) (2000) largely embodies and reproduces stereotyped messages about sport, physical education and young people and this has in many ways exacerbated the situation referred to above. Clearly, physical education could and should have an important part to play in contributing to 'the denial of ideologies of femininity' (Scraton, 1987: 183) and heterosexuality. Talbot (1995) pointed out that:

> The P.E. National Curriculum offers unprecedented opportunities to extend the boundaries of girls' and boys' perspectives and achievements, for example by:
>
> challenging sex and gender stereotypes, and traditional notions about 'appropriate' activities for girls and boys.
>
> (17)

Despite these 'unprecedented opportunities', the boundaries appear largely undisturbed. Recent research by Gilroy and Clarke (1997) and Drinkwater (2001) suggests that many girls remain locked into traditional and stereotyped notions of femininity and physicality. Thus, girls and women who step outside these boundaries run the risk of the label lesbian being levelled at them. The power of the lesbian label to keep women and girls in their place should not be underestimated. Such a label acts as a 'put down' to all women and limits their sexual and sporting freedom. This fear of being labelled lesbian 'ensures that women do not gain control over their sporting experience or develop their physical competence beyond what is acceptable in a sexist culture' (Griffin, 1998: 49).

## Social relations between teachers and pupils and the power of the peer group

Having illustrated something of the power of the official curriculum to reproduce dominant ideologies of masculinity and femininity we next consider how social interactions between teachers and pupils and between pupils and other pupils within both the formal and informal routines and rituals of physical education also contribute to this reproductive process. The intention is to reveal how these interactions involve the communication both explicitly and implicitly of a particular set of values about 'normality'.

As Fernandez-Balboa (1993) has pointed out the hidden curriculum 'shape[s] and mediate[s] our values, experiences, and practices as teachers and students; affect[s] *what* and *how* we teach and learn, and ultimately influence[s] our roles in and assumptions about society' (222). These assumptions may lead teachers to have different expectations of the abilities and behaviours of boys and girls. Thus, it is not only the content of the curriculum but also the organisation of the timetable which conveys certain messages to pupils about the relative status of the activities. In particular grouping policies may impact negatively on children's self-esteem and confidence. Studies comparing girls' with boys' attitudes have found that girls dislike mixed physical education more than boys (Lirgg, 1993) and that these feelings increase as they get older (Mason, 1995; Milosevic, 1995). Further, the wearing of physical education kit whilst useful insofar as it meets safety regulations also conveys messages and values about conformity and thereby contributes to a denial of individuality – being different is often simply not allowed. Research also suggests that many girls are reluctant to wear kit that exposes the body or parts of it especially when boys are present (Drinkwater, 2001).

Clearly, the hidden curriculum is not unitary but operates on different levels and in different ways. Hence, it is not only the actions of teachers that communicate norms and values to pupils for as Laker (2000) reveals:

> … pupils also have a part to play in establishing a status quo and their reactions to, and treatment of other pupils … demonstrates what they think is important and what their sub-cultural norms and values are.
>
> (48)

Accordingly, sporty girls come up against the culture of femininity which as we have demonstrated is at odds with the culture of physical education, thus sporty girls run the risk of negative and intimadatory comments not only from their female peers but also from their male counterparts. Cockerell and Hardy (1987) show how:

> … girls find themselves in the dilemma that in order to 'succeed' as far as the teacher is concerned, they need to demonstrate the 'masculine' traits of skill, physical perseverance and fitness; while to 'succeed' in terms of their male (and female) classmates, they need to "… preserve their carefully constructed feminine image".
>
> (Cockerell and Hardy, 1987: 149)

As Cockburn (forthcoming) adroitly comments to 'achieve in one aspect is to fail in the other because of the polarised dichotomy of gender identities on offer to them [girls] in public and popular discourse[s]'. Consequently, girls who participate in traditionally-defined male activities such as football can often become the targets of abuse. Drinkwater (2001: 50) provides a vivid example of this from her exploration of adolescent girls' experiences of physical education. She describes how girls playing football were often called 'mushbirds', a derogatory term meaning half boy, half girl. One of her respondents revealed how she had 'stopped playing football at lunch times cause I got a lot of abuse for it … you know lezzie and things like tha'. Boys too may be open to ridicule and censure from their peers when they display an interest in or aptitude for activities such as gymnastics or dance that have not traditionally been associated with normalised images of masculinity. Indeed, Drinkwater's research reveals 'that boys who don't like competitive sport were viewed with almost total disbelief and were regarded as somewhat deviant' (50). This process is not simplistic; pupils may resist and challenge these stereotypes but it is no easy process. It is however beyond the bounds of this chapter to do more than allude to the contestations.

## The multi-dimensional nature of the hidden curriculum

Although we have so far in the main examined the transmission of ideologies of femininity and masculinity and social relations between teachers and pupils to illustrate the pervasive nature of inequitable practice within physical education we recognise the highly complex and multi-dimensional nature of the hidden curriculum that exists in many of the day-to-day aspects of physical education teachers' work. As Laker (2000) confirms:

> The 'hidden curriculum' refers to what is taught to pupils by the way the school operates, by the way the teachers behave and by the interactions that take place on a daily basis in school.
>
> (47)

Thus we need to recognise the power of the teacher to transmit and reinforce particular norms, values and practices. Physical education is a highly structured and ordered subject wherein pupils have to learn a considerable number of routines be they around the rules and regulations of the particular activities on offer or those that pertain to behaviour in the 'gymnasium'. Accordingly, they have to learn for example to respect authority, to work together cooperatively, to wait their turn and to recognise the hierarchies of power that exist within the classroom. The work ethic conveyed therefore is one largely of conformity.

If we are to begin to interrupt the divisive reproduction of inequitable practice, attention also needs to be given to the ways in which physical education teachers determine the curricular and organisational choices on offer and the pedagogical strategies they use to deliver and assess pupil learning. It is to the ways in which one of the major curricular initiatives in contemporary physical education draws teachers into processes that have been complicit in reinforcing the hidden curriculum of the formal curriculum that this chapter now turns. It does so by examining the changing nature of teachers' work and the continued expansion of examination physical education. This focus will be illustrative of the contested nature and hierarchy of knowledge within the curriculum as a whole and more specifically how it manifests itself in the prevailing practices of physical education.

In the sections that follow we make use of research by Nutt (1988 and 1999) that makes a valuable contribution to our understanding of the hidden curriculum and draw in particular on the voices of student teachers, teachers and mentors to illustrate the emerging issues. The unattributed respondent quotations that follow arise from these sources. Like Tinning (1990) we believe that we need forms of enquiry that reveal the forms of consciousness which pervade assumptions and everyday practices relating to issues such as the nature of teaching, the purpose of schooling, curriculum content and school organisation. By offering us a deeper understanding of what is going on in the workplace, research of this kind has undoubtedly extended our knowledge of the implicit values communicated by physical education programmes (Bain, 1985). Moreover, it has enabled us to gain a deeper appreciation of the complexities that attend the development of occupational identities at a time of rapid organisational change and cultural tension as well as creating an awareness of the consequences for the social and physical identities of the young people with whom we work. Further, this analysis would seem timely given recent debates 'as to whether GCSE Physical Education should remain an optional extra in school Physical Education programmes or should become a foundation subject provided to all pupils aged 14–16' (Stidder, 2000: 163).

## Understanding the changing nature of physical education teachers' work

For some time, teachers have had to contend with a succession of government sponsored reforms, but, in the political rush to bring about change, teachers' concerns have been largely dismissed and their opinions neglected and over-ridden. The consequence of these reforms has been an intensification of their workload (Hargreaves, 1994) within a context increasingly structured by notions of accountability and in which a number of central state policy initiatives have functioned to alter fundamentally the nature of teaching. Understandably many teachers feel overwhelmed by the intense pace of change in schools and perceive that 'the job that they were trained to do, as teachers in front of children, marking books, preparing lessons, has dramatically and quickly changed' (Robinson cited in Price, 1990: C3). Ball (1994: 64) suggests that, 'the meaning of the 'teacher' and the nature of teaching as a career appears to be at stake.' Apple's (1986) conceptualisation of the fundamental reorganisation of teachers' work invites us to view teaching as a 'labour process' in which the patterns of control, relationships and values in education are increasingly being shaped by the power of state policies and institutional micropolitics.

Despite its imputed curricular marginality, physical education teachers have not been immune to the forces generated by professional and structural changes. Indeed, precisely because of its marginal status (Hoyle, 1986; Sparkes, 1994), they appear particularly prone to the pressures that have attended a period in which the curriculum (content and pedagogy), the 'market' (league tables) and fundamental changes to management structures have come to represent powerful sources of control over their work (Ball, 1994).

Several aspects of the prevailing culture within physical education seem worthy of study. For instance, initiatives associated with the development and implementation of the NCPE, the high profile accorded the politics of sport in schools and the growth and expansion of examinations in physical education have all emerged as factors that might yet determine the future direction for the subject and the professional identity of physical education teachers. Our view is that since subjects carry multiple messages and are communicated by the ways in which we select, organise and evaluate our work, the hidden curriculum of the formal curriculum should not be ignored. Hence our interest in the increasing importance accorded to the development of examinations at GCSE and A Level. It is a dimension of physical education teachers' work that lacks the media attention created by the 'moral panic' surrounding school sport and the failure internationally of our national teams and is rarely included in visions of the subject's future role within the curriculum. Yet, the impact of examinations on the future direction of physical education and the consequences for the entitlements of all young people could yet be significant. As one head of department explains:

> The National Curriculum can now take care of itself. We are more concerned with making sure that we have our A level teaching sorted. It's one hell of a workload for the department and for some of us it is going to require real graft to get up to date with some of the syllabus. It's going to be a real challenge but one that I am looking forward to. ... I'm sure it's going to give this department real impetus and status. It's the only way forward really, isn't it?
>
> (Nutt, 1999)

## 'Examining' the hidden curriculum of the formal curriculum

The year on year increase of candidates for GCSE Physical Education and A Level PE/Sports Studies (Stidder, 2000) appears to confirm the view that examination courses might indeed be acting as a countervailing tendency to forces that threaten to pull the subject apart (Hoyle, 1986). Certainly, examinations in physical education, particularly at A Level, have come to represent a highly competitive addition to the key stage 4 and post-16 portfolio of many schools with financial benefits to be gained from recruitment to these courses under formula funded schemes. As one teacher revealed:

> The PE A Level was introduced because the college was losing pupils in the sixth form. This meant losing a substantial amount of money. We were also losing around 10–12 students from the year 11 who were very talented sports people who contributed greatly to college sport and who wanted to continue their studies in a sport/leisure industry direction, but were not able to.

This coincides with the view that alongside the curriculum, the market has emerged as a major force in controlling and reconstructing teachers' work. Kickert (1991) concludes that whilst teachers appear to have been granted greater professional discretion, the shifts that have seen constraints replaced by incentives, prescription replaced by accountability and coercion replaced by self-steering and the appearance of autonomy, the pressures exerted upon curricular and pedagogical decisions have, if anything, increased. We contend that these decisions transmit compelling messages that the central content of the main school subjects are principally ordered around the hegemony of the intellectual cognitive domain of propositional knowledge[1] and accessed by public examinations.

However, it would be wrong to conclude that the continuing expansion of examination courses at GCSE and A Level is merely a function of strategic compliance on the part of physical education teachers. The development of examinations has been used to present evidence of increasing subject maturity, occupational professionalism and enhanced subject status (Carroll 1986, 1998; Nutt 1988). As the following responses illustrate, some teachers are motivated by their perceptions of the benefits to be gained by developing examination courses.

> Whatever the arguments for examinations in PE they present real opportunities for the kids.

> Brilliant as academic recognition. It offers pupils the opportunity to learn more about the subject academically and practically and for those pupils who want to continue in the sport and leisure industry, it offers a sound basis.

However, the social reality for some teachers has prompted a more circumspect view. In particular, they have recognised that the quest for academic credibility and enhanced professional status is replete with tensions and barriers for teachers and pupils alike. It is on a consideration of some of the deep-seated consequences of examinations that this chapter now focuses.

## Examinations, 'deprofessionalisation' and physical education

It is the multi-disciplinary nature and depth of many examination courses at A Level that has raised a number of substantive issues that strike at the heart of prevailing definitions of professionalism. In particular, evidence is emerging that not all physical education teachers can justifiably make claims to a form of occupational professionalism based upon their monopoly and autonomy of expert knowledge (Rothman, 1984). As the following teachers admitted:

> I'm OK with the contemporary stuff but the psychology is really demanding. I find it difficult let alone the kids. I guess I am learning as we go along. You know, keeping one step ahead of them. The most difficult thing is finding practical ways of introducing the concepts.

> I am not sure if I am competent enough to teach the A Level especially in the classroom environment. I will need a lot more experience, and this might be done by going on courses, support from other teachers and support from within the department.

In response, teachers have adopted a range of pedagogical and organisational coping strategies that could be seen to run counter to claims that the teaching of A Level programmes are evidence of their professional maturity and ability to teach high status forms of knowledge. For instance, Kirk *et al.* (1986) argue that attention must be given to the kinds of interactions which take place between teachers and learners and how propositional knowledge is communicated in the classroom. In particular, they point to what is described as the indiscriminate borrowing of the less satisfactory features of other traditionally high status school subjects such as:

> ... content dominated courses, didactic teaching styles, and passive non-participatory students. In addition, the effect of testing on the conduct of lessons is often to direct student attention away from the qualitative dimensions of subject matter and towards obtaining only the information or 'facts' necessary to pass the exam. Ultimately, the students' conceptions of formalised, inert and redundant school knowledge are confirmed and legitimated through the emphasis on testing. The examination becomes the main justification for the 'educational' process, and this in turn works to abrogate the 'personal' from teaching, and to restrict the range of teaching practices to those most suited to accomplishing the end of passing students through examinations. (176)

What is described is representative of a technocratic model of teaching and learning (see Bain, 1990) in which ends or goals are taken for granted and attention is focused on the development of increasingly effective and efficient means for achieving those goals. Moreover, the forms of pedagogy employed and the use of technological criteria to judge the efficiency and effectiveness of teaching has led to a strong framing and classification of constituent knowledge in which the observable, objective and quantifiable has been elevated above the experiential, subjective and qualitative dimensions of knowing. The hidden curriculum of the formal curriculum is clear; the intellectual-cognitive domain is the most important. Such a situation gives rise to questions not only about the stratifying of knowledge and what is valued and privileged but also about issues of access and specialisation (Young, 1998). Indeed, Carroll (1998: 344) has noted 'the gender differential in examination entries. ... [He] showed that there were twice as many males as females entered for GCSE and A level PE examinations consistently over the years and across all examination boards.' He concludes that it would appear that examinations reflect and reinforce gender-stereotyping in physical education. We strongly support Carroll's (1998: 345) call for more work in this area especially 'in view of the increasing importance of examination subjects in relation to career routes, and PE's value in terms of leisure opportunities.'

This technological approach has strengthened and legitimated views that the curriculum can be compartmentalised and 'delivered' by teachers with the appropriate expertise; the sources of which may be existing members of the physical education staff. Indeed, evidence is emerging from Nutt's (1999) research that, on occasions, the principal role for physical education staff is to attend to organisational issues and the teaching of practical course components while course leadership and the 'high status' academic content is covered by colleagues from other subject areas. But, whilst a commitment to the notion of a 'whole school' approach has encouraged many physical education teachers to articulate the benefits to be gained by working together as a team and exploiting the complementary expertise of their colleagues, problems clearly exist. As one head of department commented:

> We really had problems in the biology area for the anatomy and physiology section. The problem was trying to put the theory into a practical context, which the biology teacher found difficult. I intend sending someone to the Winchester 'summer school' so that we can develop more of an 'in house' team.

Thus, claiming and retaining ownership of A Level courses appears to be emerging as a priority amongst many schools committed to the protection of their new found 'status'. Whilst in-service A Level courses for teachers are clearly playing their part in the 're-skilling' process, there is an increasing awareness that the restructuring of teacher education is creating a supply of newly qualified teachers (NQTs) with academic and professional backgrounds consistent with the needs of many schools. As one head of department confirmed:

> We could really do with someone who has got a sports science degree to deliver the anatomy and physiology side of things. Ideally with experience with the A Level or to have come from college with a MSc. in Sports Science and then done a PGCE, so they could teach the scientific part of the A Level.

## Shifting trends in initial teacher training (ITT)

Since successive British governments have progressively reconstructed the relationship between schools and teacher education providers (see for instance DfEE Circulars 9/92, 14/93 and 4/98), there has been a sharpening of the practical training emphasis with trainees now required to spend a greater proportion of their time gaining 'hands-on' experience. Consequently, schools and teacher training providers are expected to be full partners in the planning, organisation and delivery of courses; in this training process physical education subject mentors undoubtedly occupy a strategic role. Their involvement comes at a time when the buoyant demand for places on courses offered by the thirty-one physical education providers in England runs counter to a nationwide 'crisis' in teacher recruitment. Of the thirty-one providers of ITT in physical education, twelve offer a four-year undergraduate programme and twenty-nine offer a one-year postgraduate course; of these, ten providers have provision for both. What is evident is the increase in one year school-based or school-centred postgraduate courses. As Ofsted (1999) pointed out, of the twenty-eight providers inspected during the 1996/97 and 1997/98 academic years 50 per cent of the postgraduate programmes were in their first three years of development. The net result of this increase in postgraduate provision is the recruitment and professional development of graduate trainees who draw heavily upon knowledge and experience gained from disparate undergraduate courses in cognate fields of study such as Human

Movement Studies, Sports Science, Recreation Studies and Sport and Exercise Sciences. Whilst an analysis of their content is likely to reveal some sharing of core knowledge and common experiences few trainees will have followed undergraduate programmes that have the conceptual, developmental and philosophical understanding of physical education and schooling that four-year teacher education courses claim to offer. The paradox here, however, is that whilst many mentors may continue to express their reservations about the limitations of one-year ITT programmes, some are evidently prepared to exploit the relevance that the constituent features of trainees' sport-related degree courses bring to their professional development. In some instances, schools are beginning to use this knowledge in the planning and teaching of their GCSE and A Level examination courses. As one mentor commented:

> She has worked really hard at her gym and dance and is doing OK. Games still needs a lot of work; particularly her knowledge of some of the basics. Strangely enough she appears to be at her most comfortable in the classroom. Some of the material she has brought from her degree is really good. We have asked her if we can use some of it ourselves; particularly the skill acquisition and notational analysis stuff.

Whilst it is to be welcomed that students are 'comfortable' teaching in classrooms what is disturbing is the apparent failure to stem the advance of technocratic ideology via the Higher Education curriculum and thereby the potential privileging of knowledge gained from sport-science-type courses. Again, we can see the influence of the hidden curriculum and the way it permeates institutions and curricular policies and how student teachers develop instrumental attitudes to their work. Fernandez-Balboa (1993) argues that if we:

> ...critically ... [analyse] the concepts and forms of our instruction and the social context in which the instruction takes place, we may be able to offset the powerful hidden influences to which we are subjected and to which we, even unconsciously, often subject others.
>
> (250)

The content of all ITT programmes warrants this kind of analysis given the crucial part it plays in the formation and reproduction of student-teacher attitudes and beliefs which are later reflected in their pedagogical practices in schools. A failure to attend to such issues will have damaging effects on young people's physical education experiences and their attitudes to life-long physical activity.

Linked to concerns about the instrumental attitudes of trainees it is evident that some are also beginning to recognise that their 'marketability' might also reside as much with the disciplines that constituted the basis of their undergraduate degree programmes as it does with demonstrating the security of their practical knowledge base across the range of activities that form the framework for NCPE. As two trainees commented:

> It was amazing there were all these B.Ed students and I was the only post-grad. I thought I had no chance but the interview went really well. I didn't have to answer many questions on the National Curriculum or assessment. They were mostly interested in my Sports Science degree and whether I would be interested in teaching some of the A level. I'm sure that my sports psychology dissertation convinced them I was a good bet. I'm really looking forward to it.

> The school is starting A level next year and they want me to do the exercise physiology. Can't wait. I couldn't ask for a better start.

Amongst NQTs there appears to be an increasing realisation that the teaching of examination classes will constitute a major part of their professional responsibilities. Moreover, there seems an acceptance that part of establishing their status as a professional and securing 'competent membership' (Denscombe, 1980) will require their commitment to a continuing professional development programme in the teaching and assessment of examination coursework. As these trainees remarked:

> The teaching of exam courses has really enabled me to use some of the work I covered in my degree. I think the kids really enjoy this work. I really get the sense that I have taught them something. I want to get a job in a school that offers GCSE and A level.

> I did this session on 'women in sport' with my year 10 GCSE group. They came up with some great ideas. It really surprised me because usually they are really difficult to motivate. My mentor was well impressed. I think I really come into my own when I am teaching GCSE.

In cases such as these it is possible that some teachers might become especially attached to the sub-group within which their professional identity is being invested. For some, the process of 'personal identification' might even involve a re-invention of their professional sense of self. These teachers remarked:

> With so much A Level work, GCSE and GNVQ, I feel more like a Sports Scientist than a PE teacher. Come to think of it, I quite like that idea.

> I see myself as a very different sort of teacher now. Of course, even after 16 years, I still enjoy the bread and butter stuff, but this A Level teaching gives me a real buzz. Getting inside all the theory, particularly things like the acquisition of skill, well, it's like having a new job.

The dangers of too strong an affiliation to the teaching of examination groups is that it might accelerate a process of 'compartmentalisation' and fragmentation. Indeed, Andy Hargreaves (1994) has described the emergence of a teaching culture characterised by strong and enduring boundaries between parts of the organisation, by personal identification with the domains these boundaries define, and by differences of power between one domain and another. It is an organisational pattern that sustains and is sustained by the prevailing hegemony of subject specialism and its marginalisation of more 'practical' mentalities; a pattern that restricts professional learning and educational change among communities of teachers, and a pattern that perpetuates and expresses the conflicts and divisions of secondary school teaching.

Precisely because conflicts evoke political behaviours that might have important educational and professional consequences, the need to focus on the impact of these 'divisions of labour' and the part that teacher socialisation plays in the process is compelling. Socialisation into groups constructs individuals' identities in particular ways and, in education, much of this comes through teachers' own school socialisation, preservice education and induction as a NQT. Since the structure of teacher preparation clearly has a powerful impact upon teachers' professional perspectives, their induction into what counts as legitimate forms of knowledge and the nature of learning ought, as we have argued, to be subjected to more in-depth critical scrutiny. In doing so we may be able to determine the extent to which responses to government directives have not only made preservice and in-service professional development complicit in reinforcing the drift towards certification but, in subtle ways, might have also fuelled a process of 'compartmentalisation'. The stance taken here is contrary to Hoyle's (1986) assertion that examinations in physical education might act as a countervailing tendency to the centrifugal forces that threaten to 'pull the subject apart'. Instead, we might like to consider the view that, set against a powerful sporting agenda and the uncertainties of NCPE, particularly at key stage 4, the continuing growth of examinations in physical education might act as the catalyst for redefining the nature and purpose of some teachers' work in schools.

## Conclusion

This chapter has demonstrated that physical education departments (and schools) are powerful social institutions wherein the hidden curriculum works both implicitly and explicitly to suppress and discourage alternative ways of being. The process of schooling defines, promotes and encourages socially acceptable ways of being, be it in terms of the knowledge that is conveyed and/or through the required heterosexual gender regimes that all are expected to conform and adhere to. Schools and physical education departments in particular sustain the hidden curriculum through the activities and specifically the examinations on offer and the materials that are used to deliver and assess it and via 'the division of labour among the teaching staff' (Acker, 1994: 93) and arguably through their NQT recruiting strategies.

However, if physical education is to take advantage of the strategic position it occupies in the lives of young people, it will surely require a vision that extends beyond the delimiting 'performance indicators' defined by the success rates of candidates registered for GCSE, A Level and other accredited courses. This is not to imply that examinations in physical education are unimportant but rather an attempt to suggest that their development is consistent with a technocratic agenda (see Bain, 1990) that has structurally reinforced a subject hierarchy favouring propositional knowledge over procedural forms of knowing. Neither is it intended to imply that the continued development of examinations will necessarily compromise any commitment towards a critical pedagogy. However, teachers engaged in the development and teaching of examination courses must begin to reconcile the tensions that will inevitably emerge between the multiplicity of role definitions and identity they are currently expected to fulfil and the statutory entitlement of all young people to an equitable physical education experience.

In short, every effort must be made to prevent schools and teachers becoming victims of forces that have little to do with the real needs of their pupils. Within this context, physical education must assume a pro-active role. At the outset, this will require conceptual clarity about the nature of physical education in our schools and the 'political capital' to secure ownership of its future direction and constituency. To do so, it will be essential that we expose and understand the vagaries of a professional sub-culture that on the surface would appear to be pro-actively working towards a position of consensus whilst at the same time continuing to wrestle with the underlying tensions that could yet 'pull the subject apart' (Hoyle, 1986).

Now that physical education has been elevated to the arena of public debate, it is hoped that there will be a greater degree of self-determination. However, if physical education teachers are to gain any genuine control over the responsibility for their own professional practice they must re-examine the hidden curriculum of education and physical education, and in the process adopt a critical perspective on their own values and beliefs. We like Kirk (1992: 53) remain convinced that 'we abandon interest in the concept … [that the hidden curriculum] expresses only at our peril.'

## Note

1 In *Ethics and Education,* Peters (1966) presents criteria that differentiates 'educationally worthwhile' and non-worthwhile activities. For Peters, worthwhile activities are 'serious' in the sense that they are morally significant. As Kirk *et al.* (1986) point out, games and other play like activities are 'hived off from the main business of life' and so the ends of such activities are morally indifferent. Peters (1966: 159) proceeds to argue that worthwhile activities are also 'serious' in that they illuminate other areas of life and contribute much to the quality of living. They have, secondly, a wide-ranging cognitive content which distinguishes them from games. Skills for instance do not have a wide-ranging cognitive content. Kirk *et al.* (1986: 176) conclude that: 'In the process of becoming an examinable subject, physical education activities can be seen to more closely resemble the propositional knowledge

that forms Peters' worthwhile activities and as a consequence, procedural knowledge associated with 'knowing how', skilful or play-like activities have been marginalised or eliminated.'

### Reflection questions

1. Justify the importance of retaining an interest in the hidden curriculum.
2. Examinations at GCSE and A Level have emerged as significant additions to the work of physical education teachers. Do you subscribe to the view that their development has challenged the status hierarchy of the formal curriculum?
3. Do you accept Carroll's (1998) view that the development of examinations in physical education have reinforced gender stereotypes within the subject?

### Tasks

1. Observe the actions of teachers and pupils in one or more physical education lessons in different environments and note any examples of the hidden curriculum in operation.
2. Fernandez-Balboa (1993) claims that the real challenge is 'to go beyond a mere acknowledging of the present conditions of ... physical education ... to make a conscious effort to change our oppressive beliefs and behavioral patterns' (249).
   In what ways do you think an understanding of the hidden curriculum can contribute to the development of a socially democratic physical education curriculum? Examine this question within the context of: curriculum content; organisational strategies; pedagogy and assessment.

### Further reading

Green, K. and Hardman, K. (Eds) (1998) *Physical Education: A Reader*. Aachen: Meyer and Meyer.

Kirk, D. and Tinning, R. (Eds) (1990) *Physical Education, Curriculum and Culture: Critical Issues in the Contemporary Crisis*. London: Falmer.
Laker, A. (2000) *Beyond the Boundaries of Physical Education: Educating Young People for Citizenship and Social Responsibility*. London: RoutledgeFalmer.

## References

Acker, S. (1994) *Gendered Education: Sociological Reflections on Women, Teaching and Feminism*. Buckingham: Open University Press.

Apple, M. (1986) Are teachers losing control of their skills and curriculum? *Journal of Curriculum Studies*, 18, 2, 177–184.

Bain, L. (1985) The hidden curriculum re-examined. *Quest*, 37, 2, 145–153.

Bain, L.L. (1990) 'A critical analysis of the hidden curriculum in physical education', in Kirk, D. and Tinning, R. (Eds) *Physical Education, Curriculum and Culture: Critical Issues in the Contemporary Crisis*. London: Falmer Press.

Ball, S. (1994) *Education Reform: A Critical and Post-Structural Approach*. Milton Keynes: Open University Press.

Carroll, R. (1986) 'Examinations in physical education: an analysis of trends and developments', in *Trends and Developments in Physical Education*. Proceedings of the VIIIth Commonwealth and International Conference on Sport, Physical Education, Dance, Recreation and Health. London: E. & F.N. Spon.

Carroll, B. (1998) 'The emergence and growth of examinations in physical education', in Green, K. and Hardman, K. (Eds) *Physical Education: A Reader*. Aachen: Meyer and Meyer.

Clarke, G. (1992) 'Learning the language: discourse analysis in physical education', in Sparkes, A.C. (Ed.) *Research in Physical Education and Sport: Exploring Alternative Visions*. London: Falmer Press.

Cockburn, C. (forthcoming) Year 9 girls' opinions of physical education: a questionnaire survey. *Bulletin of Physical Education*.

Cockerell, S.A. and Hardy, C. (1987) The concept of femininity and its implications for physical education. *British Journal of Physical Education*, 18, 4, 149–151.

Denscombe, M. (1980) The work context of teaching: an analytical framework for the study of teachers in classrooms. *British Sociology of Education*, 1, 279–292.

Department for Education and the Welsh Office (1992) Circulars 9/92 and 35/92: *Initial Teacher Training (Secondary Phase)*. London: HMSO.

Department for Education and the Welsh Office (1993) Circular 14/93: *Initial Teacher Training (Primary Phase)*. London: HMSO.

Department for Education and Employment (1998) Circular 4/98: *Teaching: High Status, High Standards*. London: HMSO.

Drinkwater, A. (2001) 'A boy wouldn't want to go out with a girl who had bigger muscles than him!' Playing the 'femininity game': the impact of stereotypical images of femininity on the physical education experiences of adolescent girls. Unpublished MA(Ed) Dissertation, University of Southampton.

Fernandez-Balboa, J-M. (1993) Socio-cultural characteristics of the hidden curriculum in physical education. *Quest*, 45, 230–254.

Gilroy, S. and Clarke, G. (1997) Raising the game: deconstructing the sporting text – from Major to Blair. *Pedagogy in Practice,* 3, 2, 19–37.

Giroux, H. (1983) *Theory and Resistance in Education: A Pedagogy for the Opposition.* London: Heinemann.

Griffin, P. (1998) *Strong Women, Deep Closets: Lesbians and Homophobia in Sport.* Champaign, IL: Human Kinetics.

Hargreaves, A. (1994) *Changing Teachers, Changing Times: Teachers' Work and Culture in the Postmodern Age.* London: Cassell.

Hargreaves, J. (1994) *Sporting Females: Critical Issues in the History and Sociology of Women's Sport.* London: Routledge.

Hoyle, E. (1986) 'Curriculum development in physical education 1966–1985', in *Trends and Developments in Physical Education.* Proceedings of the VIIIth Commonwealth and International Conference on Sport, Physical Education, Dance, Recreation and Health. London: E. & F.N. Spon.

Kickert, W. (1991) Steering at a distance: a new paradigm of public governance in Dutch higher education. Paper for the European Consortium for Political Research, University of Essex, March 1991.

Kirk, D. (1992) Physical education, discourse, and ideology: bringing the hidden curriculum into view. *Quest*, 44, 35–56.

Kirk, D., McKay, J. and George, L.F. (1986) 'All work and no play? Hegemony in the physical education curriculum', in *Trends and Developments in Physical Education.* Proceedings of the VIIIth Commonwealth and International Conference on Sport, Physical Education, Dance, Recreation and Health. London and New York: E. and F.N. Spon.

Laker, A. (2000) *Beyond the Boundaries of Physical Education: Educating Young People for Citizenship and Social Responsibility.* London: RoutledgeFalmer.

Lirgg, C.D. (1993) Effects of same-sex versus coeducational physical education on the self-perceptions of middle and high school students. *Research Quarterly for Exercise and Sport*, 64, 324–334.

Mason, V. (1995) *Young People and Sport in England, 1994.* London: Sports Council.

Milosevic, L. (Ed.) (1995) *Fairplay: Gender and Physical Education.* Leeds: Leeds City Council Department of Education.

Nutt, G. (1988) The emergence of examinations and accreditation in physical education: a critique. Unpublished M.Sc. Project, Loughborough University of Technology.

Nutt, G. (April 1999) Examining the changing nature of PE teachers' work. Paper presented at the PEA (UK) Centenary Conference, University of Bath.

Ofsted (March 1999) Proceedings at the Ofsted/HMI Initial Teacher Training Inspections 1996–98 Dissemination Conference, Newman College, Birmingham.

Peters, R.S. (1966) *Ethics and Education.* London: Allen and Unwin.

Price, C. (4 May 1990) True confessions. *Times Educational Supplement,* C2.

Rothman, R. (1984) Deprofessionalization: the case of law in America. *Work and Occupations*, 11, 183–206.

Scraton, S. (1987) '"Boys muscle in where angels fear to tread" – girls' sub-cultures and physical activities', in Horne, J., Jary, D. and Tomlinson, A. (Eds) *Sport, Leisure and Social Relations.* London: Routledge and Kegan Paul.

Scraton, S. (1992) *Shaping up to Womanhood: Gender and Girls' Physical Education.* Buckingham: Open University Press.

Scraton, S. (1993) 'Equality, coeducation and physical education in secondary schooling', in Evans, J. (Ed.) *Equality, Education and Physical Education.* London: Falmer Press.

Sparkes, A. (1994) *Understanding Teachers: A Life History Approach.* Educational Research Monograph Series, Research Support Unit, School of Education, University of Exeter.

Stidder, G. (2000) GCSE Physical Education for all: a step in the right direction. *Bulletin of Physical Education*, 36, 3, 159–177.

Talbot, M. (1995) 'Gender and national curriculum physical education', in Milosevic, L. (Ed.) *Gender and Physical Education: A Collection of Discussion Documents Research Papers and Practical Guidance.* Leeds: Leeds City Council Department of Education.

Tinning, R. (1990) *Ideology and Physical Education: Opening Pandora's Box.* Deakin: Deakin University Press.

Whannel, G. (1983) *Blowing the Whistle: the Politics of Sport.* London: Pluto Press.

Young, M.F.D. (1998) *The Curriculum of the Future. From the 'New Sociology of Education' to a Critical Theory of Learning.* London: Falmer.

# 10 Critical pedagogy: what might it look like and why does it matter?

*Doune Macdonald*

## Introduction

I first heard the term 'critical pedagogy' when I returned to university to undertake an honours degree after teaching health and physical education for four years. Several academic staff and postgraduate students met regularly to discuss the concept in a basement room that was cold and windowless. The meetings I attended spoke of hegemonic capitalism, patriarchy, domination, inequality, alienation, democracy and empowerment. To identify with a critical pedagogy seemed a serious, gloomy and somewhat confrontational business. This was in 1986 and it was the early days of scholarship in critical pedagogy in Australian health and physical education. It took me several years not to fear it, to understand its significance, digest its strengths and weaknesses and find a way of working with it that I felt was practical and positive. The aim of this chapter is to de-mystify critical pedagogy and introduce a range of contexts and practices where critical pedagogy can be used to engage more people in physically active, healthy lifestyles.

The chapter begins with a discussion of what is meant by critical pedagogy through addressing the concepts of pedagogy, paradigms and critical theory. As critical pedagogy has been accused of being long on criticism and short on suggestions, the chapter will draw on three case studies to bring to life the critical questions, pedagogies and reflections that should be central to the professional practices of teachers, coaches, administrators, sport scientists and tertiary educators. Case Study 1 reports on a project in a physical education teacher education (PETE) programme that sought to shift tertiary practices towards a critical agenda. It describes in some detail what a critical pedagogy might look like in action and indicates how a leader/instructor might go about adopting relevant critical pedagogies in their own practices. Case Study 2 focuses on differing approaches to instruction in an adult community leisure programme to demonstrate the potential impact of differing pedagogies. Lastly, Case Study 3 shifts the focus to children's sport participation and the practices that are anti-ethical to a critical pedagogy. It invites you to consider the impact of pedagogical practices that are reproductive of injustice as a prelude to considering why the practices of critical pedagogy are important.

The chapter will close with some propositions concerning the relevance and possible future of critical pedagogy in the field of physical education and sport. While critical pedagogy work in the physical activity field has been somewhat limited, the argument will be made that critical perspectives in the field are necessary if it is to make more friends and fewer enemies of postmodern participants. More specifically, notions of care, collaboration, community renewal and meaningful change will be explored.

## What is critical pedagogy?

In order to move towards an understanding of critical pedagogy we will address the preliminary question of what is meant by 'pedagogy'. Recognising that there are different views about pedagogy, the second preliminary question will discuss 'What is a paradigm?' in order to consider the different concerns, principles and practices of pedagogies as they are aligned to a particular paradigm. This then sets a platform from which we can explore the critical theory paradigm and, in turn, critical pedagogy.

In educational theory pedagogy typically refers to the 'art' or 'science' of teaching. In order to study pedagogy within this chapter, I will use a multi-dimensional view of pedagogy, comprising instruction, learning and curriculum, and premise my arguments on pedagogy being socially constructed and culturally-specific processes and practices (Kirk *et al.*, 1996). Pedagogy therefore entails a 'selective tradition of practices and conventions ... [and] insofar as such selections serve the interests of particular classes and social relations, decisions about ... pedagogy are ultimately ideological and political' (Luke and Luke, 1994: 566).

While pedagogy is typically linked to instruction, curriculum and learning in institutions such as schools, teaching and learning pedagogy occurs throughout the community in homes, clubs, gymnasia, theatres, playgrounds, coaching clinics, rehabilitation centres and so on. Consider the myriad of settings in which you have been engaged in a pedagogical process. How and why have the pedagogies differed?

Luke and Luke's (1994) definition of pedagogy alerts us to pedagogies reflecting and generating particular ideological and political positions. As such, pedagogies can be aligned to particular research and educational communities that share similar conceptions of proper questions, methods, values, techniques and forms of explanation. Such communities can be described as paradigms. Thus, a paradigm is a world-view or belief system that frames what is important, legitimate and reasonable.

> At a most fundamental level different paradigms provide particular sets of lenses for seeing the world and making sense of it in different ways. They act to shape how we think and act because for the most part we are not even aware that we are wearing any particular set of lenses.
>
> (Sparkes, 1992: 12)

Three paradigms continue to dominate ways of thinking about pedagogy: positivist, interpretive and critical. Those whose research and teaching is aligned to the positivist paradigm value the psychological traditions of experimentation, measurement of variables, objectivity, universal theories, prediction and certainty as a way of finding the 'right' practices and procedures to benefit human kind. As Kirk (1989) noted, this paradigm is:

> guided in particular by a belief in the need for objective measurement of teaching and learning in real-life situations, which can be achieved through empirical observations of life in classrooms and in the gym, the construction of standardised instruments to collect data from these observations, and the often sophisticated deployment of statistical techniques in the analysis of the data.
>
> (124)

An instructor committed to a positivist pedagogy would therefore value the refinement of technical skills such as clear instructions, high 'time on task', and frequent feedback.

The interpretive paradigm emerged as a force in the nineteenth century as a response to the positivists' search for an objective reality. Interpretivists argue that the laws of investigation in the natural sciences dealing with inanimate objects are not suited to understanding human beings with their variety of backgrounds, interests, emotions, and values. 'Since human beings are thinking, conscious, feeling, language and symbol-using animals' (Sparkes, 1992: 25), interpretivists seek to understand social reality as a process that is individual and context-specific through largely qualitative techniques. As such, an interpretive pedagogy attempts to develop a sensitivity to the individual learners, their interests, needs, and motivations, in relation to the specific learning context.

While the above two paradigms have dominated research and practice in the physical activity field, they have been criticised for failing to address systematic patterns of, for example, sexism, racism and poverty that limit people's life chances, health and well-being.

> Positivist theories, by failing to recognise the importance of interpretations and meanings that individuals employ to make their reality intelligible, fail to identify the phenomena to be explained. In consequence, the kind of theories that they produce are often trivial and useless, even though they may appear to be sophisticated and elaborate.
>
> (Carr and Kemmis, 1986: 103)

In contrast, the interpretive paradigm does encourage detailed understanding of particular social contexts and individuals' experiences within them. However, a shortfall is its failure to account for the unequal power relations that construct the social reality 'and so tells us little about how individual and group behaviour is influenced by the way in which society is organised' (Sparkes, 1992: 39).

This brings us to the third paradigm with which we are most interested. It is critical theory, or rather a collection of critical theories, that are premised on the following beliefs:

1. some groups in society are powerful while others are powerless;
2. powerful groups have a vested interest in maintaining their power and social institutions tend to support this *status quo*;
3. powerless groups have a vested interest in social change;
4. the role of critical theories is to problematize the *status quo* and to ask 'why' questions in order to change the world;
5. changing individual and group consciousness is a pathway to social change (after Griffin, in Sparkes, 1992: 40–41).

Thus, critical theories are not only about the study of limiting relationships, structures, and conditions based on social class, gender, sexuality, disability, age, race/ethnicity, and/or geographical location but also about the need for action. To arrive at what is right and just in a given situation, The Frankfurt School of critical theorists argued for an approach that emphasised practical theory or praxis directed towards self-empowerment, social transformation, and emancipation (Carr and Kemmis, 1986).

Before moving into a more detailed discussion of critical pedagogy, a caveat should be offered. Positivist, interpretivist and critical theory paradigms do not necessarily exist as mutually exclusive. In our research and practice it might be useful to draw on the principles and/or methods from a number of perspectives. For example, in your pedagogy you might be interested in monitoring and refining your technical skills in providing feedback while also being concerned about occurrences of bullying and the low levels of participation by women. Indeed, Sparkes (1992) has argued for a polyvocal community in which all paradigms provide whatever they can offer. 'If one voice, or paradigm, dominates then there is a real danger that we end up just speaking to ourselves … that can lead to a form of tunnel vision' (Sparkes, 1992: 48). (For a more detailed account of these paradigms, see Chapter 3.)

There are multiple versions of what may be understood as critical pedagogy under the umbrella of critical theory. However, there is a commonality across interpretations which suggests that it 'is primarily concerned with the kinds of educational theories and practices that encourage both students and teachers (or leaders) to develop an understanding of the interconnecting relationships among ideology, power and culture' (Leistyna and Woodrum, 1996: 3). What knowledge and skills are being valued in this learning context? Who/which groups do these benefit? Who and what controls the place, direction, style of communication and timing of learning? To what ends? Does the learning improve the life chances of all those involved in the learning process? In short, Kanpol (1998) suggests that 'one of the central components of critical pedagogy is in fact to challenge and eventually alter oppressive structural constraints in a practical way' (64). In relation to schooling, McLaren (1998) defines critical pedagogy as a 'way of thinking about, negotiating, and transforming the relationship among classroom teaching, the production of knowledge, the institutional structures of the school, and the social and material relations of the wider community, society, and nation state' (45). He sees schools as a particularly significant site in cultural reproduction as they are an introduction to, preparation for, and legitimation of particular forms of social life. Therefore, a critical pedagogy:

1. places a decreased emphasis on the technical and instrumental aspects of instructors' work;
2. views knowledge and instruction as problematic;
3. questions the ethical, social and political contexts in which instruction occurs;
4. places increased emphasis on developing critical and reflective capacities in learners;
5. listens to learners' 'voices' thereby shifting the traditional balance of power in learning environments;
6. aims to create social change towards more just and inclusive practices (e.g. Ellsworth, 1989; Gitlin, 1990; Kanpol, 1998; Kincheloe and Steinberg, 1998;[1] Kirk, 1986; Wink, 2000).

For Wink (2000)[2] a critical pedagogy generates a questioning frame of mind, a reflective approach to our actions and the actions of others, and a commitment to do something. It encourages intellectual risk taking, and accommodates and critiques different points of view. Therefore, the commitment to a truly emancipatory pedagogy requires the caring for and caring about the needs of learners and the development of skills of critical insight, emotional sensitivity, negotiation and compromise (Rovengo and Kirk, 1995). If a critical pedagogy is adopted, this is said to represent a significant shift from a pedagogy characterised by the transmission of existing knowledge, as is the case in most instructional settings, to a pedagogy which is concerned with the production of knowledge and socially just outcomes. Case Study 1 is an attempt to describe a shift in pedagogy from a more traditional mode to one that reflects the principles of critical pedagogy. While the site is a physical education teacher education (PETE) programme, the process of change could be applicable across a range of physical activity instructional contexts. Case Study 2 then attempts to capture the impact that a critical pedagogy might have in a recreational setting. Together the two cases are intended to exemplify what a critical pedagogue might do, what a critical pedagogy might look like, and what might be the consequences. The reflective questions at the end of each case are a way of helping you ask 'critical' questions.

## Case Study 1: Creating a critical pedagogy in PETE3

### *Setting the scene*

The quality of teaching in tertiary institutions, linked with the quality of professional practice of university graduates, has come under scrutiny nationally and internationally. Tertiary institutions are under pressure to graduate students who are not only technically and intellectually competent but who are also likely to practise in their chosen profession in a socially responsible way whether they be medical practitioners, social workers, exercise scientists or teachers (Lawson, 1997). A vibrant higher education system is said to fulfil:

> its obligations to the community through its traditional roles ... while acting as a centre for the critical social and cultural analysis and debate of important issues [it] is therefore one of the indispensable elements in a civilised society.
> (Higher Education Council, 1990: 1)

Therefore, educators involved with physical education teacher education (PETE) have argued for a critical pedagogy in their programmes to counter the mis-education which can occur in and through physical education (PE) such as exclusion on the basis of gender, sexuality, body shape, ability and ethnicity (see Evans, 1993; Fernandez-Balboa, 1995, 1997; Macdonald, 1993). A challenge for us as PETE faculty was how to help PETE students (and ourselves), who are embedded in the rationalist enterprise of universities, to develop a socially critical perspective. Thus, the purpose of this case study is to report on an action research process involved with the design and implementation of a critical pedagogy in order to illustrate the possibilities and pitfalls. It is offered as a case in PETE in which students were introduced to a pedagogy that centred around socially critical subject matter, negotiation, reflection and praxis within the constraints of a large, conservative university. As you read you could be mindful of what principles and practices dominate your university programme and where there might be spaces to make the programme more inclusive. The PETE programme was one professional preparation stream within a four-year applied science degree. The sixty-seven third-year PETE students who participated in the study were, in the majority, 20 to 22 years of age, and consisted of thirty-eight white males and twenty-eight white females, together with one Aboriginal female.

The university subject that provided a focus for our critical project, Curriculum Issues in Health and Physical Education (HPE), was undertaken by students in the first semester of their third year. The main purpose of the subject was to give students the opportunity to recognise and evaluate key influences in the development of HPE curricula. Anecdotal records, students' written work and formal subject evaluations collected prior to this study, suggested that the students valued technical knowledge associated with curriculum issues, felt that the subject was too remote from the 'real' task of teaching and relied too heavily on complex theoretical concepts introduced in a didactic mode.

### *Action research cycles*

The project evolved through three cycles of activity in line with an action research methodology. Action research is a process driven by the questions raised within a specific setting (What is happening now? In what ways is it problematic?) and that involves all participants in systematically and collaboratively planning, acting, reflecting and refining a series of strategies (Carr and Kemmis, 1986). The first cycle was devoted to reflecting upon anecdotal evidence concerning students' previous engagement with curriculum study and capturing, from the existing literature, practices and priorities that were characteristic of a critical pedagogy. From this information base, a conceptualisation of the content knowledge and pedagogy for the curriculum subject was distilled. Cycles two and three (the subject taught in consecutive years) represent the struggle to promote the integration of theory and practice in order to enhance the understanding of implementing a critical pedagogy. The subject's staff (the tutor and I) engaged in the teaching and learning processes of the subject as well as observing the students' engagement with critical pedagogy strategies.

Following the granting of university ethical clearance, two cohorts of students enrolled in the subject across consecutive years were asked if they were willing to be participants. Faculty and students negotiated that all lectures and tutorials could be audiotaped and transcribed for later analysis. Students who volunteered to be key informants were interviewed ($n$ = 16) using a loosely-structured interview schedule three times during each semester in which the subject was taught. When other students expressed strong positions or concerns with respect to their experiences, they too were invited for interview ($n$ = 5). Students' reflections were generated in their written work and excerpts were extracted as data. As teachers of the subject, we kept reflective journals in which we detailed our informal interactions with the students and problematised our thinking about the direction of the subject matter, research processes and questions, reflections on the lectures and tutorials, and the constraints and possibilities we encountered.

### *Cycle 1*

We generated from the literature and our reflections the following attributes upon which we proceeded to design, implement and critique the subject: socially critical subject matter; negotiation; reflection; and pedagogy as praxis. The following cycles briefly introduce the attributes by drawing on the subject's design and implementation, the participants' reactions, questions arising and recommended changes. Throughout, we tried to be critical of our own agendas through asking questions such as, 'how do we know what we are doing is right?'

### *Cycle 2*

In an attempt to challenge the taken-for-granted assumptions and dominant educational practices favoured by the students, class topics embraced issues such as 'What is the function of PE in schooling?' Questions were designed to assist students in raising their 'awareness and skepticism about "factual" knowledge' (Fernandez-Balboa, 1997: 128). Students addressed these questions through, for example, contrasting their own school experiences with those of their peers. As a means of linking the critical pedagogy to the popular beliefs about physical education, we also introduced newspaper articles and video material into the teaching and learning process to assist students to 'read the media's texts and images critically' (Fernandez-Balboa, 1997: 130). However, the students' preference for a knowledge base that was technical in nature, more readily consumed and grounded in the familiar was a recurring theme (Tsangaridou and O'Sullivan, 1997). One student (Cameron) rather resentfully suggested that the subject was 'Not important anyway. I'll study for more important exams, like biomechanics.' We questioned that if technical subject matter and skills met the students' needs but slowed the pace of their critical inquiry, was this wrong? In whose hands should rest a decision for what is 'right' for the students?

One of Ellsworth's (1989) most poignant criticisms of critical pedagogy has been that the empowerment of students was illusory and our negotiations with the students aimed to address this challenge. Negotiation suggests regular and respectful communication in which stakeholders have a share of power in decision-making and communication processes (Zeichner and Liston, 1986). Negotiation with the students in the first year of the project centred on the process of arriving at the subject's assessment profile. Students were introduced to a range of traditional and innovative assessment instruments for consideration. In small groups, each arrived at a preferred list of assessment items and then the class came together to finalise an assessment profile.

The keeping of journals by students was a key strategy in supporting and encouraging their critical reflective inquiry. It was suggested in the assessment profile that these journals should embrace a reflection of the week's work through showing evidence of critique and questioning, introducing and analysing relevant personal experiences and, through this, representing a developing understanding of curriculum as praxis. Students were given some questions to help guide their reflections and they were also encouraged to generate and respond to their own questions. The journal was a cornerstone of the subject as it was intended to provide students with an opportunity for personal expression and a synthesis of their experiences over the past week. Yet, it became apparent that much of their writing (and thinking) was at the level of technical, non-integrated description and summary rather than a thoughtful reflection of their encounter with the subject (Tsangaridou and O'Sullivan, 1997). Many of the students failed to write in their journal on a weekly basis, preferring to make hurried entries just prior to its submission for assessment.

The final attribute of critical pedagogy that helped us shape our subject was praxis, interpreted as the marriage of theory and practice, thought and action (Grundy, 1987). In order to meet many of the criticisms of critical pedagogy, the implementation of praxis can be a powerful principle to foster in that it aims to combat abstract intellectualism. Praxis draws on individuals' perspectives, critical reflection and informed action to understand and refine professional practice. In year one of the project, praxis was developed through: discussion of the experiences students were having in the companion practice teaching subject; task-based learning (e.g. preparing a situational analysis of a school in which they did their small group teaching); and role plays. Despite these initiatives, the comment was made that: 'We need to have things link together a bit more. Maybe more links directly to schools' (Jill). Another student remarked: 'We didn't always have the opportunity to do things we learnt about' (Sandy).

*Cycle 3*

As a response to our experiences with the students in the first year and from our reflections on those experiences, the subject's structure in the second year was altered. We effectively doubled the contact hours for the subject each week on the presumption that more time would be available to explore socially critical themes and for us to be more supportive of the students' struggles with the approach. We also attempted to de-emphasise the language (but not the emphasis) of sociology and critical pedagogy in an effort to encourage students to 'jump' the terminology barrier to begin engagement with the ideas being introduced. To do so we were conscious of unpacking the terms using relevant examples from films (e.g. 'Stand and Deliver', 'Heartbreak Kid').

In the second year we weighed the benefits of student selection of assessment against the benefits of a more structured assessment programme which we believed would enhance their conceptual understanding of curriculum issues. Consequently, the students' role in negotiated assessment was changed (although students still decided on the assessment criteria and item weightings) and we tried to create as many opportunities as possible for the students' voices to shape the agenda. One student (Barbara) remarked: 'As a group, I think the students ... have some authority. I think it's important and it keeps us happy. If we couldn't have our say we'd really get frustrated.'

Another dimension that we attempted to bring into focus in the second year was genuinely giving all students encouragement to take part in discussions. Of particular interest to us was the strength of women's voices within the group as research had suggested that it may be difficult for female students to find space in which to speak confidently (Dewar, 1991; Macdonald, 1993). Five female students ventured some suggestions to us to facilitate all students feeling comfortable speaking in the group.

An outcome of our experience in the first year was the decision not to include a reflective journal in the subject the next year. We understood that socially critical and transformative practitioners are those who can theorise their practice (Giroux and McLaren, 1996; Schon, 1989) and the journals were not helping students with this. Therefore, we set tasks that required students to address curriculum issues using their practice teaching schools as sites for data collection and reflection, thereby accounting for 'the primacy of student experience' (Giroux and McLaren, 1996: 322). The reflective component of the task asked the students to reflect on their implementation in terms of 'What did the students learn?' (i.e. overt and hidden), and 'What have you learned about the status of PE in your school?' It seems that the importance of real-life settings and concrete experiences cannot be underestimated in the promotion of students' reflective activity (Tsangaridou and O'Sullivan, 1997).

Throughout the refining of the subject we were constantly faced with the dilemma of balancing utilitarian knowledge with socially critical emphases and meeting the organisational requirements of the university. However, a number of the processes and strategies described above laid a strong foundation for ongoing critical approaches across the PETE programme.

**Reflection questions**

1 Consider the process that we employed in creating and refining a critical pedagogy.
2 What were the strengths and weaknesses in this process?
3 What might a critical pedagogy look like in your programme?
4 What processes could you employ in your current programme to shift it towards a critical pedagogy?
5 How would you and your peers respond? Why?

## Case Study 2: Community-based physical activity programme

### *Setting the scene*

The following case study should be of particular interest to those concerned with the failure of health promotion strategies to impact upon community physical activity patterns. To be more effective strategies need to account for at least five inter-related factors: biological, lifestyle, environment, social and economic, and use of and access to health services (Downie, Tannahill and Tannahill, 1996). Interventions have been criticised for their failure to account for issues of race, class and gender and for overlooking other powerful, and potentially damaging discourses, such as those associated with age and body image (Bunton *et al.*, 1995). In this study, Jane and Steven use different pedagogies to promote physically active lifestyles at a community group meeting. While both are technically competent, Steven is more concerned with the unique social context, giving voice to the participants, and introducing strategies that can be empowering and sustainable. The consequences of this critical pedagogy draws on the inspirational book by Meme McDonald (1992) entitled *Put Your Whole Self In* about a group of elderly women.

### *Community-based seminar*

Jane works as a recreation officer for a local council. She is a confident and well-organised speaker who has been asked to address a community group on promoting physically active lifestyles. She arrives at the venue in enough time to introduce herself to the host of the session, Marjorie Okes, check that the overhead projector (OHP) is in place and that she is familiar with how to work the videocassette recorder. After being introduced to the audience, comprising males and females covering a range of ages and ethnic backgrounds, she proceeds to deliver her talk on the deleterious effects on health of insufficient exercise, barriers to participation, and the most effective patterns of exercise to generate health benefits. Some members of the audience take notes while the remainder listen quietly. Being practised at this type of presentation, Jane talks clearly, animatedly and logically, using the OHP to help structure the presentation and provide emphasis for key points. The brief videotape excerpt on physical activity and heart disease provides a variation in her delivery. At the end of the hour, Jane thanks the group and alerts them to some brochures that outline local facilities and programmes.

The session on promoting physically active lifestyles was to be repeated one month later for different members of the same local community. Jane was busy and asked her colleague, Steven, to present. Steven was pleased to help and asked Jane for some information on the characteristics of the participants. She could only describe what her audience physically looked like, so Peter rang the community group to get a sense of who would be attending. He was interested to know the number of men and women, their ages, and to gain a general understanding of their socio-economic status, ethnicity and lifestyle patterns.

As was Jane, Steven was fully prepared, arrived early and rearranged the furniture into small groups. After being introduced to the participants, Peter asked each to give their name and share why they were interested in the topic. It seemed that all of the participants knew that they should exercise but they were unsure of what they could do, transport arrangements, costs and the like. Steven asked each participant to imagine what their ideal, physically active lifestyle would look like, and to list what was preventing this occurring. Participants were then asked in small groups to share their goals and barriers. The whole group came together to discuss their goals so that Steven could advise them of appropriate patterns for the activities relative to their age, previous lifestyle and general health. The small group were asked to record the barriers each member perceived and together they considered which were insurmountable and which were achievable and how. The session closed with a group of older women, led by Marjorie Okes, deciding they would enjoy some hydrotherapy if they could get a venue that was convenient and at a reasonable cost.

### *Community-based action*

The older women now formed the core of a self-help group and regularly undertook warm water exercise sessions and massage together. Lena says:

> If I didn't find Marjorie [and the group] I don't know what would happen to me now. I have to be honest. Marjorie put the life back into me. The massage gave me the opportunity … If I didn't join the group I would be stuck in my wheelchair … I am more alert with my brain. More clear. With MS you see, you have the brain damage. So the group helps me not only physically but mentally … We don't feel we are sick people here. We feel we are just people. It's no medical people around here at the massage. It's just us … You see when I started going they say to me, 'Lena, if you want to get your massage you have to help and do somebody else.'
>
> (McDonald, 1992: 93)

Marjorie recalls:

> I remember the night I was asked to speak at the Mary Owen dinner. I brought a bunch of us from the Northcote Hydrotherapy Group along. I got them in for five dollars rather than the thirty dollars full price … And I told [the dinner] how we're all pensioners and how we do exercises in the pool, and then on to massage, and how we get little bits of money here and there … How we organise ourselves with Stella doing the newsletter, Elsie organising bus trips, Joyce is the secretary and I am chief funding hunter. How most of us are in our seventies and eighties and live in our own homes. And we're no longer nobodies living between four walls in a street with no one to talk to. We're important people now … We're doing it for ourselves. We don't take it sitting down. We talk back. And then I said: 'A group of these women are here tonight.' Well, the crowd in the hall rose to their feet and cheered and gave them a standing ovation. It was absolutely terrific. You see, everyone in that room felt part of us winning.
>
> (McDonald, 1992: 111–112)

**Reflection questions**

1. Steven and Jane had different ways of thinking about their pedagogical work. How was Steven's approach more reflective of critical practices?
2. The self-help group also involved its own pedagogies. Did these have a critical dimension?
3. What were some of the significant outcomes for the participants in the self-help group?

## Why are critical pedagogies important?

We live in times of increasing uncertainty as to how to 'fix up' schooling, health, poverty, alienation, violence, to name a few issues of concern (Kanpol, 1998). To 'fix up' requires sensitivity to what the problems are, where power lies, what the consequences of inaction are, and how change can be instigated. These questions are central to a socially critical agenda and require professionals (teachers, coaches, recreation officers, exercise scientists, etc.) who are skilled in asking such questions and responding with democratic strategies to produce inclusive and just outcomes. Conservative, technocratic approaches to pedagogy (which narrowly conceptualise teaching and learning as a discrete and scientific undertaking) that dominate instructional settings embrace depersonalised methods for educating learners that are often manifested in the regulation, standardisation and reproduction of practices, curricula and programmes. Instructors who work within the traditional pedagogy paradigms 'with its model of teacher as knower/lecturer and students as passive recipient of information inevitably reproduce and maintain particular forms of identity, meaning, authority, and interaction, whether they are aware of it or not (Leistyna and Woodrum, 1996: 4). In contrast is the position that the teacher/instructor is a reflective intellectual who can undertake the transformative challenge of empowering learners and thereby shifting sedimented institutional practices 'toward rationally constructing future social conditions which promote enlightened democratic participation of the citizenry' (Harris, 1994: 99). A reflective teacher/instructor resists a blueprint for practice. Rather they are aware of how language shapes patterns of power and privilege, the social implications of their practices, and the policies that shape their work, and take initiative in positive social change (see Kincheloe and Steinberg, 1998; Smyth *et al.*, 2000).

While our main concern here is with the transformative impact of critical pedagogy on students, participants and clients, it should be noted that a critical pedagogy also has significant implications for your career. As suggested above, without asking critical questions about your own work context (What are the goals of my workplace? Do I have authority to make professional decisions? Am I addressing the needs of all participants?) you are in danger of becoming de-skilled, losing your professional authority, autonomy and decision-making capacities. Collins (1999) talks about meaningful work where we are creators of knowledge and initiatives in conjunction with colleagues and participants using participatory rather than coercive pedagogical techniques. In a study of experienced health and physical education teachers, Macdonald (1998) found their greatest satisfaction was derived from creating and implementing programmes and projects that their students found rewarding. Their frustrations came from the loss of authority and autonomy associated with the imposition of 'top down' policies and procedures.

So, apart from making your work more meaningful, why does critical pedagogy matter? Different instructional sites and contexts in the physical activity field have different challenges in terms of positive outcomes for all participants. As discussed in other chapters, socio-cultural research now suggests that most physical education programmes tend to favour mesomorphic, able-bodied, heterosexual, white males through, for example, the selection of subject matter, teaching methods and assessment procedures, and the learning environment and teacher-student interactions (see Tinning, 1990). These 'unintended outcomes of the schooling process' (McLaren, 1998: 186), referred to as the hidden curriculum, embrace tacit messages conveyed through the language, interactions, organisation, knowledge, skills and learning material selection, expectations and reward of the learning context. It could be argued that these patterns of privilege also exist in physical activity settings outside school. Referring to all spheres of human activity, O'Sullivan (1999) argues:

> The position of centrality is occupied by western culture (the developed minority world), white, heterosexual men. The marginal position is occupied by non-western (the underdeveloped minority world), people of colour, women, children and persons of gay and lesbian sexual orientation.
>
> (131)

Using a critical pedagogy a teacher's/instructor's challenge is to expose and examine the hidden curriculum in their programmes and practices. Many sport, recreation and education authorities are currently working towards more inclusive practices and programmes by addressing the needs and interests of girls, indigenous populations, students from non-English speaking backgrounds, those students with disabilities or those who have skills which lie outside the traditional sports-based programmes. Case Study 3 provides a snapshot of a typical school's sports afternoon and the hidden curriculum that it entails. It is intended to paint a picture of why critical pedagogy is important to our field.

## Case Study 3: School sport programme

### *Setting the scene*

As might be the tradition in your country, time during the school week in Australia is devoted to the playing of team sports supervised by teachers, coaches, parents, or sport development officers. At Norton Primary School, the number of Year 6 students keenly engaging in the sports programme is declining. What follows is an account of a sports afternoon that conveys the typical pedagogies and interactions between the leader and pupils and between the pupils themselves. To many of you this might seem an unrealistic and negative portrayal of what you remember as the best time of the school week! Yet, in a few words it tries to represent the research on questions of content, method and interaction in children's physical activity settings. As you read, identify what is unintentionally being learned by the participants.

### *Friends and enemies in school sport*

It is the first sports afternoon of a new term and the pupils meander onto a soccer field, the designated meeting point. Some of the boys keenly grab the soccer balls and run to the goals passing and kicking amongst themselves. Other pupils are muttering, 'not soccer, it's too much running' and 'it's a boys' game. Why can't we do something inside?' Khawla, an 11-year-old Muslim girl, stands quietly while another pupil, Trent, a somewhat overweight boy sits under a nearby tree. According to Muslim faith, Khawla should wear her shalwar during the school day, participate in physical activity separately from males, avoid physical activities considered masculine, and change her clothing in privacy.

The leader, Ryan, calls all pupils into a group and declares that it looks like soccer would be a popular choice of sport for the next ten weeks. A mixture of cheers and silence follows. To get started, the leader asks the class to jog up to the goal posts and sprint back. 'Come on you slow coaches,' Ryan calls, 'You're not trying hard enough!' As the class slowly dribbles back they are asked to do ten push-ups and 'twelve for the people who were too lazy to run!' The class giggles while they watch their peers struggle with the push-ups. Ryan asks the class to group themselves into four teams in a relay formation to practise a soccer dribble and pass drill. Nathan, a soccer enthusiast, is asked to demonstrate a dribble and pass technique while Ryan points out some key points of technique. Pupils then have a few minutes to practise the drill before they have a race against the other teams. The 'enthusiasts' team enjoy the activity but don't find it sufficiently challenging and soon drift off to practise kicking goals. After a couple of races with the 'enthusiasts' (boys') team winning, it's time for a modified game to get everyone involved. To create some 'balance' in skill, the leader asks the winning and losing relay teams to form the one team for the game.

The skilled players on each team take centre positions and are very vocal in directing their classmates about who should stand where. Others scatter themselves around the outskirts of the field. Play starts but within seconds there is a collision between two boys fighting for the ball. One boy is quite shaken and asks to sit out for a while. 'Girl!', is mumbled by a team-mate but Ryan chooses to ignore the remark. Play continues with much vigour in the centre of the field and Ryan is vocal in encouraging the skilled players to 'Stay with your opposite!' and 'Don't look at your feet!' Other players are brought into play intermittently but their errors are met with groans of disappointment by their peers. Play continues for twenty minutes until the bell goes. Ryan congratulates the winning team and says that the other players need to practise at home so that they are ready to win next week!

Back at her desk in an English class, Skye Gibson pens the following poem about her school sport experiences (Pallotta-Chiarolli, 1998):

Sitting, watching, waiting
Sitting, watching, waiting, I see the others play.
They wouldn't ever ask me for I'm not as good as they.
I'd thought I'd heard them say my name
But they had made another claim.
One day I will be picked in a team
However silly it may seem.
Not today though, no. No way.
I just sit and watch and wait and see the others play.

Sitting, watching, waiting, I see the others play.
But something's different, yes it is… someone is away.
I listen very carefully and then I hear my name
I go over very happy, not feeling quite the same.
As the ball is thrown around the court I try to run in fast
But even though I try so hard I always get there last.
Happier than ever now I run back up the court
Making feeble grabs at the ball, not caring what they thought.

The next day feeling different, to the court I make my way.
The others start to whisper but I don't hear what they say.
Waiting for my name to be called my smile is slowly lost:
I will get in a team I thought with all my fingers crossed.

> But as I begin to count the girls I see to my dismay
> That girl that was away that day is back again today.
> I guess my moment's over and in my seat I stay.
> Sitting, watching, waiting, I see the others play.
>
> (162)

**Reflection questions**

1. What was the possible impact of the pedagogies employed in the school sport programme on the various pupils in the class?
2. What critical pedagogy strategies could be employed to maximise the participation of each pupil in school sport?
3. What might be the long-term benefits of employing a critical pedagogy?

The case has been made that children's sport requires 'fixing'. Research suggests that children's participation in organised sport is declining from primary years through to adulthood with lower participation rates for girls as compared to boys and, in particular, for girls from minority backgrounds (see Booth *et al.*, 1997; Management and Consulting Services, 1991). A contributing factor is the pedagogies typically employed by coaches/leaders. For some young people the experience of physical activity was positive but for many others it was about 'waiting for a go, being rejected by the team they aspired to, being belittled when they made a mistake' (Management and Consulting Services, 1991: 5). For girls from ethnic minorities, barriers include having 'nobody to go with', language, religious requirements, over-competitiveness, and lower skill levels (Vescio *et al.*, 1999). Further, research on young people's club sport in Australia indicated that junior sport participants tend to come from two-car, two-parent families who are predominantly well-paid, white colour workers (Kirk *et al.*, 1997). Are you learning how to 'unpack' these issues of gender, ethnic and income-based exclusion in order to expand the participation base in community sport? Are you sensitive to the barriers that many children may face in sustaining their involvement in sport? How might you as a coach or leader structure club competition to ensure a broad base of participation?

Health statistics suggest that exercise messages and programmes have also failed to engage the majority of the population. Regular exercise can provide direct benefit for disease prevention and management in the priority areas of cancer control, cardiovascular health, injury prevention and control, mental health and diabetes. Yet physical inactivity is a major contributor to the burden of all illness in developed countries (Morrow and Blair, 1999). In Case Study 2, Jane typified the technocratic pedagogies that, when employed at the local level, limited participants' input and ownership in exercise programming, and ultimately their potential to change their lifestyles.

There is also a place for critical pedagogy in our society to help 'physical activity consumers' analyse messages about dieting options, exercise regimes, weight control products, lifestyle choices and commercialised sports as part of our physical culture (Kirk, 1998). We need a population to be critical consumers of physical culture, to be able to appraise media messages about health and body shape, gym membership, fitness programmes, school physical education or community recreation initiatives. As critical pedagogues, one of our jobs is to provide a lens through which people can judge the educational, health, social, political and economic impact of the cultural artefacts associated with sport, physical recreation and exercise. Thus, in answer to the question, 'why are critical pedagogies important?', one response might be, 'because it makes a difference' (Wink, 2000). It can make a difference to children's love of movement, an adult's well-being or a nation's health expenditure as it invites us to ask important questions and take steps towards individual, community and institutional change.

## Conclusion

Versions of critical pedagogies have been adopted, altered, and/or extended in a number of different ways. This final section will introduce challenges to critical pedagogies from postmodern perspectives together with some intiatives that demonstrate the varied potentials of critical pedagogies in line with the changing terrains of schools and communities.

Some scholars argue that critical pedagogies have not been sufficiently relevant or effective in enacting change in a post-modern world (see Ellsworth, 1989). A criticism of critical pedagogy is that it has failed to account for individuals who have harnessed personal power, who have overcome gender, race or class barriers, who have constructed their lives differently in the shifting structures of a post-modern world. In such a world shaped by new technologies, global capitalism and rapid social change, the individual is not seen as a stable 'self' with particular life trajectories, but is continually being 'constructed' in ways that are unique. A totalising, or grand theory, that relies upon structures such as class, sex and race as does critical theory, is not sufficiently sensitive or sophisticated to understand and address complex issues of personal experience and diversity. 'Universals are thus rejected in the name of difference and diversity, and the uncertainty of knowing the world in a fixed and assured way' (Leistyna *et al.*, 1999: 341). With reference to young people and learning, Giroux (1996: 61) suggests it is:

> useful for educators to comprehend the changing conditions of identity formation within electronically mediated cultures and to appreciate how they are producing a new generation of youth which exists between the borders of a modernist world of certainty and order, informed by the culture of the West and its technology of print, and a postmodern world of hybridized identities, electronic technologies, local cultural practices, and pluralised public spaces. (61)

There is debate about whether you can be a post-modern critical pedagogue given that critical pedagogy foundations were in the grand narratives of class, race and gender oppression (see Collins, 1998; McLaren and Farahmandpur, 2000). Others argue that the theories overlap and that a twenty-first century pedagogue should trespass and borrow in whatever ways help to improve educational outcomes (see Fullan, 1999). Those who argue that critical pedagogy can adopt a post-modern perspective see it asking questions about (deconstructing) differing values, assumptions and interests 'in bodies of knowledge so that they are able to recognise whose interests have been advanced at the expense of others' (Leistyna *et al.*, 1999: 341). This focus on meaning-making and life experiences moves to centre stage the oppression of individuals rather than groups of people. What is shared across perspectives, however, is a commitment to social justice.

Lawson's work (1999) provides a good example of how the principles of critical pedagogy are being applied in socially just community renewal projects. He argues that 'social trust in other people, professionals and universities is at an all time low' (139). In response he argues for universities and professions to overcome their unhelpful fragmented, specialised structures and, instead, work towards members of the helping professions collaboratively solving real community problems. Given the middle to high socio-economic background of the majority of university students (Macdonald *et al.*, 1998), much could be gained by students working in physical activity contexts where questions of social equity are part of the daily struggle. The label of 'critical pedagogy' is not explicit in Lawson's extensive writings on this topic. However, underpinning his argument is the conviction that for too long our field has not addressed the under-served. Professionals in exercise, physical education and sport may have served well the talented, able-bodied, skilled, physically fit, educated, middle classes. But what about the majority of our population? He suggests we need the knowledge and skills to work across professional boundaries and, in conjunction with communities, create sustainable programmes that address their needs. If our field fails to be 'committed to and accountable for identifiable, achievable social responsibilities' (Lawson, 1999: 138) he suggests we will become obsolete.

Again, while not labelling her work critical pedagogy, Ennis (1999) is drawing upon critical pedagogy principles of challenging the *status quo*, shared ownership, building community, inclusion, social change and empowerment in her work with young urban African-Americans. One reference point for Ennis's work is the Challenge to Care in Schools (1992) by Noddings, who outlines a school system that seeks to optimise individual students' strengths. These strengths should be developed through caring, not competition. Her argument is based on the human need to care and be cared for in the sense that 'we need to be understood, received, respected, recognised' (xi). She stresses the importance of not sentimentalising but rather rethinking education in terms of content and pedagogies that centre on what students care about, respects the range of students' capacities, and addresses the 'persistent undervaluing of skills, attitudes, and capacities traditionally associated with women' (xiii). Noddings' philosophy has recently been adopted by physical educators such as Catherine Ennis (1999) in her work with disengaged students. In some senses she is building on the pioneering work of Hellison (1995) with his self-responsibility model for working with 'at risk' young people. In one programme, Sport for Peace, Ennis and her colleagues planned a curriculum approach that combined the tenets of sport education and social responsibility models of physical education with peace education, conflict negotiation and care and concern for others. Ennis (1999) suggests that:

> Teachers who express concern for students, who care about their successes and their failures and who extend a helping hand and a second chance create bonds of sincerity and authenticity that in turn build student respect, trust, and mutual caring. There relationships empower both students and teachers, leading to shared expectations for success ...
>
> (168)

Are you ready to ask difficult questions, to care, to collaborate, to act and to change? It seems that wherever you turn in the contemporary literature in our field there are calls for leadership, partnerships, community action, and improved social outcomes.[4] In the USA the National Coalition for Promoting Physical Activity's initiatives include:

- Develop state and community coalitions
- Create health communication campaigns
- Promote political action and advocacy

(Morrow and Blair, 1999: 181)

The need for a critical pedagogy within and beyond tertiary education and schools that leads to social change seems strong and loud. Fullan (1999) has articulated several lessons that might help us to understand and act to produce meaningful change. These lessons include:

- Change is a journey not a blueprint
- Individualism and collectivism must have equal power
- Both top-down and bottom-up strategies are necessary
- Every person is a change agent
- There is no single solution: craft your own theories and actions by being a critical consumer

(18)

Thus a critical pedagogue's mandate is to develop a personal and collective consciousness as a platform for managing and creating change within a post-modern world (Fernandez-Balboa, 1997).

'How should you live?' How should you work?' These questions underpin Giddens' (1991) notion of life politics. He understands that the fullest possible life embraces a sense of human need that appreciates diversity, subjectivity, community and the environment. What will be the life politics that guide your future lifestyle and work? The following are some closing questions that might shape your work in a range of pedagogical settings.

1 What subject matter/issues are the learners addressing? How and why have these been selected? Whose interests do they serve?
2 How is the learning structured? What role does the teacher/leader take? What roles do the participant/learners take? Whose voices are heard?
3 What might be the impact of the episode on the participant/learners in the short and longer term?
4 Does the episode contribute to a more just society?

These questions attempt to make the familiar strange and the strange familiar (McLaren, 1998) thereby better preparing you to work towards the well-being of all.

## Notes

1 Part 2 of Kincheloe and Steinberg's (1998) text offers 11 chapters that each describes an approach to critical pedagogy. The foci include putting critical pedagogy into practice in a special education, mathematics, science, art and English classrooms, as well as using critical pedagogy techniques to deconstruct textbooks, the media and computers in schooling.
2 Wink's (2000) 'real world' guide to critical pedagogy provides an excellent overview of its theory, practice and significance in a style that is engaging for both novice and more familiar readers of critical theory.
3 The text of this case draws heavily on a paper by Macdonald and Brooker (1999) published in the *Journal of Sport Pedagogy*. The journal paper gives a fuller analysis of the data and the ensuing decisions.
4 A special edition in 1999 of the journal *Quest*, 51(2) contains many stories of action in schools and communities that aim to touch humanity.

## Tasks

1 In a small group, discuss how critical pedagogy strategies and practices might impact upon student relationships in terms of gender, ethnicity and body shape.
2 Your school's sports coaches are interested in critical pedagogy and have come to you for help. How would you advise them?

**Further reading**

Kincheloe, J. and Steinberg, S. (Eds) (1998) *Unauthorized Methods: Strategies for Critical Teaching*. New York: Routledge.
Tinning, R., Macdonald, D., Wright, J. and Hickey, C. (2001) *Becoming a Physical Education Teacher*. Sydney: Prentice Hall.
Wink, J. (2000) *Critical Pedagogy: Notes from the Real World*. New York: Addison Wesley Longman.

## References

Booth, M., Macaskill, P., McLellen, L., Phongsavan, P., Okely, T., Patterson, J., Wright, J., Bauman, A. and Baur, L. (1997) *NSW Schools Fitness and Physical Activity Survey*. Sydney: NSW Department of Education and Training.

Bunton, R., Nettleton, S. and Burrows, R. (1995) *The Sociology of Health Promotion*. London: Routledge.

Carr, W. and Kemmis, S. (1986) *Becoming Critical: Education, Knowledge and Action Research*. Geelong, Victoria: Deakin University Press.

Collins, M. (1998) *Critical Crosscurrents in Education*. Malabar, Florida: Krieger.

Dewar, A. (1991) Feminist pedagogy in physical education: promises, possibilities and pitfalls. *Journal of Education, Recreation and Dance*, 62, 6, 68–71 and 75–77.

Downie, R., Tannahill, C. and Tannahill, A. (1996) *Health Promotion: Models and Values*. Oxford: Oxford University Press.

Ellsworth, E. (1989) Why doesn't this feel empowering? Working through the repressive myths of critical pedagogy. *Harvard Educational Review*, 59, 297–324.

Ennis, C. (1999) Communicating the value of active, healthy lifestyles to urban students. *Quest*, 51, 164–169.

Evans, J. (Ed.) (1993) *Equality, Education and Physical Education*. Lewes: Falmer Press.

Fernandez-Balboa, J-M. (1995) Reclaiming physical education in higher education through critical pedagogy. *Quest*, 47, 91–114.

Fernandez-Balboa, J-M. (1997) 'Physical education teacher preparation in the postmodern era: toward a critical pedagogy', in Fernandez-Balboa, J-M. (Ed.) *Critical Postmodernism in Human Movement, Physical Education and Sport*, 121–139. Albany: State University of New York Press.

Fullan, M. (1999) *Change Forces: The Sequel*. Lewes: Falmer Press.

Giddens, A. (1991) *Modernity and Self-Identity: Self and Society in the Late Modern Age*. Stanford: Stanford University Press.

Giroux, H. (1996) *Fugitive Cultures: Race, Violence and Youth*. New York: Routledge.

Giroux, H. and McLaren, P. (1996) 'Teacher education and the politics of engagement: the case for democratic schooling', in Leistyna, P., Woodrum, A. and Sherblom S. (Eds) *Breaking Free: the Transformative Power of Critical Pedagogy*, 301–331. Cambridge: Harvard Educational Review.

Gitlin, A.D. (1990) Educative research, voice and school change. *Harvard Educational Review*, 60, 443–466.

Grundy, S. (1987) *Curriculum: Product or Praxis*. Geelong, Victoria: Deakin University Press.

Harris, K. (1994) *Teachers Constructing the Future*. London: Falmer Press.

Hellison, D. (1995) *Self and Social Responsibility*. Champaign, IL: Human Kinetics.

Higher Education Council (1990) *Higher Education: The Challenges Ahead*. Canberra: Australian Government Publishing Service.

Kanpol, B. (1998) Confession as strength: a necessary condition for critical pedagogy. *Educational Foundations*, 12, 2, 63–76.

Kincheloe, J. and Steinberg, S. (Eds) (1998) *Unauthorized Methods: Strategies for Critical Teaching*. New York: Routledge.

Kirk, D. (1986) A critical pedagogy for teacher education: toward an inquiry-oriented approach. *Journal of Teaching in Physical Education*, 5, 230–246.

Kirk, D. (1989) The orthodoxy in RT-PE and the research/practice gap: a critique and an alternative view. *Journal of Teaching in Physical Education*, 8, 2, 123–130.

Kirk, D. (1998) Educational reform, physical culture and the crisis of legitimation in physical education. *Discourse: Studies in the Cultural Politics of Education*, 19, 1, 101–112.

Kirk, D., Nauright, J., Hanrahan, S., Macdonald, D. and Jobling, I. (1996) *The Sociocultural Foundations of Human Movement*. Melbourne: Macmillan.

Kirk, D., Carlson, T., O'Connor, A., Burke, P., Davis, K. and Glover, S. (1997) The economic impact on families of children's participation in junior sport. *The Australian Journal of Science and Medicine in Sport*, 29, 2, 27–33.

Lawson, H. (1997) Children in crisis, the helping professions, and the social responsibilities of universities. *Quest*, 49, 8–33.

Lawson, H. (1999) Education for social responsibility: preconditions in retrospect and in prospect. *Quest*, 51, 116–149.

Leistyna, P. and Woodrum, A. (1996) 'Context and culture: what is critical pedagogy?', in Leistyna, P., Woodrum, A. and Sherblom, S. (Eds) *Breaking Free: the Transformative Power of Critical Pedagogy*, 1–7. Cambridge: Harvard Educational Review.

Leistyna, P., Woodrum, A. and Sherblom, S. (Eds) (1996) *Breaking Free: the Transformative Power of Critical Pedagogy*. Cambridge: Harvard Educational Review.

Luke, A. and Luke, C. (1994) 'Pedagogy', in Asher, R.E. and Simpson, J.M. (Eds) *The Encyclopedia of Language and Linguistics*, 566–568. Tarrytown, New York: Elsevier Science/Pergamon.

Macdonald, D. (1993) Knowledge, gender and power in physical education teacher education. *Australian Journal of Education*, 37, 259–278.

Macdonald, D. (1999) The 'professional' work of experienced physical education teachers. *Research Quarterly for Exercise and Sport*, 70, 41–54.

Macdonald, D. and Brooker, R. (1999) Articulating a critical pedagogy in physical education teacher education. *Journal of Sport Pedagogy*, 5, 1, 51–63.

Macdonald, D., Abernathy, P. and Bramich, K. (1998) A profile of first year human movement studies students. *Chronicle of Physical Education in Higher Education*, 9, 2, 16–19.

McDonald, M. (1992) *Put Your Whole Self In*. Melbourne: Penguin.

McLaren, P. (1998) *Life in Schools: An Introduction to Critical Pedagogy in the Foundations of Education*. New York: Addison Wesley Longman.

McLaren, P. and Farahmandpur, R. (2000) Reconsidering Marx in post-Marxist times: a requiem for postmodernism. *Educational Researcher*, 29, 3, 25–33.

Management and Consulting Services (1991) *Sport for Young Australians*. Canberra: Australian Sports Commission.

Morrow, J. and Blair, S. (1999) Promoting the Surgeon General's report on physical activity and health: activities of the NCPPA. *Quest*, 51, 178–183.

Noddings, N. (1992) *The Challenge to Care in Schools: An Alternative Approach to Education*. New York: Teachers College Press.

O'Sullivan, E. (1999) *Transformative Learning: Educational Vision for the 21st Century*. London: Zed Books.

Pallotta-Chiarolli, M. (1998) *Girls' Talk*. Sydney: Finch.

Rovengo, I. and Kirk, D. (1995) Articulations and silences in socially critical work on physical education: toward a broader agenda. *Quest*, 47, 447–474.

Schon, D. (1989) *Educating the Reflective Practitioner*. San Francisco: Jossey-Bass.

Smyth, J., Dow, A., Hattam, R., Reid, A. and Shacklock, G. (2000) *Teachers' Work in a Globalizing Economy*. London: Falmer.

Sparkes, A. (1992) *Research in Physical Education and Sport: Exploring Alternative Visions*. London: Falmer Press.

Tinning, R. (1990) *Ideology and Physical Education: Opening Pandora's Box*. Geelong, Victoria: Deakin University Press.

Tsangaridou, N. and O'Sullivan, M. (1997) The role of reflection in shaping physical education teachers' educational values and practices. *Journal of Teaching in Physical Education*, 17, 2–25.

Vescio, J., Taylor, T. and Toohey, K. (1999) An exploration of sports participation by girls from non-English speaking backgrounds. *ACHPER Healthy Lifestyles Journal*, 46, 2–3.

Wink, J. (2000) *Critical Pedagogy: Notes From the Real World*. New York: Addison Wesley Longman.

Zeichner, K.M. and Liston, D.P. (1986) An inquiry-oriented approach to student teaching. *Journal of Teaching Practice*, 6, 1, 5–23.

# 11 Political involvement in sport, physical education and recreation

*Barrie Houlihan*

## Introduction

Few debates stir more passion than that concerning the relationship between politics and sport. The debate is less concerned with determining whether sport and politics should mix as it has long been accepted, albeit reluctantly on the part of some, that there is an intimate relationship between the two spheres of social activity. Rather, the contemporary debate is focused on the nature of the relationship between politics and sport and questions such as how, to what extent, and for what purpose should governments be involved in sport. However, before proceeding to consider the debates about the role of government and the state in sport it is important to acknowledge that although this chapter is primarily concerned with the relationship between politics and sport there is a further dimension which focuses on politics in sport.[1] While the former focus emphasises the role of government and public policy the latter directs attention towards the control and deployment of resources within sports organisations.

A focus on politics in sport concerns the use of power within clubs, leagues, governing bodies of sport and international sports bodies such as the IOC and the international federations and reflects a definition of politics which ignores a distinction between the public and private spheres and argues that politics is present wherever disagreement and differential access to resources such as wealth, knowledge and authority are present (see Renwick and Swinburn 1987; Ponton and Gill 1993; Houlihan 2000). Politics is present in any organisation that makes decisions affecting the opportunities or life-chances of individuals or groups and as such would include decisions made by national governing bodies about player eligibility and the decision by FIFA to award the 2006 World Cup to Germany rather than South Africa.

The distinction between politics and sport and politics in sport is not watertight especially when many voluntary and private sports organisations are so heavily dependent on the state. With this caveat in mind the primary focus for this chapter is on the role of government and the state in sport, and on public policy. For present purposes, public policy refers to the choices regarding the deployment of resources made by the state. However, the concepts of 'public' and 'policy' are highly ambiguous and contested. For example, the courts in the UK have been deliberately reluctant to intervene in disputes arising from violence on the field in sport. In general, the courts have left it to national governing bodies (NGBs) to impose punishments for violence by one player on another in sports such as soccer and rugby for example. Whether a serious assault by one professional soccer player on another during a match is qualitatively different (i.e. a private matter) from a similar assault involving the same adults on the street (an accepted public matter) is a moot point (see Pateman, 1983; Pahl, 1985; Habermas, 1989 for a fuller discussion of the relationship between public and privates spheres). The concept of 'policy' is similarly ambiguous. Hogwood and Gunn (1984) identified ten different uses of the concept including policy as decisions of government, programmes, outputs, outcomes and process. In addition, policy might be indicated by action (i.e. the deployment of tangible resources such as money), but also by inaction (i.e. the decision to do nothing). Finally, policy may be simply aspirational with little realistic expectation or intention that the aspiration will be realised.

Further complications in the study of the politics of sport policy arise from globalisation and from the different ways in which power in the political process can be exercised. Globalisation is a much abused term and will be used here to refer to the extent to which national political and sports systems are increasingly subject to the influence of external governmental and non-governmental organisations. At the extreme there are those who argue that the nation-state is in terminal decline. In a number of countries the dominance of neo-liberal politics is resulting in the state being 'rolled back', or 'hollowed out' while at the same time being outflanked by unregulatable finance capital with the consequence that the proper theorisation of the policy process is now at the global level. Deacon *et al.* (1997) in their conclusion to a study of the impact of globalisation in social policy argue that 'Global social policy as a practice of supranational actors embodies global social redistribution, global social regulation, and global social provision and/or empowerment, and includes the ways in which supranational organisations shape national social policy' (195). Yet such a swift marginalisation of state influence on policy, characterised as 'state denial' by Weiss (1998) fails to take account of 'the variety and adaptability of state capacities' (Weiss 1997: 4). As Dearlove (2000) observes even if one accepts the political power of finance capital 'it cannot shape the policies of nation states directly in an unmediated way' (114). What is undeniable is that domestic policy processes in general and domestic sport policy in particular are less discrete than in previous periods and more permeable by supranational interests. Furthermore, while state adaptability and capacity may still be substantial they now have to be deployed increasingly within a global policy arena. As will be shown below, aspects of sport policy including the regulation of the sale of broadcasting rights, doping by athletes and the movement of players between clubs are all debated and resolved at an international level where individual states are still important, but are no longer the determining, policy actors.

Power is the central concept in the study of politics and policy-making and is of particular relevance to an examination of sport policy. Within pluralist theory power is assumed to be a reflection of resource control and is displayed in an open debate between interests on policy alternatives. For example, the assumption would be that the decision by the UK government to allocate public expenditure above the rate of inflation to sport in the July 2000 public expenditure review reflected not just the preferences of 'new Labour', but also the pressure exerted by NGBs, the UK Physical Education Association and other physical education teachers' lobbying groups, and the media. For Lukes (1974) the pluralist model of power needed to be complemented by additional, more subtle models which emphasised the less transparent use of power. Bachrach and Baratz (1970), for example, drew attention to bias within policy-making systems which favoured some interests at the expense of others to the extent that some interests and issues were effectively excluded from the political agenda. Bachrach and Baratz referred to 'non-decisions' which they defined as 'a decision that results in the suppression or thwarting of a latent or manifest challenge to the values and interests of the decision-maker' (7). In sport, examples of non-decisions would include the extent to which the needs of disabled athletes in the UK were ignored for much of the last forty years, and, at the international level, the slow progress of women towards equal access to the Olympic Games – a process that still has some way to go. Both these examples illustrate the capacity of powerful interests, able-bodied athletes in the former example and male athletes and administrators in the latter, to exclude issues and interests from the policy agenda.

At a deeper level still Lukes (1974) argued that there lay a third dimension of power which was embodied in the capacity to control ideas to the extent that groups who might legitimately be expected to possess a sense of grievance over their treatment or access to resources appear content. According to Lukes 'A may exercise power over B by getting him to do what he does not want to do, but he also exercises power over him by influencing, shaping or determining his very wants [by for example] the control of information, through the mass media, and through the process of socialisation' (23). For example, the participation level of women from Muslim countries in the Olympic Games is very low: indeed, many Muslim countries send all male teams to the Games. That there are few signs of significant protest from among Muslim women might be taken as evidence of the effectiveness of socialisation into traditional values and gender roles and an illustration of the third dimension of power and the importance of studying the manipulation of myths, symbols and language.

In each of the three dimensions of power identified by Lukes the state plays a central part not only in determining the redefinition of a private issue as a public problem and thus promoting some issues while suppressing others, but also in developing and maintaining the deep structure of values and attitudes in society. Consequently any study of public policy and in particular any examination of the motives of government involvement in sport, needs to be alert to the multi-dimensional nature of power and the role of the state as a key policy actor in a range of policy arenas that are increasingly international in character.

## Motives for state involvement in sport

There are a variety of explanations for state interest in sport the first of which is that of seeking to use sport as a means of achieving social control in relation to the working class in general and, more recently, in relation to young urban males in particular. Hargreaves (1986) for example, argued, not only that 'cultural elements' which would include sport 'constitute absolutely fundamental components of power networks' but also that 'sport was significantly implicated in the process whereby the growing economic and political power of the bourgeoisie in nineteenth-century Britain was eventually transformed into that class's hegemony in the later part of the century' (8, 7). The imperatives of capitalist production required the disciplining of the new urban working class in part through the elimination of what were perceived to be anarchic rural pastimes and sports and the introduction of sports which would complement and reinforce the attitudes and patterns of behaviour required by the factory system. The church and the school system, both private and state, were, for Hargreaves, central agents of social control.

More recently in the mid and late twentieth century the persistence of the motive of social control was still evident for example in the view expressed in the influential Wolfenden Report (1960) that 'if more young people had opportunities for playing games fewer of them would develop criminal habits' (4). In the 1980s sport was perceived as a potentially effective way of dealing with urban unrest. The series of urban riots of the early 1980s prompted the Action Sport programme in London and the West Midlands (Macintosh and Charlton, 1985). Almost twenty years later, Policy Action Team 10, set up following the report of the Blair government's Social Exclusion Unit, confirmed the continuing commitment to using sport as an agent of social renewal and social engagement for 'those who feel most excluded, such as disaffected young people and people from ethnic minorities' (DCMS, 1999: 5).[2]

That successive governments have treated sport as a convenient policy response to urban unrest and that sport is still prominent in the National Curriculum for Physical Education might indicate the pursuit of a class-based hegemonic enterprise, but it might equally indicate a much more open and fluid pattern of policy-making which incorporates elements of moralistic rationalisation derived from the assumption that sport builds character; elements of policy diffusion i.e. policies borrowed from other countries; elements of political expedience, in so far as sport-based projects have good publicity value and are relatively quick and cheap to implement, and also elements of policy learning from examples of successful sports-based social engineering projects, including many of the Football in the Community schemes and the 'Burngreave in Action' project in Nottingham which has achieved an increase in changes in attitudes towards physical activity and health within a deprived inner city area. Among the variety of motives that governments have for investing in sport it is undoubtedly accurate to claim that a regular motive is one of manipulation of attitudes and values often under the guise of moral improvement. This, however, does not necessarily constitute support for the theorists of class hegemony whose claims should be treated with some scepticism for three reasons. First, it is not possible to establish conditions under which the hegemony hypothesis might be falsified; second, and more specifically, the assertion that attempts to establish class hegemony are contested and subject to occasional setback leads to the tautologous position according to which both defeats and victories for dominant class interests are claimed as evidence in support of the hegemony analysis;[3] the process by which dominant class interests, even if amenable to precise specification, are articulated is rarely delineated (Abercrombie *et al.*, 1980).

The second major motive for government involvement reflects, as did the first, the adaptability of sport as a tool for achieving a wide variety of non-sports policy goals and refers to the justification of investment in sport by reference to health objectives. In recent years governments have been lobbied to invest in sports services because of the mounting evidence of a less active lifestyle among children and the rise in obesity among the young with the consequent risks to cardio-vascular health (Sports Council and HEA, 1992; Reilly *et al.*, 1999; Sport England, 2000).

A third reason for government intervention in sport is because of a growing awareness of its important diplomatic symbolism epitomised by the Cold War rivalry between the US and the former Soviet Union. Somewhat surprisingly sports diplomacy has lost none of its significance to governments in the post Cold War period (Houlihan, 1994). While negative diplomacy, such as boycotts, is less common the positive diplomacy arising from international sporting success and the hosting of major sports events has intensified as illustrated by the £10 million that the UK government spent in its abortive attempt to persuade FIFA to award the 2006 World Cup to England and the threats of legal action against FIFA by the South African government who were unhappy at losing out to Germany due to the abstention of the New Zealand representative. The willingness of governments to humble themselves before the IOC and FIFA through lavish hospitality and the strategic deployment of presidents, prime ministers, royalty and supermodels is a reflection of the value that governments place on international sport.

In recent years an increasing number of governments have seen in sport a valuable tool for stimulating urban regeneration. The failure of attempts to regenerate declining regions through the encouragement of new manufacturing ventures in the 1970s led to greater attention being given to job creation in the service sector and in the 1990s the potential for sport and sports tourism to stimulate the revival of downtown areas and create jobs. While sports projects, especially stadium development, have been a common element in regeneration strategies for downtown areas in the US it was the impact of Barcelona's successful bid to host the Olympic Games on its renewal that alerted the British and other European governments to the potential contribution of sport. It is argued that the development of major sports facilities and the hosting of prestigious sports events not only increases sports tourism for the duration of the event (Mules and Faulkner, 1996; Crompton, 1995), but also supports longer-term regeneration through its contribution to the 're-imaging' of the city (Roche, 1992).

Sports tourism also has a more generalised impact on a national economy. The impact of Euro96 on the UK economy was considerable. It was estimated by the

British Tourist Authority that each of the 250,000 overseas visitors would spend an average of £500. It was further estimated that additional income from tourism during the competition accounted for an increase of 0.25 per cent to the UK's exports for the second quarter of 1996 (UK Sport, 1999a, 1999b). One of the responsibilities of UK Sport is 'to promote the UK or any part of it as a venue for international sports events' and as Richard Callicott, UK Sport's Chief Executive, noted its role is to 'create and ensure a central focus and point of reference for all bids' (1999b: 9). Confirmation of the current priority given to sports tourism by the government is that lottery funding has been allocated to support UK Sport's Major Events Strategy.

The final major motive for state involvement in sport is the belief that international sporting success can both reflect and enhance a country's prestige. The heavy investment made by many of the former communist states, especially the GDR and the USSR, provide ample evidence of the value placed on Olympic success. In the former GDR its international athletes were 'diplomats in tracksuits', but their outstanding success in Olympic competition was said to be based as much on systematic doping as on the enormous state investment in training facilities and coaching (Strenk, 1980; Franke and Berendonk, 1997). Morton (1982) crisply summed up the attraction of international sporting success to the former Soviet Union:

> At home foreign sporting triumphs, officially presented as proof of socialism's superiority over capitalism, are primarily used to stimulate feelings of national pride and Soviet patriotism to aid in preserving national unity … Abroad, USSR athletes competing frequently and winning games, medals and championships project a positive, vibrant image of success and strength which can be transferred to the Soviet Union.
>
> (210)

However, it is not just the former communist states that sought to utilise sport to enhance their prestige. The governments of Canada, the US and most western European countries invested heavily in élite sport prompted by exactly the same motive. Few industrialised states have not established an elaborate publicly-funded system of élite talent identification and development involving specialist sports schools and academies and heavy direct public subsidy to athletes. Indeed most western élite sports systems are copies or at least close adaptations of the Soviet model refined in the 1960s.

In summary, states and their governments become involved in sport for a wide range of reasons few of which relate to the intrinsic benefits and values of sport. States have traditionally treated sport as a convenient and malleable instrument for the achievement of non-sporting goals such as socialisation, improved health, job creation, urban regeneration or the enhancement of international prestige. It is a moot question whether governments are capable of treating sport as anything other than an adaptable, high profile and relatively inexpensive policy instrument. This question will be examined in the next section, which provides an analysis of policy statements on sport by two recent British governments.

## From Major to Blair: continuity and change

Throughout the 1980s sport languished on the margin of politics and on the rare occasion when it did move to centre stage it was the result of crisis and embarrassment rather than success and celebration. Prime Minister Margaret Thatcher had little empathy with sport and generally saw public expenditure on sport (and indeed other cultural services) as consumption and as a cost rather than as an element of the productive economy and an investment. For her, mass participation was a service for which the user should pay while élite sport, especially soccer, was more a source of problems than a source of pride. In the mid-1980s fifty-five people died in a fire during a soccer match at Bradford City's ground, hooliganism at domestic matches was a regular occurrence, and thirty-eight Italians died during the European Cup Final between Liverpool and Juventus at the Heysel stadium as a result of trying to escape attacks by Liverpool fans. The Heysel disaster defined the attitude of the Thatcher government to soccer and coloured her attitude to sport in general. As Szymanski and Kuypers (1999) note 'Margaret Thatcher knew little about football and cared even less, but was concerned that the perception of widespread national disorder would damage her government's reputation' (51). Four years later the Hillsborough tragedy in which ninety-six fans lost their lives marked the lowest ebb of British sport. During this period government policy toward sport oscillated between neglect, as exemplified by the gradual reduction in resources available to the Sports Councils and local authorities for sports services, and sporadic, ill-thought-out policy initiatives best illustrated by the abortive football club membership scheme. The membership scheme was included in the Football Spectators Act 1989 and gave power to the relevant minister to designate certain matches as open only to 'authorised spectators', predominantly those who were members of membership schemes. A number of clubs introduced limited membership schemes for their fans, but the proposal was abandoned following criticism from Lord Justice Taylor, who chaired the inquiry into the Hillsborough disaster. Lord Justice Taylor questioned the capacity of computer-based technology to cope with membership swipe cards and supported police concerns that the scheme would lead to a greater likelihood of disturbances outside the ground. The failure of a similar scheme in Holland sealed the fate of the proposal which was quietly dropped (Houlihan, 1991).

The replacement of Thatcher by John Major as prime minister and leader of the Conservative Party marked a watershed in sport policy. Not only was Major a sports enthusiast, but so too were a number of members of his Cabinet. Among the more significant changes introduced by the Major government were the elevation of sport to a Cabinet level service through the creation of the Department of National Heritage in 1992 and the support that the government provided for a national lottery to provide additional funding for a range of 'good causes' including sport. Of especial significance was the publication of the first policy statement on sport by a government for twenty years. *Sport. Raising the Game* was instrumental in confirming and adding momentum to the recent direction of policy which was essentially away from support for mass participation in preference for an increased emphasis on élite development and school sport (Department of National Heritage, 1995). However, of especial note was the degree to which the Major years was one of the few periods since sport entered the policy agenda of government in the 1960s that there had been a recognition of the intrinsic merits of sport. In addition to the orthodox range of motives John Major emphasised the capacity of sport to 'enrich and elevate daily life' and to produce 'pure enjoyment for those who play and those who watch' (DNH, 1995: 2).

The policy statement reflected many of the motives mentioned above. In John Major's introduction to the statement he refers to sport's capacity to build character and to teach 'valuable lessons which last for life'; to achieve social integration as a 'binding force between generations ... [and as] one of the defining characteristics of nationhood and of local pride'; and to reinforce the sporting heritage of the country that 'invented the majority of the world's great sports' (DNH, 1995: 2–3). The vehicles for realising these policy goals were élite success and the revival of school sport. An élite British Academy of Sport was proposed, modelled on the successful Australian Institute of Sport, which would provide the highest quality training, coaching and sports science facilities. The provision of world-class support and facilities for élite athletes was to be supported by a series of building blocks the most important of which was a revival of school sport. John Major declared that his intention was to 'put sport back at the heart of weekly life in every school' (DNH, 1995: 2), an objective which was to be achieved through a broad range of policy instruments. On the one hand there were a series of incentives such as the award of the Sportsmark to recognise schools with outstanding provision, and funding for in-service training for teachers, and on the other hand a series of constraints including OFSTED inspection and most importantly of all a revised national curriculum for physical education which not only provided for an enhanced role for sport, as opposed to physical education, but which also emphasised the centrality of 'traditional team games and competitive sport' (DNH, 1995: 7).

Although the motives embodied in *Sport. Raising the Game* were conventional, distinguished from previous interventions in sport policy largely by the commitment of financial and legislative/regulatory resources, it is important to note the elements of previous sport policy that received little endorsement or mention. Sport For All, the slogan of sport policy adopted by the Sports Councils for much of the 1970s and 1980s, and the commitment to promote mass participation in sport received only passing comment as did local authorities, the primary agents for achieving mass participation. In part this omission reflected the view of the government that the facility infrastructure for mass participation was now in place and that management and policy leadership could be left to local authorities. However, the scant reference to the contribution of local government, which spends over £800 million each year on sport, was a reflection of the Conservative government's longstanding antipathy towards local authorities.

The incoming Labour government of 1997 was surprisingly hesitant and faltering in its initial attempts to impose a 'new Labour' stamp on sport policy. The pre-election policy statement *Labour's Sporting Nation* (Labour Party, 1996) confirmed the broad priorities of *Sport. Raising the Game*. The twin emphases on school sport and improved support for élite athletes remained intact with the vague commitment to return the ideal of Sport For All to the heart of government policy being the only innovation. Many of their predecessor's school sport policies were left in place, such as the Sportsmark awards, the introduction of specialist sports colleges, and the commitment to concentrate support for élite athletes. Sportmark awards are given to those schools that meet a series of criteria regarding the breadth of their curriculum, the time allocated to physical education and sport, and the quality of resources available. Specialist sports colleges are schools which have gained approval to specialise in physical education and sport. The colleges are given additional funding directly by government and are allowed to select up to 10 per cent of their intake on the basis of ability in sport. It is intended that the colleges will form an integral part of the evolving system of high performance talent identification and development and work closely with their regional centre of the UK Sports Institute.

Unfortunately, Labour's first three years in office are best characterised as a period of muddle and retreat. The muddle was over the location of the proposed British Academy of Sport (now retitled the UK Sports Institute (UKSI)). After a protracted period of bidding between competing centres the government announced that the UKSI would be located in Sheffield only for the decision to be reversed in the face of governing body opposition and a revised model proposed which would provide a series of regional centres with Sheffield as the administrative hub. However, within a short time the plans were altered again this time transferring the administrative functions from Sheffield to London. The policy retreat was in the area of school sport where the government suspended the National Curriculum for Physical Education (NCPE) in primary schools for two years in order to create space in the timetable for the literacy and numeracy hours. More generally, the Minister of Sport, Tony Banks, devoted much of his time to the attempt to bring the 2006 World Cup, and its attendant economic benefits, to England.

It was only in 2000 that the Labour government managed to establish a distinctive sport policy which it could link to some of its core electoral themes, particularly that of social inclusion. In mid-2000 *A Sporting Future For All* was published (DCMS, 2000) which established a clear policy profile for the new government. Although the policy statement retained the Conservative government's twin emphases on school sport and élite achievement the Labour document restored support for mass participation as a central objective. Like the Conservatives, Labour acknowledged the central importance of schools to its policy ambitions: 'It is school where most of us get our first chance to try sport' (3), but rather than rely primarily on constraints such as curriculum reform and OFSTED inspection the Labour government made greater use of inducements including investment in school sports facilities, the designation of 110 specialist sports colleges (SSCs) and the appointment of 600 school sport coordinators. Also unlike the policy in *Sport. Raising the Game* the Labour strategy integrated, more explicitly, objectives for school sport with those for élite sport by linking the specialist sports colleges to the UKSI network regional centres.

The commitment to establish the UKSI network and to continue the World Class Programmes, which provide a range of services to élite athletes including direct financial support, remained intact. Apart from linking the regional centres to the SSCs the policy statement required 'governing bodies to create a national talent development plan' part of which would involve identifying the 'most talented 14 year olds' and offering them a place at one of the SSCs (DCMS, 2000: 15, 16).

Apart from integrating school sport with élite development more tightly the statement also sought to link school sport, and especially facility provision, more effectively with the development of an infrastructure of community facilities. Funding for facility development will come from changes to the criteria for allocating National Lottery income with £125 million available from the New Opportunities Fund for green spaces and a requirement that 75 per cent of Lottery income be devoted to developing community sport. In addition, the government proposed that those sports with significant broadcasting income should devote at least 5 per cent of that income to the development of grassroots facilities and 'wherever possible, this new investment should be targeted on schools' (DCMS, 2000: 12).

There are many valuable insights to be gained into the policy process and the politics of sport from a comparison of the policies of the Major and Blair governments. Allowing for the fact that both governments were firmly rooted in the centre ground of British politics the first observation concerns the difficulty of making radical shifts in policy in the short term (i.e. four to five years). At the heart of the problem of policy change, even of the small-scale incremental kind, is the complexity and extensiveness of the network of organisations that has to be mobilised in order to effect change. Nowhere is this clearer than in school sport where the Sports Councils deal with a vast number of independent or at least relatively autonomous bodies. The steady decline in the influence of local education authorities means that governments and the Sports Councils need to liaise with individual schools and their boards of governors. In addition, the Sports Council has to work with around thirty national governing bodies each of which has its own internal decision-making process. Finally, implementation of the policy also relies on the cooperation of over three hundred local authorities each of which has its own political priorities set by its elected members.

Both governments sought to effect policy change through a combination of constraints or sanctions and inducements. The Major government used constraints in the form of change to the physical education curriculum and OFSTED and HMI inspection, but also used inducements in the form of the Lottery, Sportsmatch (where the government matched donations from private sponsors), and tax deductible sponsorship. In similar fashion the Blair government has imposed constraints, for example in the form of requiring NGBs to devise talent development strategies as a condition of grant aid and imposing tighter controls on the sale of school playing fields, and created inducements by earmarking Lottery funds for priority schemes, providing funding for newly created SSCs, and a particularly favourable comprehensive spending review in 2000 largely directed towards school and community facilities.

Apart from illustrating the variety of policy instruments available for the implementation of government policy a comparison of the two policy statements also provides an insight into the scope for policy learning, best illustrated by the increasingly sensitive use of Lottery finance to achieve policy objectives. Over the last three years the criteria for Lottery grants have been changed to enable more precise targeting of specific geographical areas and socio-economic groups. Other illustrations include the more painful lessons learnt during the shift in policy from a centralised UK Sports Institute to a regionalised network. Finally, policy learning is also taking place concerning the far more intractable problem of raising the profile of physical education and sport in the school curriculum. Sportsmark, Sportsmatch, OFSTED reports, the formulation of the National Curriculum for Physical Education and more recently the establishment of specialist sports colleges, the series of TOPs schemes[4] and the appointment of 600 school sport coordinators are testament to the incremental approach adopted by policy-makers.

The extent of policy diffusion is also striking, but not surprising. Most governments when faced with a new problem rarely approach it in the fashion suggested by the classical rational model of decision-making. It is much more common for governments to take policy shortcuts such as asking which other problem is this new one similar to and how have other countries responded which have encountered this problem. For example, many of the current responses to the problem of doping in sport are adapted from the longer established attempts to tackle recreational drug use, the UK Sports Institute is modelled on the Australian Institute of Sport, while the specialist sports colleges have a pedigree that stretches back to the 1960s Soviet Union.

This brief review of the two most recent policy statements on sport suggests three important conclusions. First, and perhaps most importantly, policy-making and implementation are often indivisible and successful implementation relies increasingly heavily on the cooperation of an extensive network of partners. However, to argue that the state has been 'hollowed out' due to the transfer of responsibilities to commercial or voluntary sector organisations and consequently has a reduced capacity for policy leadership is highly debatable as one can argue, more persuasively, that rather than being hollowed out the state has been extended and that while it may have less responsibility for direct service delivery it is more influential because of the complex and extensive pattern of organisations that are dependent on state resources. For example, the major NGBs are involved in an increasingly close and prescriptive relationship with the Sports Councils where grant aid is predicated on compliance with Council (and government) policy objectives in areas such as provision of coach and youth development and contributions to social inclusion. Second, while the government's reach might be extended through the increasing use of regulation and grant aid its capacity to respond speedily to a changing environment has diminished due to the range of organisations involved in delivering any one policy objective and their capacity to prevaricate. For example, the apparently simple and clear-cut objective of increasing the quality of the British squad for the Olympic Games involves negotiations with the British Olympic Association (one of the few national Olympic committees that is independent of government), twenty-seven or so NGBs for Olympic sports, the Lottery distribution panel for sport, and the host organisations of the regional centres of the UK Sports Institute. Thus not only are governments severely constrained by the decisions of their predecessors, but existing policies also have their own momentum which takes time to redirect. The final observation is to note the importance of factors outside the domestic political system. In all the policies referred to above the non-domestic political environment has acted as a resource for domestic policy-makers which has enabled them to borrow successful policies from other countries. However, as will be shown in the next section the non-domestic political environment is acting increasingly as a constraint rather than a resource.

## The broadening context of sport policy-making

Three issues in sport policy, the construction of the National Curriculum for Physical Education (NCPE), the eligibility of players, and anti-doping strategies, will be examined to illustrate the manner in which domestic processes are affected by the international context.

At first sight the design of the NCPE should be subject to little influence from outside the UK. Curriculum design is, at first sight, a purely domestic matter and not subject to any international agreements or treaties. Set against the background of the ideological debate about the role of education initiated by the Thatcher government in the early 1980s, the 1988 Education Reform Act included in its provisions the decision to establish a national curriculum.[5] The decision to design a national curriculum was informed in part by the government's concern that education should make a more explicit contribution to the acquisition of vocationally relevant skills and thereby enhance Britain's international economic competitiveness. Moreover, as Deacon *et al.* (1997) make clear, in the 1980s social policy in general was sharply informed by the fundamentalist neo-liberalism which emanated from powerful international bodies such as the International Monetary Fund, the World Bank and, though to a lesser extent, the Organisation for Economic Cooperation and Development which permeated domestic policy debates through the formation of a powerful community of ideas or epistemic community.

Although the physical education curriculum working group was one of the last to be established by the secretary of state the fact that physical education had been included as a foundation subject was greeted with much relief among physical education teachers and advocacy groups. However, the real battle was not over the status of physical education in the national curriculum but the subject specific content. Three reasonably distinct clusters of interests emerged during the debate on curriculum content, the first of which included the major NGBs whose main concerns included the preservation of the time allocation for sport and physical education, the promotion of skills acquisition and development as a central theme of the NCPE, and the revival of extracurricular sport. The second cluster included physical education teachers and related advocacy groups, most notably the UK Physical Education Association, who shared some of the concerns expressed by the NGB cluster, especially regarding the defence of curriculum time, but who were generally opposed to the undermining of physical education by an over-emphasis on sport. The third interest, the British Sports Council, was during this time the weakest interest as it had only recently accepted that sport and recreation for school-age children was a legitimate concern. Under the terms of its Charter and due to the fairly rigid demarcation between government departments the British Sports Council had had little opportunity or encouragement to seek a leading role in policy for this age group.

The Interim Report produced by the NCPE working party highlighted the divisions between the first two clusters of interests. The Report was heavily criticised for being overly academic and for giving too little emphasis to 'doing sport' (Talbot, 1995). The criticism was led by the secretary of state for education and the minister for sport and was strongly supported by the major NGBs though not initiated by them as the NGBs played a largely supporting role in this phase of policy-making. The final version of the NCPE, published in 1991, reflected a retreat on the part of the working party and a substantial compromise with the 'sports' interests as it gave prominence to the acquisition of sports-specific skills and especially to competitive sports.

The process by which the NCPE was formulated reflected the government's concern, or more accurately that of a few key ministers, to impose a particular vision of sport on schools. From the first step of selecting the membership of the curriculum working party, through the response to the Interim Report, and the monitoring of implementation by the School Curriculum and Assessment Authority the government managed the process of policy-making. As Evans and Penney (1995) observe, the government 'intentionally and cynically ... intervened in the making of the national curriculum for physical education for the purposes of promoting its own "restoration interests"'(184). In short, the government, in the form of key government ministers, supported by NGB interests, engineered a situation through which they were able to juxtapose the practice of competitive sport with physical education and argue that the former would lead to positive social, economic and personal outcomes whereas the latter, at best, lacked clarity of purpose and, at worst, undermined competitive values.

By way of assessment of the policy process for the NCPE there are many respects in which the government of Margaret Thatcher was moving in parallel with other neo-liberal governments such as those in New Zealand, the US and some Canadian provinces where the policy was typified by strengthening provincial/state or central direction of the curriculum towards greater vocationalism coupled with delegation of control over finance to school boards or governors (Houlihan, 1997). The concern with international economic competitiveness, the critique of public sector professions such as teachers, and the concern with the achievement of international sporting success were all ideas that informed neo-liberal policy and were not unique to Britain or to the Conservative government. Thus although the formulation of the NCPE was largely a domestic issue it was nonetheless informed and mediated by a series of international debates on the relationship between education and the economy, professional autonomy, and the role of international sport.

The second example concerns the Bosman case and the way in which the judgement by the European Court of Justice (ECJ) had major implications for domestic clubs and leagues and imposed an issue on the UK domestic policy agenda. Jean-Marc Bosman, a Belgian footballer, was offered a new contract at a lower wage by his club RC Liège. After refusing the new contract RC Liège placed him on the transfer list and he was offered employment by US Dunkerque. However, RC Liège refused to process the transfer as there were doubts about the capacity of US Dunkerque to pay the fee. Bosman took his case to the European Court of Justice and argued successfully that the transfer system violated his rights to freedom of movement under Article 48 of the Treaty of Rome. The case had widespread and well-known implications. In brief it allowed soccer clubs within the EU to ignore the UEFA regulation that limited the number of non-national players that a club could field to three plus two assimilated players. The case gave a significant stimulus to the accelerating commercialisation of soccer and led to clubs in Spain, Italy, France and England rapidly increasing the number of non-national players in their squads.

From the point of view of the UK government the intervention by the ECJ had few immediate implications as it was content to continue to treat the question of team composition as a matter for UEFA and individual clubs provided they operated within the Department for Education and Employment's (DfEE) regulations regarding the granting of work permits to non-European Economic Area (EEA) players.[6] However, over the next four years the implications of the Bosman case were to force two closely-related issues onto the government's policy agenda. The first arose from the difficulty of maintaining the then current criteria for granting of work permits to non-EEA soccer players and the second concerned the growing demand for protection of 'home-grown' soccer talent. As regards the first issue the UK had some of the most stringent regulations in the EEA on the granting of work permits. The Overseas Labour Service of the DfEE would grant a work permit only if a player was internationally established and if his job could not be fulfilled by an EU citizen. 'Internationally established' was usually defined as requiring a player to have played in approximately 75 per cent of his country's international matches. There had been little controversy surrounding the stringency of the criteria for granting work permits before the Bosman ruling. In the immediate years following the Bosman case the scramble for élite EU players appeared to make the work permit criteria redundant. However, as the cost of attracting the limited number of high quality players in the EEA escalated clubs began to look beyond the EEA with the consequence that work permit criteria became an increasingly sensitive political issue. This was of especial importance to the élite clubs which wanted to protect their commercial interests and, for many, those of their shareholders. Clubs from the lower divisions were also keen to recruit from the non-EEA market in order to enhance the strength of their squads and offer their supporters the same internationalised product as their

Premiership counterparts. Largely in response to lobbying from Football League clubs the government decided, in July 1999, to relax the criteria for granting work permits. As Ferragu (1999) notes 'It was believed that relaxing the rules would even out the opportunities available to clubs' (3).

While the clubs might have been happy with the change in work permit rules other interested parties, concerned with the protection of home-grown talent, were not. The Professional Footballer's Association argued that the change was a further disincentive to clubs to nurture and employ domestic talent, a situation that would be to the long-term detriment of the interests of the national team. The Football Association shared this general concern and suggested that Premier League clubs should be limited to two non-EEA players and First Division clubs be limited to one. Balancing a concern with the development of local sporting talent with the commercial interests of clubs was, and continues to be, a difficult issue for government. That it should be a concern of government at all is surprising and reflects the extent to which the current government of Tony Blair has sought to associate itself with the 'people's game'. Since coming to office in 1997 the government has sought a role in shaping soccer first through the establishment of the Football Taskforce which reported, *inter alia*, on commercialisation and racism, and most recently with the establishment of the Football Foundation to support the development of grassroots soccer and of the Independent Football Commission to act as a 'watchdog' body on behalf of fans.

In part, the addition of the issues of work permit regulations and the development and protection of home-grown talent to the government's sports policy agenda is a reflection of its populist stance on sport and culture, but it also indicates the extent to which the government's control over the sports agenda has been weakened by the growing interest of non-domestic policy actors such as the EU. Moreover, not only is there evidence of a dilution of domestic control over the setting of the UK sport policy agenda, but there is also evidence that the range of policy responses to issues on the agenda is being increasingly constrained by non-domestic actors. For example, while the UK government appears to be content to leave soccer clubs to cope as best they can with the more open market in players that resulted from the Bosman judgement other countries, most notably France, and organisations such as UEFA and FIFA are lobbying hard for a modification of EU regulations on freedom of movement of labour to limit the number of non-national players that a club can field.

The growing involvement of the EU in sport is also a factor in anti-doping policy-making, the third and last example in this section. Since the traumatic events of the late 1980s when the Seoul Olympic Games were marred by Ben Johnson's drug-assisted victory in the 100 metres, the discovery by the subsequent commission of enquiry in Canada of extensive systematic doping within its élite squad, and a similar scandal at the world renowned Australian Institute of Sport, anti-doping efforts have been slowly transformed from a series of disparate, country-specific, *ad hoc* and largely ineffective responses to a much more integrated global endeavour (Houlihan, 1999). The UK government was one of the first to accept the issue of doping in sport as a matter of public policy and used a variety of policy instruments, including legislation, imposing conditions on the award of grant aid to NGBs, and education campaigns, to strengthen anti-doping efforts at the domestic level. However, as it became clear that the problem was outgrowing the domestic context the government, through UK Sport, became involved in an increasingly elaborate network of international collaborative arrangements, including the Council of Europe's Anti-Doping Convention, the International Anti-Doping Arrangement and a series of bi-lateral agreements which involved sharing information, agreements to test each other's athletes, and attempts to devise common procedures and penalties for dealing with doping infractions. Most recently, the International Olympic Committee, a group of countries, of which the UK was one, the EU and the Council of Europe established a new body the World Anti-Doping Agency (WADA). WADA will be responsible for leading and coordinating the global anti-doping effort and will, *inter alia*, seek to achieve agreement and consistency on such awkward issues as a definition of doping, an agreed list of banned substances and practices, and agreement on penalties. In effect, WADA will become the lead policy body not only for the international federations and the IOC, but also for governments on a series of issues which had previously been treated as domestic matters thus redefining the role of governments, including that of the UK, to joint policy-makers and important agents of implementation of WADA policy rather than independent agents.

Although in all three examples in this section the state retains an important role in determining policy on a variety of sports issues it is undeniable that its role has greatly changed and that rather than sports issues being largely the preserve of domestic policy actors and processes they are much more likely to be resolved, or at least addressed, at an international level. Such a development requires states and indeed other domestic policy actors to reorientate their activities to suit an increasingly internationalised policy-making process.

## Conclusion

The gradual increase in the importance of the international environment for domestic policy suggests that we need to examine policy-making as a dual level process where domestic and international processes intersect and affect each other. A trend toward the internationalisation of sport policy-making highlights the importance of a strong set of domestic policy actors capable of participating effectively at the international level and defending, when necessary, domestic interests and priorities. Unfortunately, analysis of the domestic policy process and the balance of influence between domestic policy actors does not provide a reassuring picture.

One strong theme running through this chapter has been the extent to which there is a general tendency among recent governments to treat sport in instrumental terms. The sentimentalism of John Major and the populism of the government of Tony Blair belie the continuing perception of sport as a resource rather than as a distinct policy field. However, such a view should not detract from the substantial benefits, for example in the form of sustained public investment in sports facilities, that have accrued from government interest in sport, even if there is suspicion regarding the motive and depth of commitment to the policy area. The impression of a largely superficial interest in, and commitment to, sport is reinforced by the degree to which policy change is the product of ministerial and prime ministerial enthusiasm or of self-contained decision-making within the Sports Councils rather than shifts within a substantive sports policy community. The decision over the location of the UKSI (to which one might add the subsequent decision regarding the redevelopment of Wembley as the national stadium), the pre-occupation of Tony Banks, the first Labour minister of sport in the Blair government, with soccer, and the prioritising of school sport, are all symptomatic of policy-making in relative isolation from the wider policy community. In large part the ability of successive governments to treat sport and physical education in an instrumental fashion and to promote and pursue arguably idiosyncratic policies reflects the weakness of the sport-related interest groups and their inability to establish an institutionalised presence in the policy process. Unlike a number of other policy areas, such as health, defence and transport, where interest groups are securely established in their respective policy communities and display a capacity to mediate public policy, sports interests have yet to achieve an equivalent degree of systematic access and influence.

At the domestic level the policy process for sport is strongly influenced by the government. Yet earlier in this chapter reference was made to the continuing debate about the globalisation of the policy process and the consequent need to review the conventional model of the sport policy process as taking place within an essentially self-contained domestic context and the need to take account of the increasing importance of policy actors and environmental aspects beyond the domestic political system. The evidence presented above provides partial support for this view. It would be quite misguided to suggest that across a range of sport, physical education and recreation issues the state and individual governments still retain the authoritative position that they once held or were capable of holding, bearing in mind the general reluctance of governments to become too heavily involved in sport until the 1960s. However, to assume that the changing role of the state has been a shift from centrality to marginality in the policy process would be wrong. The state is still a central policy actor except that it is having to operate in an increasingly complex, fragmented and differentiated policy environment. Of particular significance is that the resources of individual states, which in the case of developed economies are substantial, can now be augmented by the collective influence of states operating through formal international organisations such as the EU and informal groupings such as the International Intergovernmental Consultative Group on Anti-doping in Sport (IICGAS) associated with WADA. Although it is possible to argue that the IGOs such as the EU and the IICGAS have the capacity to mediate state interests as well as simply reflect them the developments at international level provide evidence of the capacity of states to adapt effectively to the globalisation of sport policy-making.

Discussion of sport policy has moved a long way from the days when politicians would have supported government involvement in sport in apologetic tones and sought to perpetuate the myth that sport was somehow outside normal political life. It is now clearly accepted by all parties and in most countries that sport is a political issue. Such a realisation should be welcomed rather than feared. Activities that are ignored by political interests are only treated in that fashion because they are marginal to social life. Sport is increasingly central in many people's lives as a source of identity, personal pleasure and well-being, and employment and income. Those interested in the future of sport should therefore welcome its political profile as there are a number of key issues that will require political action if they are to be resolved including equity in access to sports opportunities, the balancing of sports media interests with those of spectators, and the maintenance of high ethical standards in sport.

## Notes

1 The term 'state' is used to refer to the range of institutions, including the central government departments, semi-independent agencies, such as the Sports Councils, and local government, whereas the term government is reserved for those elected politicians that hold ministerial posts, with those, in the UK, that are members of the cabinet being of especial importance. The state is relatively permanent whereas, in democracies at least, governments come and go. For a discussion of the relationship between the state and government see Heywood, 1994: 36.

2 On its election in 1997 the Labour government gave priority to overcoming what it referred to as 'social exclusion' which was defined as an inability to participate in mainstream social and economic activities. Social exclusion might be the result of a variety of factors including poverty, ethnicity, urban degradation, language and location. The government argued that as social exclusion was often multi-dimensional an integrated, cross-departmental (or as the government termed it a 'joined up') solution was required. As a result each service department was asked to review its work and suggest how it could contribute to the achievement of greater social inclusion. Within the DCMS, Policy Action Team (PAT) 10 was established and reported to the Social Exclusion Unit in July 1999.

3 See Morgan, 1994 and MacAloon, 1987 for discussions of the tautologous aspects of hegemony theory.

4 TOPS schemes are managed and coordinated by the Youth Sport Trust and are designed to improve the quality of the teaching of physical education and sport in schools. There are a series of TOPS schemes aimed at different age groups. A priority for the Youth Sport Trust is improving the quality of teaching in primary schools where there are very few

specialist physical education teachers. The TOPS scheme provides training, equipment and a series of outline lesson plans to support the non-specialist teacher.

5 For a fuller discussion of the policy-making process for the NCPE see Penney and Evans, 1999; Evans, Penney and Davies, 1996; Houlihan, 1997.

6 The European Economic Area comprises the fifteen members of the European Union plus Norway, Iceland and Liechtenstein.

## Reflection questions

1. Evaluate the argument that governments see sport as a convenient tool for responding to other non-sporting problems.
2. Discuss the view that British sport policy is more often made in the institutions of the European Union, in the board rooms of multinational broadcasting companies, or in the offices of the international sports federations and rarely in Britain.
3. 'The sooner we abandon the fiction of physical education in schools and call it sports coaching the better'. Discuss.

## Tasks

1. Using the websites of the major political parties compare current sport policy with that set out in the *Sport. Raising the Game* (DNH, 1995). Has policy changed? How would you account for the degree of change?
2. Using the European Union website identify the range of issues on which the EU is currently active. What might be the consequences of EU activity for sport in Britain?

## Further reading

Penney, D. and Evans, J. (1999) *Politics, Policy and Practice in Physical Education*. London: E. & F.N. Spon.

Houlihan, B. (1997) *Sport, Policy and Politics: A Comparative Analysis*. London: Routledge.

Hylton, K., Bramham, P. and Nesti, M. (2001) *Sports Development: Policy, Process and Practice*. London: Routledge.

## References

Abercrombie, N., Hill, S. and Turner, B.S. (1980) *The Dominant Ideology Thesis*. London: Allen & Unwin.

Bachrach, P.S. and Baratz, M.S. (1970) *Power and Poverty, Theory and Practice*. New York: Oxford University Press.

Callicott, R. (22–24 September 1999) The economic importance of major sports events. Paper to the conference, The Role of Sport in Economic Regeneration: Durham.

Crompton, J.L. (1995) Economic impact analysis of sports facilities and events: eleven sources of misapplication. *Journal of Sport Management*, 9, 1.

Deacon, B., Hulse, M. and Stubbs, P. (1997) *Global Social Policy: International Organisations and the Future of Welfare*. London: Sage.

Dearlove, J. (2000) Globalisation and the study of British politics. *Politics*, 20, 2, 114.

Department for Culture, Media and Sport (DCMS): Policy Action Team 10 (1999) *Arts and Sport: A Report to the Social Exclusion Unit*. London: DCMS.

Department for Culture, Media and Sport (DCMS) (2000) *A Sporting Future For All*. London: DCMS.

Department of National Heritage (DNH) (1995) *Sport. Raising the Game*. London: DNH.

Evans, J. and Penney, D. (1995) Physical education, restoration and the politics of sport. *Curriculum Studies*, 3, 183–196.

Evans, J., Penney, D. and Davies, B. (1996) 'Back to the future: education policy and physical education', in Armstrong, N. (Ed.) *New Directions in Physical Education: Change and Innovation*. London: Cassell.

Ferragu, B. (1999) Recent development in the UK work permit scheme for footballers. *Sports Law, Administration and Practice*, 6, 6.

Franke, W.W. and Berendonk, B. (1997) Hormonal doping and androgenization of athletes, a secret program of the German Democratic Republic government. *Clinical Chemistry*, 43, 7, 1262–1279.

Habermas, J. (1989) *The Structural Transformation of the Public Sphere: An Inquiry into a Categorisation of Bourgeois Society*. London: Polity Press.

Hargreaves, J. (1986) *Sport, Power and Culture*. Cambridge: Polity Press.

Heywood, A. (1994) *Political Ideas and Concepts: An Introduction*. Basingstoke: Macmillan.

Hogwood, B. and Gunn, L. (1984) *Policy Analysis for the Real World*. Oxford: Oxford University Press.

Houlihan, B. (1991) *The Government and Politics of Sport*. London: Routledge.

Houlihan, B. (1994) *Sport and International Politics*. Hemel Hempstead: Harvester-Wheatsheaf.

Houlihan, B. (1997) *Sport, Policy and Politics: A Comparative Analysis*. London: Routledge.

Houlihan, B (1999) *Dying to Win: Doping in Sport and the Development of Anti-Doping Policy*. Strasbourg: Council of Europe Publishing.

Houlihan, B. (2000) 'Politics and Sport', in Coakley, J. and Dunning, E. (Eds) *A Handbook of Sport Studies*. London: Sage.

Labour Party (1996) *Labour's Sporting Nation*. London: The Labour Party.

Lukes, S. (1974) *Power: A Radical View*. Basingstoke: Macmillan.
MacAloon, J. (1987) An observer's view of sport sociology. *Sociology of Sport Journal*, 4, 103–115.
Macintosh, P. and Charlton, V. (1985) *The Impact of Sport For All Policy, 1966–1984, and a Way Forward*. London: Sports Council.
Morgan, W.J. (1994) *Leftist Theories of Sport: A Critique and Reconstruction*. Urbana: University of Illinois Press.
Morton, H.W. (1982) 'Soviet sport reassessed', in Cantelon, H. and Gruneau, R. (Eds) *Sport, Culture and the Modern State*, 209–219. Toronto: University of Toronto Press.
Mules, T. and Faulkner, B. (1996) An economic perspective on major events. *Tourism Economics*, 12, 2.
Pahl, J. (Ed.) (1985) *Private Violence and Public Policy: The Needs of Battered Women and Responses of the Public Services*. London: Routledge.
Pateman, C. (1983) 'Feminist critiques of the public and private sphere', in Benn, S.I. and Gaus, G.F. (Eds) *Public and Private in Social Life*. London: Croom Helm.
Penney, D. and Evans, J. (1999) *Politics, Policy and Practice in Physical Education*. London: E. & F.N. Spon.
Ponton, G. and Gill, P. (1993) *Introduction to Politics*. Oxford: Basil Blackwell.
Reilly, J.J., Dorosty, A.R. and Emmett, P.M. (1999) Prevalence of overweight and obesity in British children: cohort study. *British Medical Journal*, 319.
Renwick, A. and Swinburn, I. (1987) *Basic Political Concepts* (2nd edn.). London: Stanley Thornes.
Roche, M. (1992) Mega-events and urban policy. *Annals of Tourism Research*, 21, 1.
Sport England (2000) *Young People and Sport in England 1999*. London: Sport England.
Sports Council and Health Education Authority (1992) *Allied Dunbar National Fitness Survey*. London: Sports Council.
Strenk, A. (1980) Diplomats in tracksuits: the role of sports in the German Democratic Republic. *Journal of Sport and Social Issues*, 4, 1, 34–45.
Szymanski, S. and Kuypers, T. (1999) *Winners and Losers*. London:Viking.
Talbot, M. (1995) Physical education and the national curriculum: some political issues. *Leisure Studies Association Newsletter*, 41, 20–30.
UK Sport (1999a) *The Economic Impact of Major Sports Events in the UK*. London: UK Sport.
UK Sport (1999b) *The Major Events Strategy*. London: UK Sport.
Weiss, L. (1997) Globalization and the myth of the powerless state. *New Left Review*, 225.
Weiss, L. (1998) *The Myth of the Powerless State*. Ithaca, NY: Cornell University Press.
Wolfenden Report (1960) Report of the Wolfenden Committee on Sport, *Sport in the Community*. London: CCPR.

# 12 Global sport and global mass media

*George Sage*

## Introduction

An understanding of the synergetic relationship between sport and the mass media in this era of globalisation requires that one have some familiarity with the organisation and roles of the media in the contemporary world order. Communication is the fundamental constituent of our social lives; it is a form of social glue bonding people together with common knowledge. Because of world-wide access to newspapers, magazines, films, television, and the internet, the mass media have become a powerful cultural source of information and public debate on matters of national and international importance, as well as a rich source of entertainment.

This omnipresence of the mass media enables the industry to be an extremely powerful source for forming values, beliefs, and organising consensus in each country of the world. Indeed, media scholars frequently call the mass media 'the consciousness industry'. Television, especially with its use of powerful images, words, gestures, settings, music and sounds has become a principal repository of ideologies (La Feber, 1999; McChesney, 1999; McChesney Wood, and Foster, 1998).

Communication in primitive societies took place during social interaction between people. As language became more complex and central to human societies, written communication became important. Beginning with the ancient Egyptian civilisation, systems of writing came to have a central cultural role in all subsequent societies. A major advancement in mass communication occurred with the invention of movable type for printing in the fifteenth century. This invention also laid the foundation for the development of book publishing and journalism. Skilled writers were in demand and a new occupational niche arose in conjunction with written communication. In the eighteenth century, technological innovations that made possible the Industrial Revolution also set in motion the development of mass communication media in the nineteenth century, starting with the telegraph, then telephony, then wireless telegraphy, and in the twentieth century radio, television, and the internet (Herman and McChesney, 1997; Sloan and Startt, 1999).

## Social roles of the mass media

The mass media have two fundamental roles: to communicate information about people and events and to provide entertainment to its consumers. In performing these roles, the media fulfill a further two less obvious, but nevertheless important, roles: social integration and social change. To the extent that communication media promote shared values and norms they contribute to social integration. But contrary to conventional wisdom and the industry's claims, the media are not neutral communicators of messages in any of its forms. The industry is involved in the everyday production and marketing of mass cultural products. Its values, norms and practices belong to a conservative ideology for interpreting and promoting culture and consciousness. Thus, the broad pluralistic mass of constituents which the media claim to represent is actually a range with discrete ideological limits. Furthermore, advertising and stockholder-conscious editors and publishers, filtering the information through a profit motive, make major decisions about media content. A careful analysis of the news pages and broadcast programmes reveals lamentably little outside the mainstream of public discourse (Cook, 1998; Fallows, 1997).

Although the media tend to be biased toward maintaining the *status quo* and promoting conventional norms and values, cutting edge research, new social practices and values, and critiques of contemporary attitudes and behaviours are also printed and broadcast, thus supporting social change. The mere reporting of new ideas and events can serve as a stimulant for reinterpretation of the world and may promote changes in many spheres of life. Nevertheless, contemporary media are not a major instrument of social change. Calls for fundamental political and economic change go largely unreported, or if reported, are treated as coming from extremists and therefore as unacceptable.

## Organisation of the mass media

Each nation in the world has its own system of mass communications. Some have a mass media solely under the jurisdiction of the government and thus publicly financed; others have a commercial system in which media organisations are privately owned and operated. Still others have a mixed public and private system of mass communications. Media in dictatorships and one-party countries tend to be under governmental control. Democratically-based countries tend to have commercial or mixed systems of mass communications. For example, both Great Britain and Australia have mixed communications systems that began as publicly financed systems but subsequently added commercial sectors. In the US, with the exception of the Public Broadcasting System (PBS) and National Public Radio (NPR), all the major mass media are privately owned (McChesney, Wood and Foster, 1998; Herman and McChesney, 1997).

The trend in most countries has been toward an increasing dominance of commercial over public control of the mass media. In the mid-1990s, British media analyst Colin Sparks (1995) claimed that the trend in British broadcasting was a shift from a public service system towards a predominantly commercial system. Media scholars Herman and McChesney (1997) argue that the current concentration of media power is built on 'through-going commercialism, and an associated decline in the relative importance of public broadcasting and the applicability of public service standards' (1).

### *Concentration of media ownership*

Accompanying the trend toward private ownership of media organisations has been a tendency toward a concentration of ownership, with fewer and fewer corporations controlling media firms. This can clearly be seen in the newspaper industry. At the beginning of the twentieth century, wherever private ownership existed, individuals or partnerships owned most newspapers, and publishers were not particularly wealthy. By mid-century, more than 80 per cent of the daily newspapers were still independently owned in western countries. But by 1999 less than 20 per cent were independently owned. The prevailing pattern for newspapers is currently one of corporate ownership. Indeed, of roughly 1,500 US daily newspapers, fifteen large newspaper chains own and control more than 50 per cent of the US newspaper circulation.

The broadcasting industry has undergone a similar pattern of increasingly concentrated ownership. Massive corporate conglomerates – mostly American based – own television and radio networks. General Electric, owner of NBC, is one of America's five largest American corporations, and it also owns CNBC and MSNBC cable channels; Walt Disney Corporation, owner of ABC, is also a leader in the entertainment industry; Viacom Corporation, owner of CBS, is one the nation's largest media conglomerates. Time Warner, owner of CNN, is the biggest media conglomerate, having far-flung enterprises in entertainment and retail sales. Billionaire Rupert Murdoch's News Corporation is a transnational media conglomerate, owning Fox network and several pay satellite services such as British-based BskyB and Hong Kong-based Star. The full extent of the ownership and control of business organisations by each of these corporations is astounding. Listing all their holdings would require several pages (McChesney, 1999).

Despite the fact that there are some 25,000 mass media outlets – newspapers, magazines, radio stations, television stations, book publishers, and movie companies – in the US, control of what people see, read and hear flows from a small, powerful handful of corporations. According to media analyst Ben Bagdikian, most media firms are owned by giant corporate conglomerates, and just six corporations now supply most of the nation's media fare. Although ownership of newspapers, magazines, book publishing, radio and TV organisations are, in theory, available to all, the reality is that ownership of mass media communication businesses is, in fact, restricted to those who have the financial means to afford the costs involved. As the media critic A. J. Liebling wryly noted, 'freedom of the press is guaranteed only to those who own one' (quoted in Kluger, 1986: 341). In the present era those who have the necessary financial resources are a few extremely wealthy individuals and increasingly large corporate conglomerates. It is they who are the power holders of the media, and it is they who fashion the daily discourse through that ownership (Alger, 1998; Bagdikian, 2000).

Collectively, the global mass media system is dominated by US-based transnational conglomerates, with another thirty to forty very large, mostly North American and western European, firms occupying what are called 'niche and regional' markets (Herman and McChesney, 1997; Cohen, 1997). These global mass media are a forum for the most powerful corporate interests. Social analyst Noam Chomsky (1987) noted that 'the media represent the same interests that control the state and private economy, and it is therefore not very surprising to discover that they generally act to confine public discussion and understanding to the needs of the powerful and privileged ... Their top management (editors, etc.) is drawn from the ranks of wealthy professionals who tend naturally to share the perceptions of the privileged and powerful, and who have achieved their position, and maintain it, by having demonstrated their efficiency in the task of serving the needs of dominant élites' (125). By communicating their definition of social reality, the global media tend to construct an image of societies and the world that appropriates their interests as the interests of everyone (Herman, 1996).

## Business connections between the mass media and broadcast sport

The mass media and sport have become mutual beneficiaries in one of capitalism's most lucrative associations. The first objective of mass media corporations is profit, and profit comes from selling the published or broadcast product to consumers and advertisers. As a business industry, the mass media has no innate interest in the commercial sport industry. Because people throughout the world read about, listen to, and watch sport in huge numbers, the sport industry is a lucrative means of making profit for the media industry. For newspapers and magazines, sport coverage helps sell these publications because many people enjoy reading about sports. The situation is different for radio and TV; sporting events (such as National Football League games or Manchester United matches) are the product being sold. Sports organisations sell their sports events to radio and television networks in the form of 'broadcast rights fees'. In fact, the search for broadcast rights revenues has come to dominate the revenue-seeking structure of the professional sport industry.

Once media organisations have bought the rights to broadcast specific sports events, they then sell the advertising time available during the 'commercial breaks' that periodically interrupt broadcast sports events to corporations wishing to advertise their products. Some media analysts claim that what radio and TV networks are actually selling to advertisers is audiences – their predicted size and demographic characteristics are assigned a monetary value by the media and sold to corporate advertisers. It is true that the larger the anticipated audience for a sports event, the larger the broadcasting rights fees charged by the networks. For whatever reason, wherever corporate advertising during sports events is popular it accounts for a substantial amount of radio and TV network revenue and abundant profits for the media industry.

Corporations spend lavishly on advertising during sports events in order to create a demand for their products. Broadcast sporting events attract large audiences because many people are interested in the beauty and drama of sports events, which many find more exciting and suspenseful than most other broadcast programming. Audiences who hear and see the associated broadcast commercials may become consumers of the products and thus help the advertisers to realise a profit. Sports are therefore a natural setting for corporate advertising.

Realising the popularity of broadcast sports, the sports industry has been successful at negotiating large contracts with media organisations for the rights to broadcast events. This, in turn, helps make commercial sports profitable. A few examples of recent contracts are listed below:

- The rights to televise national football league games from 1998 to 2006, as well as the 1997 Super Bowl, were sold to several networks for $17.6 billion; about 65 per cent of all revenues of NFL teams comes from the sale of television rights.
- The national TV and radio rights to Major League Baseball were sold to NBC, Fox, FSN and ESPN for $4.2 billion over ten years (1996–2005), making the annual income for each team from these contracts over $13 million. More than half the teams can pay their entire annual player payrolls solely from national broadcast revenues (Martzke, 1999). In the Autumn of 1999 CBS signed an eleven-year TV broadcast rights contract with the NCAA that begins in 2003 for $6.2 billion for the Division I men's basketball tournament; this was a 252 per cent increase over the previous contract (Wieberg, 1999).
- NBC paid $705 million in broadcast right fees for the 2000 Sydney Summer Olympic Games, $793 million for the 2004 Summer Olympics in Athens, and $894 million for the 2008 Summer Olympics.

It can be seen that the networks, the superstations, the cable sports stations, and local TV stations have presented commercialised team sports with a veritable bonanza of dollars. Contracts like these have made the commercial sports industry very profitable, resulting in expanded franchises, higher salaries and all-round plush lifestyles for many in the industry (Quirk and Fort, 1999).

### *Overlapping ownership between media organisations and sport organisations*

The financial association between the media and commercial sports goes beyond broadcast rights fees and advertising revenues; the media and sports have intimate ownership connections as well. Several owners of professional sport teams are also owners, or major shareholders, of media corporations. Table 5 illustrates well the close business ownership associations between media organisations and sport organisations. Rupert Murdoch, the media mogul with arguably the greatest global media empire, has called sports the 'cornerstone of our worldwide efforts' (quoted in Knisley, 1995: S–2).

*Table 5* Media corporations that have ownership stakes in professional US sport teams

| *Corporation* | *Teams* |
|---|---|
| Walt Disney | NHL's Mighty Ducks, MLB's Anaheim Angels |
| Time Warner | MLB's Atlanta Braves, NBA's Atlanta Hawks, NHL's Atlanta Thrashers |
| News Corp. | MLB's Los Angeles Dodgers, minority ownership in NBA's New York Knicks and NHL's New York Rangers |
| Tribune Co. | MLB's Chicago Cubs |
| Comscast-Spectacor | NBA's Philadelphia 76ers, NHL's Philadelphia Flyers |
| Cablevision | NBA's New York Knicks, NHL's New York Rangers |
| Paul Allen Group | NFL's Seattle Seahawks, NBA's Portland Trail Blazers |
| Ackerley Group | NBA's Seattle SuperSonics |

### *Indirect media and sport business linkages*

Beyond the direct financial association between the mass media and sport, there are several other indirect financial linkages. Commercial sport receives an enormous amount of free publicity via the media. The media coverage itself tends to promote sports – its leagues, teams, athletes and coaches – as typical sports coverage is put out in a blatantly booster manner, designed to hype interest in the athletes and teams. Newspaper sport sections are, in subtle ways, an advertising section for commercial sports. Radio and television segments dealing with sports news are essentially advertising for commercial sports. Indeed, many sports news announcers act like cheerleaders for the local professional sports teams, often referring to them as 'our team'. No other privately owned, profit-making industry – which the commercial sport industry is – receives as much free publicity for its product. Of course, the reciprocal business aspect of this is quite clear: the more interest generated in commercial sports, the greater the profits for the mass media (Lowes, 1999; Rowe, 1999).

## Historical and contemporary linkages of sport and the mass media

There is a long history of connections between sport and the media. In many ways advances in communication technology were major factors in the rise of modern sport. Without the mass media to promote sporting events, broadcast the events and report the results to masses of widely-scattered people, it is unlikely that modern commercial sport would have grown in popularity. On the other hand, without sports to write and broadcast about, public consumption of mass media products would have been more muted.

### *Print media*

According to some historians, newspaper coverage of sport can be found as far back as the eighteenth century. Michael Harris (1998) found that 'cricket was drawn into the content of the London newspapers' by the mid-eighteenth century as part of the 'widening circle of commercialization within what might ... be described as the leisure industries' (19, 24). As professionalised forms of sport began to attract wider popular attention around the mid-nineteenth century, newspapers began periodic coverage of sports events, and by the 1890s a separate sports section had become a regular feature of many newspapers. Throughout the twentieth century newspaper coverage of sports increased. Currently, sports coverage in some of the world's most popular newspapers constitutes as much as 50 per cent of the space devoted to local, national and international stories. All sports newspapers, such as *Britain's Sport*, which was launched as a daily in 1991, and *Sport First*, a national Sunday newspaper that began in 1998, are growing in popularity throughout the world. Studies in Australia and the US indicate that sports journalists are the largest single specialty in the journalism industry (Henningham, 1995; see also Salwen and Garrison, 1998).

Books on field sports, horse racing and popular games have been published for over 200 years. One of the most famous of these is Joseph Strutt's *Sports and Pastimes of the People of England*, published in 1801. It is a volume of over 300 pages describing everything from children's games to an incredible variety of adult games and sports. The first massive sports book wave began around the mid-nineteenth century. How-to books on every popular sporting activity appeared, and a youth literature centred around sporting activities contributed significantly to interest in sports among adolescents of the later nineteenth century (Sloan and Startt, 1999). The most prolific of the American youth literature authors was Gilbert Patten (whose real name was Burt L. Standish) who wrote a series of books about Frank Merriwell, a fictitious schoolboy athlete. In the early twentieth century the Merriwell stories sold about 135,000 copies weekly.

A bewildering array of journals and magazines specialising in sports were being published in the early nineteenth century, with almost every sport having its own publication, and many of the magazines specialising in chronicling the activities of athletes and sports teams. These publications have continued to proliferate, so much so that wherever magazines are sold, one-third to one-half of the shelf space is taken up by sports titles. In the US, the first prominent sports journal, the *Spirit of the Times*, began publication in 1831. Another nineteenth century sports magazine, the *Sporting News*, began publication in 1886 and continues today to be one of the most successful sport magazines. Founded in 1954, *Sports Illustrated* is currently the largest-selling sports magazine worldwide, with a circulation of around 3.5 million copies weekly.

### Broadcast media

While books about sports, sport magazines, and sports sections of newspapers continue to have significant linkages to the mass media, it is radio, and television, especially television, which now dominate the media-sport nexus. Only a couple of decades separated the invention of wireless broadcasting in the 1890s and the appearance of radio sportscasts in the 1920s. Broadcasts of sport events and post-game reports of results quickly became one of radio's most popular functions. But radio's popularity as a medium for sport information and entertainment was dealt a serious blow by the introduction of network television in the 1950s. However, over 500,000 hours of sport are still broadcast via radio annually in the US – everything from sport talk and call-in shows to play-by-play reporting. In 1998, there were 237 sports talk radio stations in the US and the number has been increasing each year (Goldberg, 1998; McCallum and O'Brien, 1998).

Currently, the predominant association between the mass media and sport is through television. Telecasting was developed during the 1930s, but its commercial use was delayed until after the Second World War. In the early 1950s commercial TV made an immediate and dramatic impact on sport. Since then the two industries have grown large and powerful together. It is often claimed that the highly successful industry of commercial sports could not exist without television and that television would have a more difficult time generating profitable revenues without the commercialised sport industry.

Spectators consume sport to a far greater extent through television than through personal attendance at events. In the US, over 2,500 hours of televised sport is programmed per year by the major commercial networks. Cable TV networks, such as the Entertainment and Sports Programming Network (ESPN, ESPN2), which reaches over 75 per cent of American homes with cable TV, broadcasts over 8,000 hours of live sports each year. Regional sports cable networks and direct satellite broadcasts (e.g. Madison Square Garden, Turner Broadcasting System, Golf Channel) are growing rapidly, and they broadcast countless thousands of hours of sport each year. Finally pay-per-view (PPV) seems poised to become an increasingly popular form of sports telecasting. All-sports news channels are the most recent innovation in sports television. ESPNews and CNN/SI began this form of twenty-four-hour sports coverage in the fall of 1996. They do not carry live sports events. Instead they telecast only sports news.

Half of the twenty-five top-rated television programmes of all time are sport events. Super Bowl telecasts usually attract between 45 and 55 per cent of the households watching TV. An estimated six billion people worldwide tuned in to at least some of the televised coverage of the 1996 Atlanta Summer Olympic Games. In the years that the World Cup is played, the month-long soccer tournament draws a total worldwide audience of up to forty billion viewers.

## Modifying sports to accommodate television's interests

Everyone has heard the saying 'He/She that pays the piper calls the tune'. It is certainly true with regard to broadcast media sport. The formula is quite straightforward: since TV networks charge corporations advertising fees based on the anticipated number of viewers – the more viewers, the larger the advertising fee – the networks are desirous that the sports events to which they buy rights fees attract huge audiences. In their pursuit of viewers, and thus larger rights fees, media networks have been able to persuade pro sport leagues and franchise owners to modify rules and schedules in the hopes of attracting a larger number of viewers. They have often found willing associates in the sports industry. Pro sport owners and leagues charge broadcasting rights fees based on anticipated audience size, so they have been willing to modify rules and schedules in hopes of increasing the number of viewers. Thus, in order to enhance viewer appeal and accommodate programming needs, both the media sport and the commercial sports industries have manipulated the structures and processes of sport. Here are some examples:

- In NFL football, rule changes, such as moving the sideline hash marks and the kickoff spot, reducing defensive backs' contact with receivers, and liberalising offensive holding have been adopted to open up the games and make them more attractive to television viewers. Other modifications have been introduced to permit more commercials – time-outs at the discretion of television officials and the two-minute warning as the game nears the end are both used as a TV time-out.
- To enhance spectator and viewer interest, NBA basketball led in the adoption of the shot clock, the slam dunk, and the 3-point shot.
- In televised golf, match play, where the golfers compete hole by hole (with the golfer winning the most holes being the winner), has largely been replaced by medal play, where golfers play the field (and the one with the lowest score over the course wins). The Skins Game, where large sums of money ride on the outcome of each hole, has become a popular form of televised professional golf. Each of these new forms of golf competition is more compatible with television coverage.
- In professional tennis, to accommodate television scheduling, tennis executives have established a tie-breaker system of scoring when sets reach six games for each contestant, thus making it easier to complete matches within a designated time period.
- Major League Baseball introduced the designated hitter and lowered the strike zone, and there is strong suspicion that the baseball itself has been modified to make it livelier. All of these changes have been motivated by an interest in increasing what spectators like to see: more extra base hits and home runs. Time-honoured afternoon world series and all-star games were switched to evenings to serve the interests of television.
- The sudden-death tie-breaking rule in football, ice hockey, and soccer, and the extended play-off system in all of the pro sports leagues, are additional examples of modifying rules to increase TV viewer interest, and make the sporting events more profitable for both TV networks and professional sports.
- During recent Winter and Summer Olympic Games, the International Olympic Committee (IOC) has agreed to reschedule championship events to accommodate television networks' desire to show them during America's prime time. Moreover, much of the Olympic Games TV coverage is now shown after the events are completed, but frequently the events are presented to television viewers without informing them of this fact, leading them to believe that they are actually seeing live events.

To summarise, television's influence on sport adaptations, modifications and scheduling is tied directly to enhancing the action for television viewers and making it convenient for bigger audiences to see the commercials being shown. This, in turn, maximises commercial sports revenue from the sale of broadcast rights and TV networks' revenue from the sale of advertising.

### *Television's own sports*

Not satisfied with the variety of 'real sporting events', and seeking a way to broadcast events having characteristics similar to sports events (i.e. competition requiring physical strength, endurance, speed, skill, etc.). TV networks created made-for-television sports events, popularly know as 'trash sports'. Made-for-television sports began in the mid-1970s with an ABC programme in which outstanding élite athletes competed in events contrived by TV executives. Winners of these events were awarded titles like 'world's best athlete'. Other made-for-television sports events followed: *Challenge of the Sexes* pitted top male athletes against top female athletes, with the males handicapped to heighten the uncertainty of the outcome; *Super Teams* pitted members of professional teams in two different sports against each other in contrived competitions.

The most popular, and long running, made-for-TV sporting event of the 1990s was *American Gladiators*. In this event, off the street competitors try to win points in a variety of physically demanding events requiring strength, agility, tenacity and guile against specially chosen 'Gladiators' with backgrounds as professional athletes and Olympic competitors. Originally conceived as entertainment for ironworkers in Erie, Pennsylvania, in 1989 the Samuel Goldwyn Company, a movie-making firm, developed the television series titled *American Gladiators*. By 1991 the series was one of the top five weekly syndicated TV programmes (Simpson, 1991). Because of the popularity of the TV series, *American Gladiators* gave rise to cross-country touring groups, and it gradually became a popular international attraction in the latter 1990s, especially in the UK and Europe.

Most of the original made-for-television sports events have disappeared from sports programming. However, with the popularity of almost any kind of competitive event, and with the all-sports TV channels needing to fill numerous hours of programming time, various made-for-television and alternative sporting events now appear. Some of these are actually legitimate sports, but often they do not have a large number of participating athletes nor a large spectator following. When they are telecast nearly every aspect of them is aimed at making them appealing to viewers, and thus to corporate advertisers and sponsors. ESPN's *X-Games* fits this genre of TV sports. Created in 1995 as a made-for-TV alternative sports festival, *X-Games* appeals to a very large, young TV-watching audience. Since the *X-Games* were created and owned by ESPN, the network does not have to pay broadcast rights fees to air them. Reruns and qualifying events fill many hours on the ESPN broadcast schedule (Walters, 2000a). *Gravity Games*, the most recent addition to this genre of sporting events, is owned by emap usa and presented by NBC. They were first held in 1999 in Providence, Rhode Island. *Gravity Games* features aggressive inline, bike, downhill skateboarding, freestyle motocross, skateboarding, street luge and wakeboarding competitions.

Beach volleyball, long a popular recreational activity throughout the world, was modified and its players glamorised and marketed as an exciting and highly competitive TV sport by networks during the late 1980s. Its TV version was an immediate hit. For many TV viewers, the main attraction of beach volleyball – especially women's beach volleyball – is its soft porn aspects of the beautiful, tanned, semi-naked bodies bouncing and falling around in the sand while TV camera operators seek to get the most provocative views of the athletes' bodies. Some media critics contend that televised beach volleyball was largely responsible for popularising the sport to the point that it was adopted as an Olympic event.

## Broadcast sport as a mediated event

A common assumption among the public is that a broadcast sport event is an objective mirror of the reality of the contest, and that, in TV for example, the framing, camera angles, use of scan and zoom, and sportscaster commentary are neutral conduits for presenting 'the facts' of the event. In reality, however, a broadcast game is an entertainment spectacle sold in the marketplace, a tool for attracting listeners and viewers so the media can broadcast commercials to the audiences they have sold to advertisers.

Ostensibly, sportscasters simply keep listeners and viewers apprised of essential information as the contest unfolds. But they do much more; they mediate a sporting event and thus create the listeners' and viewers' experiences of the event through their intervention. Because of sportscasters' mediation, a sporting event becomes a collage of happenings and thus 'reality' is socially constructed by the sportscasters, who decide what to reveal to listeners and viewers, and how. What they reveal and what they conceal becomes, in effect, the 'event', and the way listeners and viewers experience it becomes their reference point for its very existence – but it is a mediated version of reality.

In a televised sports event, cameras, camera angles, producers' choices of focus and sportscasters' interpretations – all of which forms the invisible apparatus of a televised presentation – interpose between the viewers and the event. Viewers do not see the entire event; instead, they see only those parts that are sifted and filtered through the broadcasting process. Spectators attending the event in a stadium or arena perceive it 'as is'. But broadcast listeners and viewers experience an event that is socially constructed by a team of broadcast professional gatekeepers and dramatic embellishers. A critic of the typical mediated broadcast content, Australian sport studies researcher David Rowe (1999), claims that 'there is no other media sports text that is subject to greater ridicule than the live broadcast commentary which describes for viewers what they are seeing' (98).

The public has many options as to what to listen to and watch, so a variety of techniques are used to attract listeners and viewers. One of the most important decisions that media executives must make is about selection – decisions about which sports events to broadcast and which sports events not to broadcast; decisions to accentuate certain aspects of the sporting event for listeners and viewers and not others. In making these decisions, broadcast coverage constructs listener and viewer interests, attitudes and beliefs about sports. One insightful description of this selection process deserves to be quoted at length:

> [Television] selects between sports for those which make 'good television', and it selects within a particular event, it highlights particular aspects for the viewers. This selective highlighting is not 'natural' or inevitable – it is based on certain criteria, certain media assumptions about what is 'good television'. But the media do not only select, they also provide us with definitions of what has been selected. They interpret events for us, provide us with frameworks of meaning in which to make sense of the event. To put it simply, television does not merely consist of pictures, but also involves commentary on the pictures – a commentary which explains to us what we are seeing ... These selections are socially constructed – they involve decisions about what to reveal to the viewers. The presentation of sport through the media involves an active process of re-presentation: what we see is not the event, but the event transformed into something else – a media event. This transformation is not arbitrary, but governed by criteria of selection, which concentrate and focus the audience's attention, and, secondly, those values which are involved in the conventions of television presentation: concentration and conventionalism.
>
> (Clarke and Clarke, 1982: 69–71)

Two examples of broadcast selection can illustrate the selection and exclusion in media sports coverage. First, male sporting events coverage dominates broadcast sports and helps reinforce cultural attitudes about gender specificity in sport and gender appropriateness of sports. Second, team sports have dominated sports broadcasts. Indeed, male team sports are TV 'authorised sports'; in many ways the media have advanced the popularity of male team sports at the expense of other forms of sport. Thus, social values are conveyed through the particular choices made by the media's selective coverage.

Once particular sports events are chosen for broadcasting, the next task is to 'hook' listeners and viewers to the broadcasts. This begins with pre-game programmes that are mostly a contrived mix of interviews, network promotions and hoopla (e.g. theme building). The main purpose of these programmes is to frame and contextualise the game by building dramatic tension artificially and solidifying allegiances, thus encouraging listeners and viewers to stay tuned to the event, while preparing them for how they should hear, see and understand it. The rhetoric concentrates listeners' and viewers' attention on the overall importance of this particular contest, individual athletes' (and coaches') personalities, 'match-ups', statistics, records and team styles of play. Rowe (1999) notes:

> Some of the more hyped-up commentaries are intended for those 'unconverted' viewers whose interest has to be stimulated by communicating a sense of high drama in the events on screen. If television sports commentators, then, are irritating a core audience while trying to lure a peripheral one … then it is hardly surprising that they are so often subject to hostile commentary themselves.
> (98–99)

In the interest of enhancing the excitement and suspense of a sports event, the processes employed by sportscasters sometimes involve altering the broadcast of an event to portray something quite different than what actually happened during the event. For example, in the women's team gymnastic competition during the 1996 Atlanta Summer Olympics, one of the American gymnasts, Kerri Strug, injured an ankle in a landing during the vault competition. In spite of the obvious pain, Kerri ran down the runway and completed her second vault. A courageous act, but at the time of her second vault there was no way of determining how her score would affect the overall outcome of the competition. However, in the delayed telecast of the meet, NBC revised the sequence of the competition and selected her performance as the last for the vaulters, and thus the culminating factor in the overall competition. Television viewers were not only led to believe that the televised event was live, but that the competition took place in exactly that sequence (Paige, 1996).

The overarching value in media sport is winning. Broadcast sports tends to be a single-minded ode to winning, so much so that almost any action in the pursuit of victory is justified; indeed, athletes are often lionised for illegal play. Sportscasters frequently declare admiringly that an athlete will do 'whatever it takes to win'. No sacrifice is too great in the interest of winning; athletes who surmount injury, endure pain and continue to play are valorised. During one NFL football game, the camera zoomed in on the heavily taped right arm of a defensive lineman. One of the sportscasters then explained that the player had incurred a compound fracture of one of his fingers – meaning the bone was sticking out of the skin. The player had gone to the bench, shoved the bone back in, taped up the finger, and returned to the game. The sportscaster then said, in a thoroughly admiring manner, 'It just goes to show how badly these guys want to win.' Another example: during an NFL game, one of the sportscasters applauded a quarterback by saying, 'Here's a guy that probably had to take a pain-killer shot in his lower back so he could play tonight.'

The selecting, screening and filtering of sport events through the images shown and the commentary given constructs broadcast sport as an entertainment spectacle. Consequently, one outcome of this process is that broadcast sport audiences become less interested in the traditional appreciation of the beauty, style, movement artistics, skill, and the technical accomplishments of the athletes, and focus more on provocative excitement and productive action, usually meaning scoring and winning. Because the definitions, values and practices of media sport commentary are privileged, they become the 'common-sense' constructions about sport that grow out of the production of broadcast sport.

### *Sportscasters: narrators of mediated sport*

Because radio and TV sportscasters are the 'tutors' for what listeners and viewers should hear, see and believe about the sports events they are broadcasting, they are extremely important in the broadcasts of sporting events. Consequently, they are carefully selected with an eye to their ability to command credibility because media organisations must rely heavily on the personae of these men and women to attract and hold listeners' and viewers' attention. So former professional and élite amateur athletes with high name recognition are often selected. As sporting celebrities, they command immediate recognition from and credibility with the listeners and viewers. Moreover, since they are part of the media sport star system, audiences of broadcast sports events are expected to rely on the interpretations and judgements of these 'certified experts' and to accept their interpretations and opinions as objective and true.

Employing former athletes and coaches to describe the technical skills, strategy and tactics used during a broadcast sporting event may seem reasonable enough, but it is important to realise that they also act to dictate moral values and to remark prescriptively on social relationships. Former sport stars are uniquely qualified for this task because they are survivors – even models – of the competitive sport meritocracy. By and large their attitudes and values are congruent with commercialised sports perspectives; they are fully integrated into the dominant values and beliefs of that system.

Preventing viewer boredom is one of the main concerns of broadcast producers, so, as noted above, a basic job of sportscasters is to keep listeners and viewers tuned in to the broadcast. To do this, they provide a commentary that heightens the drama of the event. One of the favourite ways of doing this is to construct themes such as 'these teams hate each other' or 'this is a grudge game'. The message in both cases: the audience can expect a hard fought contest with lots of fierce action. Another favourite tactic of sportscasters is to highlight 'match-ups' between players on opposite teams. This sets up a kind of one-on-one competition on which the audience can focus. A third technique used by sportscasters is framing the game as an extremely crucial game for both teams (even if they are both hopelessly out of championship contention); heightening the significance of the game enhances audience interest (or so it is believed). Other sportscaster techniques are personal interest stories, recitation of statistics and records, anticipation of what to expect, dramatic embellishments of the action, and second-guessing. All these narratives are designed to keep audiences tuned in to the broadcast.

Sportscasters have another important job, which is selling the sport organisations and league for which they are broadcasting. Game commentary is frequently commercial hype for the league and the sport organisation for which the sportscasters are broadcasting. For example, sportscasters frequently bestow effusive accolades on the athletes, teams and leagues for which they are broadcasting. Another favourite 'sales' practice of sportscasters is to create attention-attracting nicknames to develop team name recognition and get fans to identify with teams or athletes, e.g. the Dallas Cowboys of the NFL have become known as 'America's Team' through sportscaster commentary.

Broadcast audiences are largely unaware that they are being subjected to advertising for the league and sport organisation that is independent of corporate product commercials for which commercial breaks occur periodically during an event. It has been suggested by more than one media analyst that an appropriate description for sportscasters would be 'sport public relations agents'.

## The internet: the newest mass communications form

The current cutting edge in communications is the internet. It is a quantum leap beyond previous forms of communication because it makes possible the inexpensive transmission of messages and images throughout the world in seconds. The internet had its origins in US Defense Department research done in the late 1960s, but by the mid-1990s it was almost entirely funded by private communications conglomerates, some of them originally founded as internet firms and some of them originally founded as media print or broadcast corporations. There have even been mergers of the two types of corporations. For example, in early 2000 American Online (AOL), the world's largest internet service provider, became the first internet firm to become a major player in the sports world with its takeover of Time Warner, the world's largest media company. Included in the deal, AOL inherited three Atlanta professional teams, their venue and various sports media properties (McChesney, Wood and Foster, 1998). By mid-2000 more than half of the US population had access to the web from their homes.

The implications of the internet as a source of sports information of all kinds are seemingly limitless. Sports business consultant, Dean Bonham (quoted in Hiestand, 2000), predicts that 'sports is going to be as valuable to the Internet, as programming, as it has been for television' (1C). Kevin Werbach (quoted in Kornblum, 2000), editor of technology insider newsletter *Release 1.0*, asserts: 'The Internet is the next mass medium, and inevitably the Web, with its incredible openness, is going to swamp the closed model of television' (3D).

Literally thousands of websites serve to inform the general public about sports. In September 2000 a website search using 'sports AND websites' with the search engine http://www.google.com produced a list of 1,140,000 websites. It is anticipated that when sports become internet programmes they will be interactive, and when that happens it will change not only the character of sports, but also how the media presents sports to mass audiences. Interactive sports on the internet will enable viewers to control the information displayed on the monitor. Showtime and Home Box Office (HBO) have offered coverage on their websites that allow users to choose various camera angles of the fight, the audio from either of the fighter's corners, various punch statistics, and a chance to score the fight and compare their cards with that of the ringside judges (Walters, 2000).

The 2000 Sydney Summer Olympics are considered to be the first official Olympic Games of the internet era. IBM's Olympics.com site reported 8.7 million visitors worldwide and had 11.3 billion 'hits' (the number of website elements seen). Other websites reported visitors in the millions as well. But according to Michael Goss (quoted in Snider, 2000b; see also Snider 2000a) of Quokka Sports, NBC's partner in NBCOlympics.com, 'the Web is never going to replace television. Understanding how these mediums complement each other is the Holy Grail' (3D).

Although there are still many technical and legal issues to resolve, the internet certainly has the potential to surpass all other mass communication forms as a source of sport information and entertainment.

## The global economy and the global media sport complex

A significant transformation in the world order has been underway during the past half century that can be characterised as a growing political, economic and cultural interdependence among the world's nations. The word most popularly used to characterise the features of this process is 'globalisation'. In economics, the adoption of a market-based economy by developed and many developing nations, as well as formerly centrally-planned economies, and the opening of international markets, have created what is increasingly being called a global economy. Some 500 transnational corporations (TNC) based in developed countries control about 75 per cent of world trade. They are the major forces contributing to this emerging global economy. This is not only because of the sheer scale of their operations, but also because of the way in which these gigantic companies integrate their administrative and production systems worldwide through rationalised economic activities, modern bureaucratic organisation, advanced communications networks and scientific data calculations. (For good general discussions of the global economy, see Gray, 1998; Greider, 1997; Hoogvelt, 1997.)

A major component in the expanding globalised economy is cultural products, such as music, art, sport and the mass media, especially film and television, which flow around the world and enhance the integration and interdependence tendencies of the world order. Films, music and television programmes are produced, marketed, sold and consumed throughout the world, and top actors, actresses and musicians are worldwide celebrities (McChesney, Wood and Foster, 1998). Sporting practices that have long existed in national cultures and communities are no longer isolated from global changes. They, too, have become an integral part of the globalised economic and cultural world, and widening global interdependency is profoundly influencing traditional sports practices and values. As British sport sociologist Joseph Maguire (1993) noted, 'sports development is interwoven with this process of accelerated globalization' (32).

Several trends highlight the interconnections between global sports development and the global economy. For example: a growing number of international sports organisations; the internationalisation of sports leagues, e.g. MLB, NBA; the international migration of sports personnel, such as athletes, coaches, trainers; increasing competition between national teams, regional championship events, such as the European Championships, Commonwealth Games, Pan American Games, Asian Games; numerous world championships, e.g. World Cup and

Olympic Games; the worldwide broadcasting of sporting events. All these trends exhibit the key economic elements of production, distribution and consumption. They all employ athletes from throughout the world, draw spectators and television audiences the world over, attract advertisers of products made throughout the world, and shape global sport consumer behaviour. These, and others, highlight the various components of globalisation in sports.

### *Global media/sport production, distribution, and consumption*

One of the dominant forces fuelling the growth of the global sports nexus is an increasing global media/sport production complex (Maguire, 1999; Rowe, 1999). This complex is composed of several key groups: media organisations and personnel, notably broadcasters and journalists; transnational product/marketing/advertising organisations, i.e. Coca Cola, Anheuser Busch, IBM, etc.; and sport organisations. Ownership and control of the global media/sport communication organisations is in the hands of the same few transnational corporations that dominate mass communications in the US, i.e. General Electric (NBC), Viacom (CBS), Disney (ABC), Time-Warner (CNN), Rupert Murdoch (News Corp. Ltd.). News Corporation's Rupert Murdoch, owner of Fox television network and a leading player in international sports television, was chosen the most powerful person in sports by the *Sporting News* four times in the six years between 1994 and 1999; he was also judged to be the seventh most powerful person in sports during the twentieth century by the same publication (*Sporting News*, 2000).

Several examples will illustrate how the global media/sport/transnational corporate complex works and how it shapes global consumer attitudes, values and behaviour. First, the global media/sports production process not only spreads American sports around the world, the commercials accompanying the televised event advertise non-sport commodities, i.e. Coca Cola, Pepsi Cola, Nike, IBM, etc. The growing global popularity of American sports such as American football, baseball and basketball in countries throughout the world is partially attributable to the various corporations whose advertising on TV is associated with sporting events.

Second, when British television began showing American football games on a regular basis in 1982, the programmes attracted an average viewer audience of 1.1 million. By 1990 the viewing audience had nearly tripled. The marketing strategies of the NFL, Anheuser-Busch and a British TV company were instrumental in this growth, and in the emergence of an American football sub-culture in English society (Maguire, 1999).

Third, in describing two studies of sport heroes among New Zealand youth, Andrews *et al.* (1996) reported that Michael Jordan was by far the number one choice of a hero among teenagers in New Zealand. According to them, New Zealand teens' 'knowledge of Jordan appears dependent upon sports highlight programs, news, and the myriad of television commercials that reveal his corporate alliances' (433). They continue, 'perhaps the most important finding was simply that all [respondents] could identify Jordan as an athlete or, at least, as an American corporate icon' (433).

There are diverse and contradictory interpretations about the influences of the globalised media sport complex on the world order. Several sport studies scholars have suggested that the social process of global sport development has created what they call 'Americanisation', a vision of a one-way cultural imperialism by which American cultural products, forms and meanings are imposed on other nations and their national culture. Thus, Americanisation is thought of as an imperialistic process involving the political, economic and cultural diffusion of American methods, values and social forms at the expense of the domestic culture. This Americanisation thesis is bolstered by the fact that during the later twentieth century there has been a strong American presence in many aspects of European, Middle Eastern and Asian economies and cultures, especially through American transnationals (e.g. Esso, Coca Cola, Heinz, Ford, IBM), who sell their products, marketing and advertising strategies around the world.

In terms of cultural pursuits, American television has had a potent impact on cultural thought and lifestyles throughout the world, with televised American sports playing a leading role in this. American global sports influence has taken several forms: the spread of American sports forms, the adoption of sports marketing strategies along American lines and the migration of American sports personnel. For some, then, the US is considered to be largely responsible for the production and distribution of the globalised sports model along with the practices and values that accompany it.

Canadian sport sociologist Bruce Kidd (1991) has argued that American cultural imperialism has served to undermine the traditional role of Canadian sporting practices in strengthening Canadian national identity. He asserted: 'Americanization exerts a heavy burden on Canadian sportspersons by greatly restricting their ability to fashion meanings and activities in their own experience' (180).

Anthropologist Alan Klein examined the political economy of baseball in the Dominican Republic and found that American major league baseball teams have had a deleterious structural effect on the autonomy and quality of baseball in the Dominican Republic. Klein (1991a; see also Klein, 1991b) claims that 'Americanization is apparent in all aspects of the Caribbean, but particularly in the Spanish-speaking islands and surrounding nations' (80). He argues that American major league baseball functions as a neocolonial enterprise, mirroring 'the political economy of other American enterprises in the Third World' (Klein, 1989: 95). In a subsequent study of baseball on the US–Mexican border, Klein (1997) makes a similar case.

Other sport sociologists have been sceptical about the Americanisation thesis. Several favour a cultural hegemony view whereby the transmission of cultural products, such as sporting practices, is more complex, dynamic and multi-directional. Rowe *et al.* (1994) argue that 'it is necessary to move beyond the simple logic of cultural domination and towards a more multi-directional concept of the flow of global traffic in people, goods, and services' (675). According to this view, all nations and their cultures have some freedom, some choice, to interpret, reinterpret, even resist, American cultural products – including sports – in their own unique ways. In their analysis of Australian sport development, Rowe *et al.* (1994) conclude that 'although Australian sport has adopted American styles of production and promotion, its subsequent corporatization and commercialization cannot be typified [as] ... Americanization or ... cultural domination [but by] a more multi-directional concept' (673). See also McKay *et al.* (1993).

In his analysis of the popular emergence of American football in Britain, Maguire (1999) acknowledged the evidence of a strong element of Americanisation, but he rejected the notion of a simplified one-way American influence on the growing popularity of this sport in Britain. He posited a process in which Americanisation is only one of several global processes in progress and he identified several conflicting global flows and resistances to cultural imperialism. He also asserts that the 'Americanization thesis arguably overstates how global media content is understood and (re) interpreted by people in different societies' (145).

Although there are differences in interpretation of the worldwide influence of American sports, there are several reasons for linking of the processes of globalisation and American global sport. As the commodification of sport has occurred in many countries, there is general consensus that the dominating force has been an explicitly American set of practices and values. The US has been the most dominant and successful twentieth-century nation, and its economic, political, military and cultural power extends throughout the world. American products seem to represent global culture most distinctly. American popular music, satellite news, T-shirt designs, Hollywood films, and commodified sports have infiltrated most countries of the world. Donnelly noted: 'What is important is that the American style of sport has become the international benchmark for corporate sport – "show-biz", spectacular, high-scoring, or record-setting superstar athletes; the ability to attract sponsors by providing desired audiences; and having the characteristics necessary for good television coverage' (246).

At the same time, most scholars acknowledge that the globalisation of commodified sport transcends the influence of the US. Rowe *et al.* (1994) say:

> Although sport around the world has adopted American styles of production and promotion, [its] corporatization and commercialization cannot be typified as the completion of the projects of Americanization or globalization. In order to comprehend the 'reach' of international images and markets, it is necessary to move beyond the simple logic of cultural domination and towards a more multi-directional concept of the flow of global traffic in people, goods and services.
>
> (673)

At a later point in their article, they argue 'there has even been a limited amount of ''Australianization", with Australian companies sponsoring sporting events in Canada, England, Japan, and the USA' (669).

From their study of American popular culture, as represented by the NBA and its corporate and intertextual alliances in New Zealand, Jackson and Andrews (1999) maintain that worldwide circulation of American sporting practices 'is not only contributing to the flow of global cultural products and practices, it is also leading to the rearticulations of national and local cultural identities … Hence, rather than causing the dissolution of local identities through the establishment of a homogeneous global culture, the NBA may actually play a role in energizing multiple popular and local cultures' (40).

## Conclusion

A synergetic relationship exists between the mass media and sport in this era of increasing globalisation. The major roles of the mass media are to communicate information about people and events and provide mass entertainment. Each nation in the world has its own system of mass communications, but the trend in most countries has been toward an increasing dominance of commercial over public control of the mass media. Along with the trend toward private ownership of media organisations there has been a movement toward a concentration of ownership, with fewer and fewer corporations controlling media firms.

The mass media and sport have become mutual beneficiaries in one of capitalism's most lucrative associations. The mass media have supported commercialised team sports with large sums of money. This has made the commercial sports industry very profitable. But, while media sport is an arena for accumulation of capital and expenditures for leisure, it is not just about the economic interests of the media and sport corporations. Because the media are effective and powerful organisations for promoting ideology, media sport is also an arena for the advancement and reproduction of political and social interests.

A notable transformation characterised by political, economic and cultural interdependence among the world's nations has been underway during the past half century. A major component in this transformation is the cultural products that flow around the world and enhance the integration and interdependence tendencies among nations. One outcome of all of this is an increasing global media/sport production complex.

### Reflection questions

1 It is often claimed that there is a symbiotic relationship between sport and the mass media, that each is dependent upon the other and that each is influenced by the other. Does this seem like an accurate portrayal? If so, what do you consider the major positive and negative features of this relationship. If you do not believe this is an accurate portrayal, describe what you consider to be a better portrayal of the relationship between sport and the mass media.

2 This chapter argues that broadcast sports are mediated events. Reflect upon the mediated features of sporting events that are recounted in the chapter. Does broadcast mediation of sporting events influence the core values of sport, such as attitudes and beliefs about winning, losing, playing fair, etc.? If you believe it does, explain.
3 In the light of the debate described in this chapter about the 'Americanisation' thesis of the influences of the globalised sport media on the world's sports development, which of the arguments for and against this thesis is more accurate from your standpoint? Explain and defend your answer.

## Tasks

1 Conduct a content analysis of the sports pages of a newspaper for one week (including photos). Determine the amount of coverage (in column centimetres) devoted to male versus female sports, white versus non-white athletes, team sports versus individual/dual sports. Develop explanations for different amounts of coverage for these various categories of sport.
2 Locate five sports-media websites. Describe the sponsoring organisations of the website, the kind of information and coverage offered by the website, the design of the website, some of the links listed, and explain how the website's coverage is relevant to one or more topics of this chapter.

## Further reading

Rowe, David (1999) *Sport, Culture, and the Media: The Unruly Trinity*. Buckingham: Open University Press.
Wenner, Lawrence (Ed.) (1998) *MediaSport*. New York: Routledge.
Alger, Dean (1998) *Megamedia: How Giant Corporations Dominate Mass Media, Distort Competition, and Endanger Democracy*. New York: Rowman Littlefield.

## References

Alger, D. (1998) *Megamedia: How Giant Corporations Dominate Mass Media, Distort Competition, and Endanger Democracy*. New York: Rowman and Littlefield.

Andrews, D.L., Carrington, B., Jackson, S.J. and Mazur, Z. (1996) Jordanscapes: a preliminary analysis of the global popular. *Sociology of Sport Journal,* 13, 428–457.

Bagdikian, B.H. (2000) *The Media Monopoly* (6th ed.). Boston: Beacon.

Chomsky, N. (1987) *Power and Ideology*. Boston: South End Press.

Clarke, A. and Clarke, J. (1982) 'Highlights and action replays – ideology, sport and the media', in Clarke, J. (Ed.) *Sport, Culture and Ideology*, 69–71. Boston: Routledge & Kegan Paul.

Cohen, Richard M. (1997) 'The corporate takeover of news: blunting the sword', in Barnouw, E. *et al.* (Eds) *Conglomerates and the Media*. New York: New Press.

Cook, T.E. (1998) *Governing With the News: The News Media as a Political Institution*. Chicago: University of Chicago Press.

Fallows, J. (1997) *Breaking the News: How Media Undermine American Democracy*. New York: Vintage.

Goldberg, D.T. (1998) Sports, talk radio, and the death of democracy. *Journal of Sport and Social Issues*, 22, 212–223.

Gray, J. (1998) *False Dawn: The Delusions of Global Capitalism*. New York: New Press.

Greider, W. (1997) *One World, Ready Or Not: The Manic Logic of Global Capitalism*. New York: Simon & Schuster.

Harris, M. (1998) Sport in the newspapers before 1750: representations of cricket, class and commerce in the London press. *Media History*, 4, 1, 19–28.

Henningham, J. (1995) A profile of Australian journalists. *ACHPER Healthy Lifestyles Journal*, 42, 3, 13–17.

Herman, E.S. (May/June 1996) The media mega-mergers. *Dollars & Sense*, 8–13.

Herman, E.S. and McChesney, R.W. (1997) *The Global Media: The New Missionaries of Global Capitalism*. London: Cassell.

Hiestand, M. (11 January 2000) AOL becomes player in the world of sports. *USA Today*, 1C–2C.

Hoogvelt, A. (1997) *Globalization and the Postcolonial World: The New Political Economy of Development*. Baltimore: Johns Hopkins University Press.

Jackson, S.J. and Andrews, D.L. (1999) Between and beyond the global and the local: American popular sporting culture in New Zealand. *International Review for the Sociology of Sport*, 34, 31–42.

Kidd, B. (1991) How do we find our voices in the 'new world order'? A commentary on Americanization. *Sociology of Sport Journal*, 8, 178–184.

Klein, A. (1989) Baseball in the Dominican Republic. *Sociology of Sport Journal*, 6, 95–112.

Klein, A. (1991a) Sport and culture as contested terrain: Americanization in the Caribbean. *Sociology of Sport Journal*, 8, 79–85.

Klein, A. (1991b) *Sugarball: The American Game, the Dominican Dream*. New Haven: Yale University Press.

Klein, A. (1997) *Baseball on the Border: A Tale of Two Laredos*. Princeton: Princeton University Press.

Kluger, R. (1986) *The Paper: The Life and Death of the New York Herald Tribune*. New York: Alfred A. Knopf.

Knisley, M. (2 January 1995) RuperTVision. *The Sporting News*, S–2.

Kornblum, J. (7 August 2000) NBC webcasts clear Olympic hurdles. *USA Today*, 3D.

La Feber, W. (1999) *Michael Jordan and the New Global Capitalism*. New York: W.W. Norton.

Lowes, M.D. (1999) *Inside the Sports Pages: Work Routines, Professional Ideologies, and the Manufacture of Sports News*. Toronto: University of Toronto Press.

Maguire, J. (1993) Globalization, sport development, and the media/sport production complex. *Sports Sciences Review*, 2, 29–47.

Maguire, J. (1999) *Global Sport: Identities, Societies, and Civilizations*. Cambridge: Polity Press.

Martzke, Rudy. (7 December 1999) Baseball, ESPN settle on $851M deal. *USA Today*, 1C.

McCallum, J. and O'Brien, R. (17 July 1998) Public dis-coarse. *Sports Illustrated*, 27.

McChesney, R.W. (1999) *Rich Media, Poor Democracy: Communication Politics in Dubious Times*. Chicago: University of Illinois Press.

McChesney, R.W., Wood, E.M. and Foster, J.B. (1998) *Capitalism and the Information Age*. New York: Monthly Review Press.

McKay, J., Lawrence, G., Miller, T. and Rowe, D. (1993) Globalization and Australian sport. *Sport Science Review*, 2, 10–28.

Sporting News (2000) The most powerful people in sports. Online Available HTTP: http//:sportingnews.com/ features/powerful

Paige, W. (25 July 1996) What you see is what already has occurred. *Denver Post*, 1D, 4DD.

Quirk, J. and Fort, R. (1999) *Hard Ball: The Abuse of Power in Pro Team Sports*. Princeton: Princeton University Press.

Roberts, G. (1997) 'Conglomerates and newspapers', in Barnouw, E. *et al.* (Eds) *Conglomerates and the Media*, 61–72. New York: New Press.

Rowe, D. (1999) *Sport, Culture and the Mass Media*. Buckingham, UK: Open University Press.

Rowe, D., Lawrence, G., Miller, T. and McKay, J. (1994) Global sport? Concern and peripheral vision. *Media, Culture and Society*, 16, 661–675.

Salwen, M. and Garrison, B. (1998) Finding their place in journalism: newspaper sports journalists' 'professional problems'. *Journal of Sport and Social Issues*, 22, 88–102.

Simpson, J.C. (21 October 1991) Real-life Davids vs. Goliaths. *Time*, 102–103.

Sloan W.D. and Startt, J.D. (1999) *The Media in America: A History* (4th ed.). Northport, AL: Vision Press.

Snider, M. (2 October 2000a) Internet deserves medal for keeping us informed. *USA Today*, 9E.

Snider, M. (9 October 2000b) Net traffic surges for summer games. *USA Today*, 3D.

Sparks, C. (1995) The future of public service broadcasting in Britain. *Critical Studies in Mass Communication*, 12, 325–341.

Strutt, J. ([1801] 1903) *Sports and Pastimes of the People of England*. London: Methuen.

Walters, J. (21 August 2000) Key punch. *Sports Illustrated*, 24.

Wieberg, S. (19 November 1999) Basketball TV deal blunts drive for a football playoff. *USA Today*, 1C.

# Index